Oxford

MAPPING THE CITY

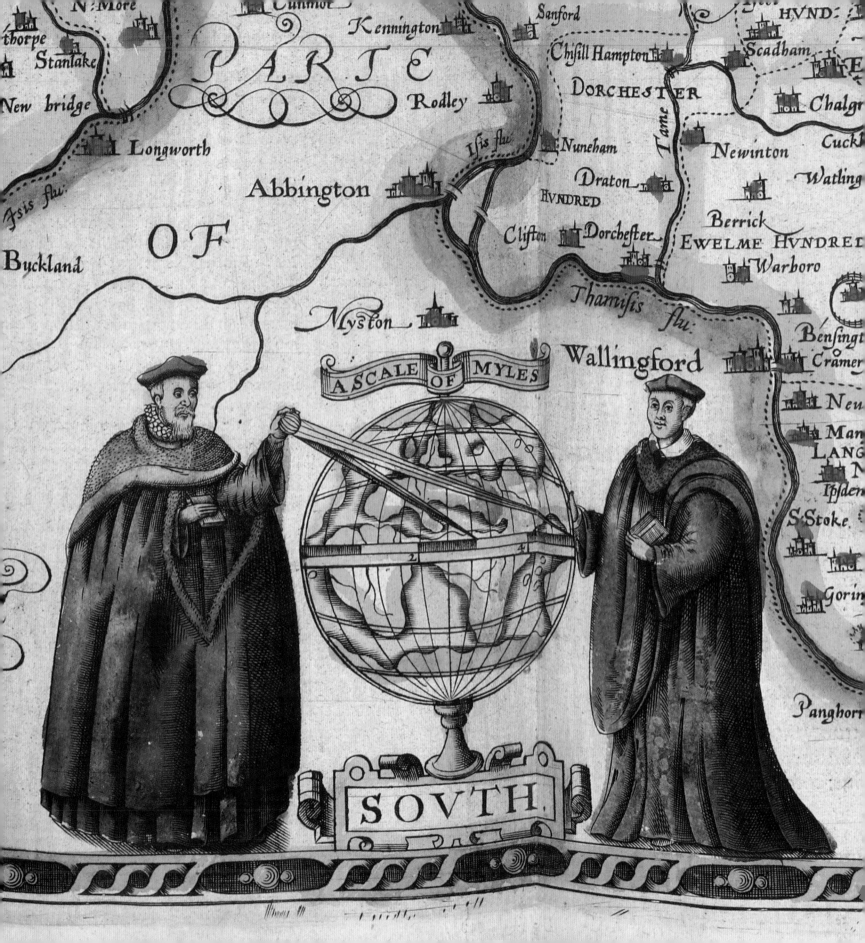

PARTE

thorpe
Stanlake

New bridge

Longworth

OF

Byckland

Kennington

Rodley

Isis flu

Abbington

Nyston

Sanford

Chisill Hampton

DORCHESTER

Nuneham

Draton

HVNDRED

Clifton   Dorchester

Tame

Scadham

Chalgr

Newinton

Cuckl

Watling

Berrick

EWELME HVNDRED

Warboro

Thamisis flu

Bensingt
Cramer

Wallingford

Neu

Man

LANG

Ipsden

S. Stoke

Gorin

Panghorn

A SCALE OF MYLES

SOVTH

Oxford

MAPPING THE CITY

Daniel MacCannell

BIRLINN

First published in
Great Britain in 2016 by
Birlinn Ltd
West Newington House
10 Newington Road
Edinburgh
EH9 1QS

www.birlinn.co.uk

ISBN: 978 1 78027 400 3

British Library Cataloguing-in-Publication Data
A catalogue record for this book is available on
request from the British Library

Designed and typeset by Mark Blackadder

PREVIOUS PAGE

Detail of John Speed, 'Oxfordshire described
with the citie . . .', from *The theatre of the
empire of Great Britaine: presenting an exact
geography of the kingdomes of England,
Scotland, Ireland . . .* (1611)

Printed and bound by Livonia, Latvia

Sacred to the memory of 9 Bear Lane
and all who sailed in her, 1993–94

Daniel MacCannell

The Publisher would like to dedicate this book,
on behalf of generations of Magdalen historians,
to Dr John Stoye, an inspiration to us all

Hugh Andrew

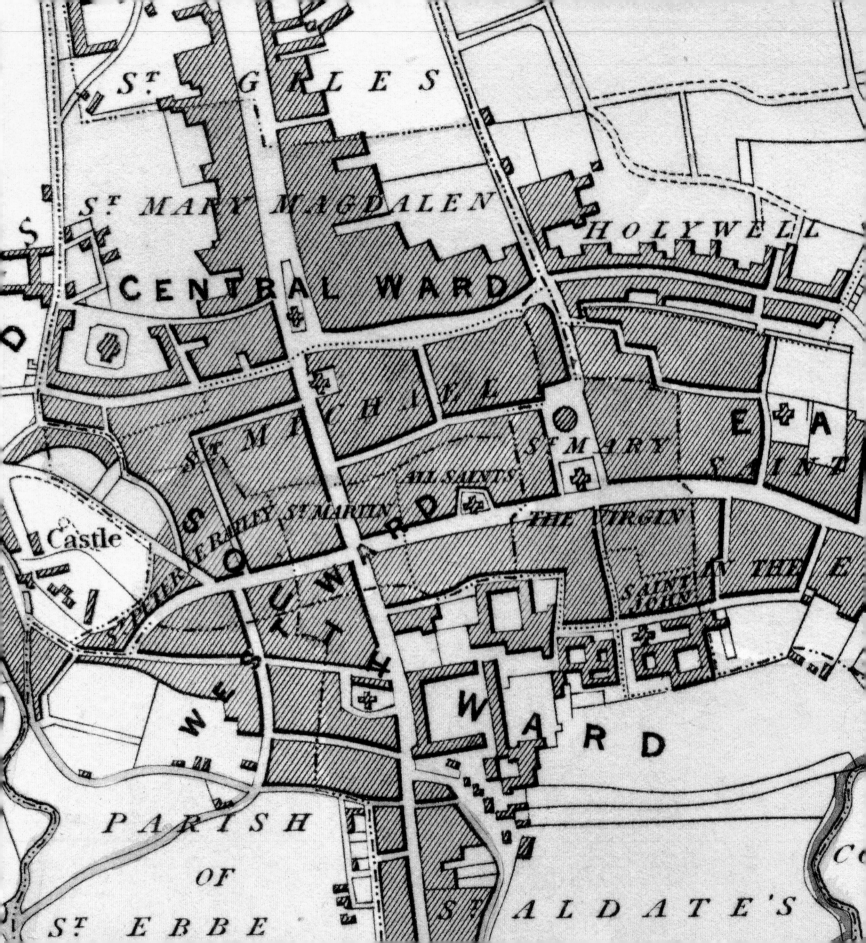

Contents

Opposite. Detail of Thomas Drummond/Robert Dawson, 'Oxford From the Ordnance Survey', from House of Commons, *Reports from commissioners on proposed division of counties and boundaries of boroughs* (1832)

CONTENTS

Introduction

Second only to London, the beautiful and strange city of Oxford occupies a central position in the history of England, despite never having been in the first rank of English settlements by age or size. By digging a great ditch from the Thames to the Cherwell, more or less along the line of present-day Broad Street, the Saxons were able to create a 'gravel island among the swamps', secure against all but the most determined assaults. By the late tenth century, when the Vikings attacked it with depressing regularity, Oxford was very much the crossroads of England: holding key positions on both the east–west land-borne trade routes between London and Gloucester, and the north–south ones between the Midlands and Southampton, to say nothing of the great highway that the Thames then was. Many of the nine million tourists who pass through the city each year suppose that it grew up around the castle or the university, but it is in fact several centuries older than either, for it had been the principal frontier town between the Saxon kingdoms of Mercia and Wessex, and more than that, 'the place where the hostile races of the land met to settle their differences' (A. Lang). It would remain on the border between the dioceses of Lincoln and Salisbury until the Reformation, and on the county boundary between Oxfordshire and Berkshire until 1974; and a sense of uncertainty regarding its precise regional identity will probably cling to it forever.

Through the 57 maps printed here, some of them for the first time, the city emerges not only as the scene of great triumphs of cartography, architecture, engineering, science, music, literature and drama, but of appalling squalor, overcrowding, terrible fires, drunkenness, disease, mob justice, political violence and religious bigotry. Oxford's wealth, defensibility, and tradition as an alternative capital of England dating back to the days of King Harold Harefoot also made it the target of military designs, domestic and foreign. This status as a stronghold, rallying point and target began long before the age of detailed city mapping – notably, in the twelfth-century civil war between Queen Maud and King Stephen – and continued right through it, as reflected in the maps we have included here from the Civil War of the 1640s and the Seven Years' War. The rise of the motorcar and aircraft industries in the early twentieth century added additional cherries to the cake, which Nazi and Soviet war planners were not slow to acknowledge.

Some maps of Oxford made for general wayfinding sought to support their sponsors by prompting consumers to visit certain businesses in the city while ignoring others. Many were created for even more specific objectives, ranging from

Opposite. Detail of Nathaniel Whittock, *Bird's-eye view of the University and City of Oxford* (1850)

the reform of parliamentary constituencies and the fair apportionment of revenue between rival railway companies to the explanation of cholera and fever epidemics, the planning of sewer systems and the battle against the Demon Drink. All such maps were valuable due as much to what they elided as what they included; indeed, a simple or even simplistic focus on a single issue was often what made a city map of this kind effective as communication, or propaganda.

As such, this book cannot present any triumphalist narrative based on ever-better surveying methods or ever-sharper detail. Even if we only consider those maps of Oxford that appear to have been made for 'general purposes' – which may mean merely that their main actual purpose can no longer be recaptured – the voyage from 'primitive' to 'modern' aesthetics and techniques was a circuitous one indeed. Down to the beginning of the Victorian era, the majority of makers of maps of the city adopted a precedent model that presumed the rightness of some or all of their forebears going right back to Radulph Aggas in the 1570s, rather than a more outward-looking vision based on the international cartographic norms of their own time. Thus in 1733 we see William Williams adopt a modern ichnographic (top-down) perspective, but keep south at the top of his map; and in 1751 and 1773, George Anderton and Barak Longmate II moving north to the top, but abandoning strict ichnography in favour of the inclusion of side views of places of worship, in the manner of Captain Sir Bernard de Gomme more than a century earlier. In the end, as we shall see, John Cleghorn [1837] simply shaded Anderton's churches in a deep black, preferring to pretend they were plan views – every one of them wrong – than to perpetuate such embarrassing early modern violations of the picture plane. Moreover, bird's-eye views of a type that was normal in the sixteenth and early seventeenth centuries have, in Oxford's case, continued to appear at regular

Oxford's walls, on its twelfth-century seal.

intervals from the 1670s down to the present day.

Historians of cartography, particularly since Brian Harley's seminal essay on the subject in 1988, have rightly concerned themselves with 'cartographic silences': the 'intentional or unintentional suppression of knowledge in maps', which may result from 'deliberate policies of secrecy and censorship' or from 'more indeterminate . . . hidden procedures or rules'. Though many and various such silences in the mapping of Oxford will be pointed out in the pages that follow, the profoundest 'silence' is the complete absence of any maps of the town during the first six centuries of its existence, except as tiny, stylised icons on maps of the entire country. The 1191 Common Seal of the town, which depicts its crenellated walls [inset], is unique in showing any building detail at all, improbable as this detail may be. Beginning in the nineteenth century, antiquarian scholars including H.E. Salter, C.W. Boase, and Herbert Hurst, and even the Wagner & Debes Geographical Establishment of Leipzig [1910], sought to redress this absence: publishing speculative maps – greatly varying in size and quality – of how Oxford might have been laid out at various specific points in previous ages.

As with any other human product, a book of this kind implies selectivity on many levels. Tempted as I was to include Benjamin Badcock's fine 1:3,200 map of the 1617 water conduit from Hinksey to Carfax (1821), for instance, I decided that the evolution of mapmaking must take priority over the history of the city per se. Logically, this also tends to rule out detailed treatment of the many avowedly 'retro' bird's-eye views of the city, many of them quite splendid, that were produced beginning with Robert Whittlesey's 1:2,520 reduction of Aggas, and including the striking late one by Nathaniel Whittock (1850) shown on pp. x and xiv. In recent years, '3-D' mapping – now with computer assistance – has again emerged at the cutting edge of cartography, often in combination with

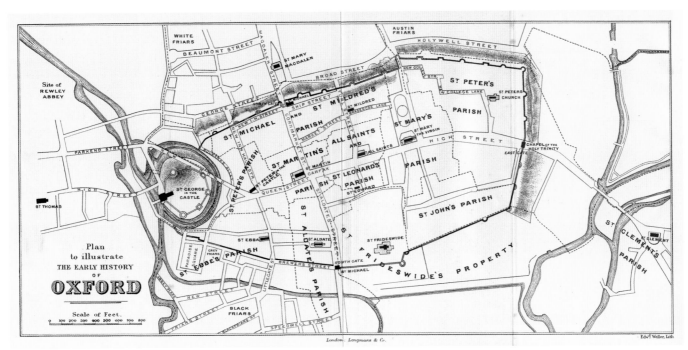

Published in 1887 in a book by Charles Boase, this map by Edward Weller overlays some key features of medieval Oxford on the city's modern streets, many of which had been renamed less than a century earlier. Queen Street was still known as Butcher Row Street and St Aldates as Fish Street in the late Georgian period, and in medieval times they were usually called Great Bailie and South Street, respectively. As such, the map seems intended to help Victorian scholars and tourists find their way to particular medieval sites, rather than to reconstruct the cultural landscape of the old town in any comprehensive way.

interactive features. But the medium-term future probably belongs to the intersection of mobile technology and inexpensive remote-sensor networks, as part of the so-called 'internet of things'; and one eminently practical example embodying such possibilities has been included as our final map.

As with any other place in Britain, detailed town plans of Oxford from the nineteenth century are so much more numerous than ones from all previous centuries combined (53 vs. 31, according to http://townmaps.data.history.ac.uk/) that a similar book of this size could readily have been written about maps of Victorian Oxford alone. In an effort to preserve some sort of balance across the 450 years during which any maps of the city have been created at all, I have perforce included the great majority of the known maps of Oxford dating from before the Restoration, while excluding the great majority produced from the accession of King George III onward: running the risk of creating an impression that early maps of Oxford were more common, or later ones rarer, than is really the case. Ordnance Survey maps, in particular, are consciously under-represented as being already very well known and readily accessible elsewhere. However, even within the pre-1660 period, I chose to omit a well-known 1643 bird's-eye view of the city by Wenceslaus Hollar (1607–1677), due to its striking inaccuracy vis-à-vis both the written records of building and other, visually similar but far more accurate views by Aggas [1578] and David Loggan [1673].

Inevitably, given that the twentieth-century city of Oxford came to include not just the medieval city and its suburbs but a large number of pre-existing villages on both sides of the Oxfordshire/Berkshire boundary, as well as a fairly distant

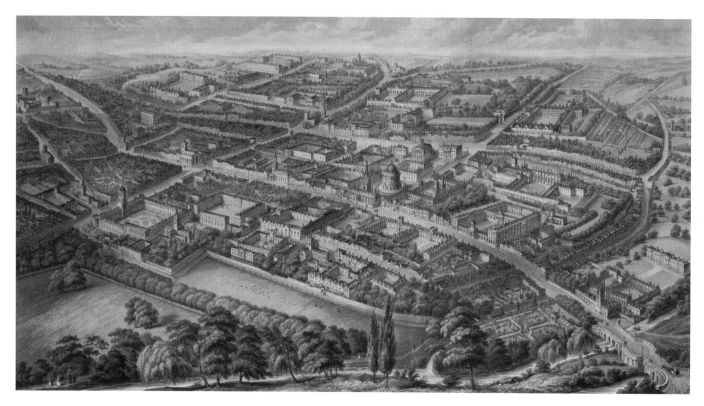

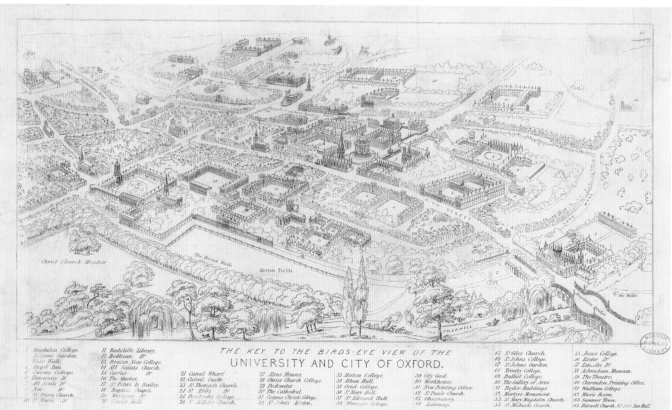

THE KEY TO THE BIRDS-EYE VIEW OF THE
UNIVERSITY AND CITY OF OXFORD.

1 Magdalen College.
2 Botanic Garden.
3 Water Walk.
4 Angel Inn.
5 Queens College.
6 University D.º
7 All Souls D.º
8 New D.º
9 S.t Peters Church.
10 S.t Marys D.º

11 Radcliffe Library.
12 Bodleian D.º
13 Brazen Nose College.
14 All Saints Church.
15 Carfax D.º
16 The Market.
17 S.t Peters le Bailey.
18 Baptist Chapel.
19 Wesleyan D.º
20 County Hall.

21 Canal Wharf.
22 Oxford Castle.
23 S.t Thomas's Church.
24 S.t Ebbs D.º
25 Pembroke College.
26 S.t Aldate's Church.

27 Alms Houses.
28 Christ Church College.
29 Peckwater.
30 The Cathedral.
31 Corpus Christi College.
32 S.t Johns Merton.

33 Merton College.
34 Alban Hall.
35 Oriel College.
36 S.t Mary Hall.
37 S.t Edmund Hall.
38 Worcester College.

39 City Goal.
40 Workhouse.
41 New Printing Office.
42 S.t Pauls Church.
43 Observatory.
44 Infirmary.

45 S.t Giles Church.
46 S.t Johns College.
47 S.t Johns Garden.
48 Trinity College.
49 Balliol College.
50 The Gallery of Arts.
51 Taylor Buildings.
52 Martyrs Monument.
53 S.t Mary Magdalen Church.
54 S.t Michaels Church.

55 Jesus College.
56 Exeter D.º
57 Lincoln D.º
58 Ashmolean Museum.
59 The Theatre.
60 Clarendon Printing Office.
61 Wadham College.
62 Music Room.
63 Holywell Church. 64 New Inn Hall.

Christ Church Meadow. The Broad Walk. Merton Fields. THE CHERWELL.

airport, the selection process raised the philosophical question of 'What is the city?', alongside the more usual question associated with projects of this kind, 'What is a map?' As with *Edinburgh: Mapping the City*, published in this series in 2014, a wide-net approach was chosen. On the city side, I have included a small selection of maps of places like Wolvercote and Iffley before their incorporation into Oxford either physically or legally, where doing so tended to provide important information about cartographic practices or the socioeconomic state of Oxford's hinterland. On the map side, we have again adopted the international History of Cartography project's definition of 'mapping', as 'graphic representations that facilitate a spatial understanding of things, concepts, conditions, processes, or events in the human world'. Oxford's astonishing concentration of fine buildings by great architects raises a further philosophical question: 'At what point does a map become so large-scale that it is essentially architectural rather than cartographic?' In the end, just a few such plans were chosen for inclusion, where they illustrated aspects of life in the city that would otherwise be difficult to convey: from storing the Victorian army's explosives, to protecting the Natural History Museum from thrill-seeking roof-climbers, to defending the St Clement's Street Car Park against public acts of homosexuality.

It is deeply regrettable that, for reasons of space and coherence, we have not been able to include maps of places other than Oxford that were created by the city's people. By the late sixteenth century, Oxford had begun producing towering figures in the international development of geography and cartography, including Richard Hakluyt (d.1616), William Camden (1551–1623), John Norden (d.1625), Thomas Pennant (1726–1798), Daines Barrington (d.1800), Hereford George (1838–1910), Sir Halford Mackinder (1861–1947) and the aforementioned Brian Harley (1932–1991). Cartography and exploration were often combined in the same person – for example, the fascinating Margaret Lowthian Bell CBE (1868–1926), who with her fellow Oxford graduate Lawrence of Arabia (1888–1935) helped establish the modern Kingdom of Jordan. It may be

Oxford has no equivalent to this diagrammatic view of Bristol drawn by its town clerk, Robert Ricart, in 1479. Indeed, no other pre-Tudor bird's-eye views or plans of English towns are known to exist.

for this reason that so many fine maps have been produced of the fictional worlds written in, or inspired by, the city: by J.R.R. Tolkien, C.S. Lewis, Philip Pullman and others. In this context, special mention is due to Pauline Baynes (1922–2008), who attended the Slade School of Art during its wartime evacuation to Oxford and, after a stint making Admiralty charts, mapped Middle Earth and Narnia for their respective creators.

The date provided at the top of each chapter is the date of survey rather than the date of publication, where the former can be determined. In the case of maps whose surveys took place over multiple years, e.g. de Gomme [1646] and Rocque [1761], the date shown is that of the survey's completion rather than its commencement. Publication dates, where known, are given at the foot of the first page of each chapter.

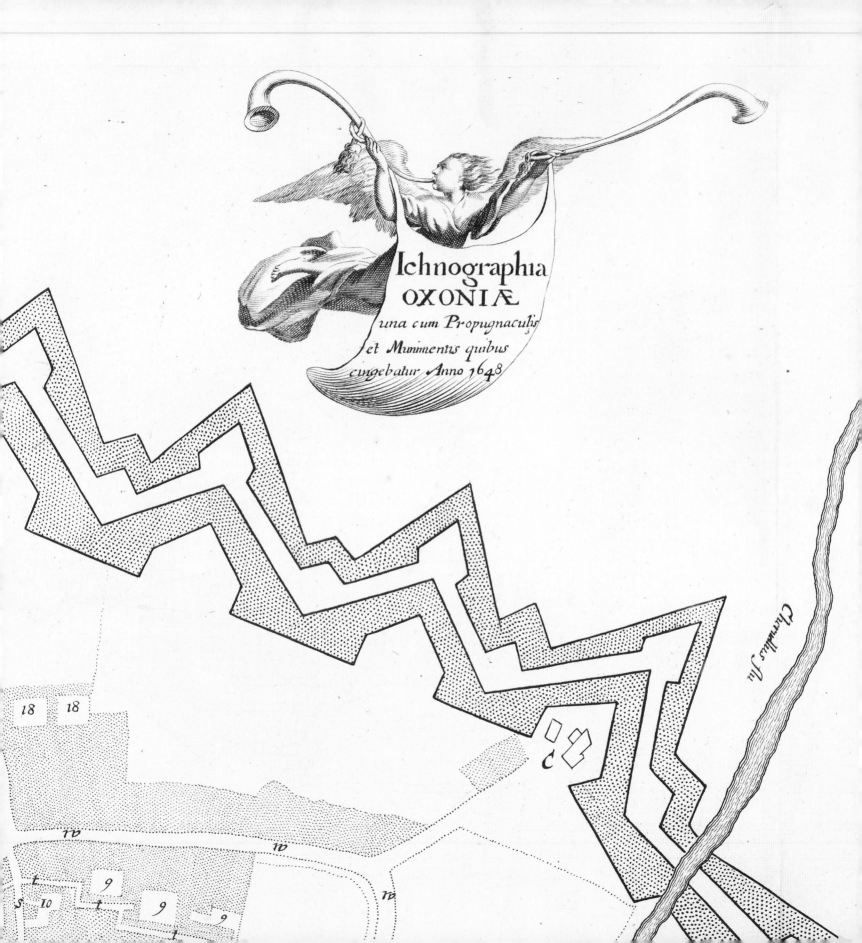

Ichnographia
OXONIÆ
una cum Propugnaculis
et Munimentis quibus
cingebatur Anno 1648

18   18

9

9   9

10

Charwellus Fl.

Acknowledgements

In a project of this complexity, thanks are due to a large number of people. First and foremost, I would like to thank Hugh Andrew of Birlinn Ltd for creating the *Mapping the City* series and inviting me to participate in it not once, but twice; to Christopher Fleet, Philip Schwyzer and Jason MacCannell, my chief mentors in matters geographic and cartographic; and to Birlinn's Andrew Simmons for his indefatigable sorting-out of problems technical, financial and administrative on the image side. I am grateful to my wife Eleanor MacCannell for consulting on various aspects of image selection and story emphasis, and to Anna Brown and Juliet Flower MacCannell for reading early drafts of the manuscript. For advice and help with more specific questions, I am also deeply grateful to Rob Braam, Peter Davidson, Lesel Dawson, Max Edelson, Tom Freshwater, Anemone Linthorst, Bryan Marshall, Henry Miller, Sue Minnick Gathman and Ben Ward; Sarah Boada-Momtahan and Phil Marston of Sanders of Oxford; David Hodgkinson of the Warwickshire Record Office; all the staff of the Oxfordshire History Centre, the British Motor Museum and the National Archives; and Lucy Warwick and Helen Gilio of the Bodleian Library. Any errors or omissions, however, remain my responsibility alone.

Opposite. Detail of Anthony à Wood, 'Ichnographia Oxonia una cum Propugnaculis bet Munimentus quibus cungebatur Anno 1648', from *Historia et Antiquitates Universitatis Oxoniensis, duobus Voluminibus comprehensae* (1674)

OXONIVM *nobile Angliæ oppidum, Septentrionalem Tamefis ripam elegantißimo atque falubri fitu illus trat.*

Depingeb. Georg. Hoef: nagle.

1568

The city meets the world

The second of the six volumes of the bestselling and enormously influential *Civitates Orbis Terrarum* ('Towns of the world') was printed in 1575 and included Oxford's first appearance in what we would now call an atlas. The use of the term 'atlas' for such books would not become current until 20 years later, however, with the publication in Duisburg of Gerard Mercator's *Atlas Sive Cosmographicae Meditationes de Fabrica Mundi et Fabricati Figura* ('Atlas or cosmographical meditations upon the creation of the universe, and the universe as created'), which despite its lofty title focused heavily on England.

Surviving medieval maps that depict the British Isles often have east at the top, perhaps reflecting the importance of the Holy Land in the geographical thought of the time. But this representational tradition (if indeed it ever was one) was soon broken as Renaissance publishers came to focus on counties, cities and various other sub-components of nations. Certainly, a northward-looking perspective has not been adopted for either of the views seen here, printed from copper plates based on drawings by Antwerp-born Joris Hoefnagel (1542-c.1600). The son of a wealthy diamond merchant, Hoefnagel was educated in France and spent much of his life in Spain, Germany and Austria, but is known to have visited England in 1568. His original Oxford picture – in brown ink and black chalk, and gridded for transfer to the plate – survives in the Royal Collection, and can be presumed to have been drawn from life at that time. In content, it differs little from the printed version shown here. A lively, unique and invaluable general impression of the city in the first decade of the reign of Queen Elizabeth I, it looks westward from a southerly part of Headington Hill, probably within the area of the present-

Joris Hoefnagel, 'Oxonium' and 'Uindesorium', from Georg Braun and Franz Hogenberg, *Civitates Orbis Terrarum*, vol. 2 (1575)

day South Park, and tends to reinforce Hoefnagel's reputation as an accurate recorder of cityscapes.

Proceeding from left to right, the first major building we see is the steepled tower of Christ Church Cathedral, as medieval St Frideswide's Church had been renamed just one generation earlier. It was not the city's first Anglican cathedral, however, as twelfth-century Osney Abbey – too far to the west of the city to be seen here – was accorded the same honour for a very brief period. Next, we see two flat-topped towers with small Gothic pinnacles at the corners. The first and more distant of these is the 1450 Great Tower of Merton College Chapel, and the larger/nearer one the Magdalen College Bell Tower, constructed beginning in 1492. The complex of walls and towers on a massive earthen mound, visible between Merton and Magdalen, is intended to represent Oxford's Norman castle, begun in 1071 by Robert D'Oyly on what was then the far western edge of the town.

Moving rightward from Magdalen to the foreground's pair of entwined trees, we see three roughly equidistant towers: the first two with steeples and the third flat-topped. The steeples belong to the parish churches of All Saints and St Mary the Virgin, both located along the north side of the High Street [p. xiii]. They appear to the right of Magdalen – which

is east of them, and also on the north side – due to that street's two significant changes of direction (that is, from west-southwest/east-northeast from Carfax to Queen's College, then west-northwest/east-southeast from Queen's to the city's East Gate, and then nearly northwest/southeast from the gate to the bridge over the River Cherwell). The flat-topped tower to the right of Mary the Virgin may then represent the Church of St Peter in the East; and the more massive square tower to the right of the same trees, a part of the city's defensive walls, which were particularly elaborate at their northeastern corner.

However, it must be said that positively identifying anything to the right of Mary the Virgin in this picture would be difficult at best, with the specific appearance of the ecclesiastical building immediately to the left of the bearded figure's outstretched hand being especially problematic. From its position alone, it might conceivably be St Cross Church, though that church's single, stumpy, battlemented tower, completed in 1464, could hardly look less like this one. Indeed, Hoefnagel's structure so resembles the abovementioned Osney Abbey that it has led a number of casual observers to incorrectly assume that his view was drawn from the north or northwest rather than the east. Such misidentifications are aided by the absence from the middle ground of the two

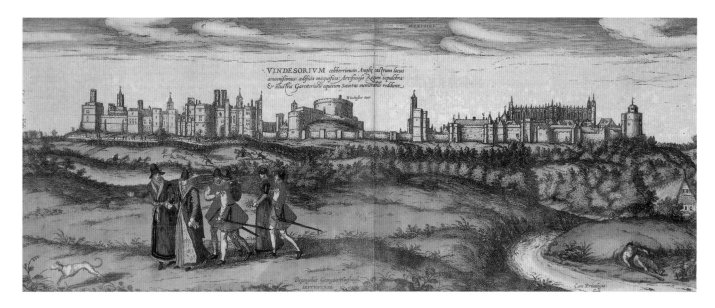

streams of the River Cherwell and the arrow-straight, 500-foot-long medieval stone bridge that spanned them until the later eighteenth century [1724]. In Hoefnagel's defence, however, the current bridge [1771] is never visible in modern photographs taken from this precise angle. J.M.W. Turner's *View of Oxford from the South Side of Heddington Hill* (1803–04) does show it, but Turner positioned himself at the extreme northern edge of South Park, and he therefore has Merton's tower peeking out from behind Magdalen's on the latter's right-hand side.

Publisher/editor Braun's brief commentary to this illustration focused on three main themes: the beauty of Oxford's site on the northern bank of the Thames, the healthfulness of the location and its abundance of food, and the fame of the city's university among Europe's educated classes. All of this carefully elided the steep commercial decline of the town since the Black Death and the Hundred Years' War, which had drastically curtailed its role in the wine trade between Southampton and the Midlands; the fact that the university was still casting about for a role in the chaotic aftermath of the Reformation; and that the Thames between Oxford and London had not been fully navigable in perhaps 200 years, and would not be reopened to barge traffic until 1635. Nevertheless, apart from

Oxford, Windsor and London, the only English towns deemed worthy of inclusion in the atlas were Canterbury, Bristol, Norwich, York, Exeter, Cambridge, Chester, Lancaster, Richmond and Shrewsbury – a blunt reminder of the critical importance of the industrial revolution to the size and location of our major population centres in more recent times. The non-European component of Braun's 'world', meanwhile, was limited to Morocco, Mexico and Peru.

It is tempting to read the colours of roofs as representing a variety of building materials – blue for slate or lead, yellow for thatch and so forth. But it should be borne in mind that the colour was applied to copies of *Civitates* after printing and by a variety of hands. I have seen half a dozen coloured copies of this plate, no two of them with the roofs coloured in a similar way; and Hoefnagel's original drawing is strictly brown-and-white, lacking even shading. However, thatched roofs and wooden chimneys could still be seen in Oxford in 1582, when an unsuccessful attempt was made to ban both.

It was Braun's idea to include human figures in each plate, albeit for military rather than educational or decorative purposes. The Turks, he reasoned, could not glean military secrets from his *Civitates* because they were barred by their religion from viewing depictions of the human form.

1578

A 'prodigy' map of a city on the brink of revival

For more than a century, cartographic depictions of the city of Oxford would be overshadowed by this striking and enormous map. Engraved in the year of the Armada by Augustine Ryther (d.1593), one of the first Englishmen to become internationally prominent in a field dominated by the Flemish, it is based on a drawing by Suffolk-born surveyor Radulph Aggas (c.1540–1621). Stylistically, it occupies a distinctive middle position between the inescapable flatness of 'stacked' medieval town views like Robert Ricart's Bristol [p. xv] or John Hooker's mid sixteenth-century Exeter, on the one hand, and true bird's-eye views that make a systematic use of perspective. Victorian author Herbert Hurst classified Aggas's Oxford a bird's-*flight* view, on the grounds that it 'gives us parallel lines only' rather than 'perspectives and vanishing points'. Certainly, its very size – four folio sheets in width and two in height – makes it difficult to process as a single object without losing sight of the details, each of which taken in isolation makes a sort of perspectival sense: quite as if the viewer is slowly floating across the city at a relatively low altitude, rather than viewing it from a single fixed point.

Though much larger in scale and therefore much richer in detail, Aggas's map is, perspective-wise, probably most similar to the map of London that was published in the initial (1572) volume of Braun and Hogenberg's *Civitates* [1568]. A *c.*1562 woodcut map of London on which Braun and Hogenberg based theirs was long said to have been surveyed by Aggas, but this is no longer believed; by Aggas's own account, his career began only in 1566, so the influence may well have operated in the other direction. The now-normal ichnographic style of mapping, in which all elements are seen as if directly from above, was in its infancy in the England of the 1570s, being applied mainly to fortified seaports. The

Radulph Aggas/Augustine Ryther, *Celeberrimae Oxoniensis academie avlarvm et collegiorvm aedificiis totivs Evropae magnificentissimis cvm antiqvissima civitate conivnctae* . . . (1588)

The map's scale, explained by the messenger of the gods.

The North Gate area, with Jesus College at upper left.

printing of English town maps was also a novelty, which had begun as recently as 1559 with Norwich, second city of the Tudor kingdom in terms of population size.

The precise nature of Aggas's relationship with Ryther is unknown. The latter may have intended his prodigious engraving of Aggas's Oxford principally as an advertisement of what he – and secondarily, the crafts of engraving and printing – could achieve. Certainly, the British Isles had no shop specialising in printed pictures before 1599, implying that the 'market' for works like Ryther's at the turn of the 1580s to 1590s was vanishingly small. Given this map's prestige value and the vast amount of meticulous labour it involved, the fact that only one impression has survived – out of a total of just three mentioned in the historical record – may indicate that only a handful were produced in the first place.

In his relatively brief but varied career, Ryther would engrave two county maps for Christopher Saxton, as well as Saxton's map of England; Robert Adams's ten charts of the 1588 Spanish invasion attempt and its aftermath; and the earliest known set of geography-themed playing cards. Responding to sharp growth in demand for surveying instruments, Ryther turned his hand to designing them and was the first of many scientific-instrument makers to become a freeman of the Worshipful Company of Grocers, second oldest of the City of London's livery companies. Shortly before he died, he engraved the nine copper plates used to print John Hamond's immense map of Cambridge.

Aggas's pretensions to exactitude were numerous and varied. He specified that this map was produced to a scale of 1:1,800 (i.e. 1 inch to 30 paces of 60 inches). Mercury, messenger of the Roman gods, is depicted wielding a gigantic pair of compasses, and beside him lies a monstrous ruler marked with perches or poles (5½ yards), paces (5 feet), and ells (the ¾ pace or '¾ yard' of 45 inches). Between 8 and 22 inches longer than the ells used in other European countries, including Scotland, the English ell was standardised around the time this map was made, via a brass version deposited

Greate Bailie and the Castle.

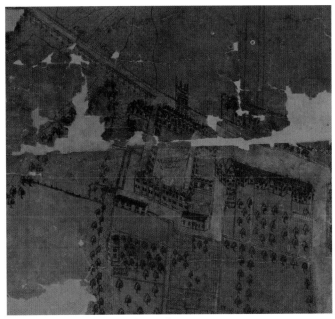

The East Bridge and Magdalen College.

with the Exchequer. Such actions were a further indication of the rapidly growing cultural and legal importance of exact measurement at this time, which from the early 1570s also led to a flurry of publications for surveyors, including Aggas's own *A Preparative to the Platting of Landes* (1596) which advocated the use of theodolites. (Maps were commonly referred to as 'platts', and less frequently 'platforms', in Elizabethan times.) However, close study of Aggas's Oxford shows it to be mostly inaccurate with respect to east–west, north–south, diagonal and vertical distances. In the majority of cases, he under-reported the distances between features by around 12 per cent. If this were the only error, it could be blamed on the use of an instrument that was inaccurate by a like amount. In a minority of cases, however, Aggas *over*-reported distances by a roughly similar amount, and in yet others, e.g. the lengths of St Mary the Virgin and the west front of Oriel College, he got it exactly right. Only haste or inattention could readily explain this combination of problems.

On the other hand, the sparse to non-existent appearance of Jesus College, founded in 1571, reflects the reality of the slow pace of construction there. The college took over the buildings of the medieval, academically defunct Great White Hall, which can be seen along the northwestern i.e. lower right part of 'Cheyney Lane', now Market Street, where it meets 'North Streate', and did not demolish it until its first quadrangle was built in the 1620s. On the whole, the appearance and placement of the buildings on the Jesus site can be taken as evidence that Aggas's survey was made before 1580; and this, combined with the allusion in the engraved map's text to his having completed it 'Neare tenn yeares paste', has led to the traditional dating of it to 1578.

More usually called North*gate* Street in the sixteenth and seventeenth centuries, North Street came to be known as Cornmarket by the early eighteenth, though grain had been sold in it since the time of Henry VIII, in a purpose-built structure invisible here due to damage. It was presumably comparable to the butchers' buildings that can be seen running down the middle of 'Greate Bailie', later called Butcher Row

Ryther's mannerist cartouche and extensive use of heraldry reflect the fashions of the age.

on the same principle as Cornmarket, and now Queen Street. In a city where most street names have changed once or twice since Aggas's day, Wood Street – so called for its timber yards – may win the prize for 'most renamed': now St Michael's Street, having been at various times Bedford Street, Bocardo Lane and an arm of New Inn Hall Street, as well as plain Michael Street.

The siting of churches just inside cities' gates was a Saxon tradition. Dating from 1040, the tower of St Michael at the North Gate is Oxford's oldest surviving building. Nothing now remains of its opposite number, St Michael at the South Gate, which was demolished during the initial building of Christ Church – still open on its north side in this view – in the early sixteenth century. It has been speculated that Oxford, like some other Saxon planned towns of its age, was originally square, with the west and east gates located near the churches of St Peter-le-Bailey and St Mary the Virgin, respectively, and that the walled area of the town then expanded dramatically in the early eleventh century, but in the east–west dimension only.

Though a southwestern candidate has also been proposed [c.1600], on balance it is likely that the original oxen-ford for which Oxford was named was located directly to the south of the city, on an important trade route to Southampton. A 'great causeway' certainly existed on the southern approach by the late eleventh century, and possibly hundreds of years earlier. Unlike Hoefnagel's [1568], Aggas's perspective is able to show us 'well-spaced dwellings and vacant plots, streets with few houses, and large gardens and orchards within the walls' (A. Crossley). As pleasant as this may seem to us today, it could have signalled to contemporaries that both the city and university had declined since the fifteenth century. This going-to-seed aspect is particularly evident in the southeastern (top left) part of the city, which had been packed with both academic and non-academic structures in medieval times. It is fascinating to compare this map directly against David Loggan's [1673], which following a century of population growth and economic expansion shows not just the filling in of gaps in street frontages, but building in what had been back gardens, as well as dramatic increases in house-heights.

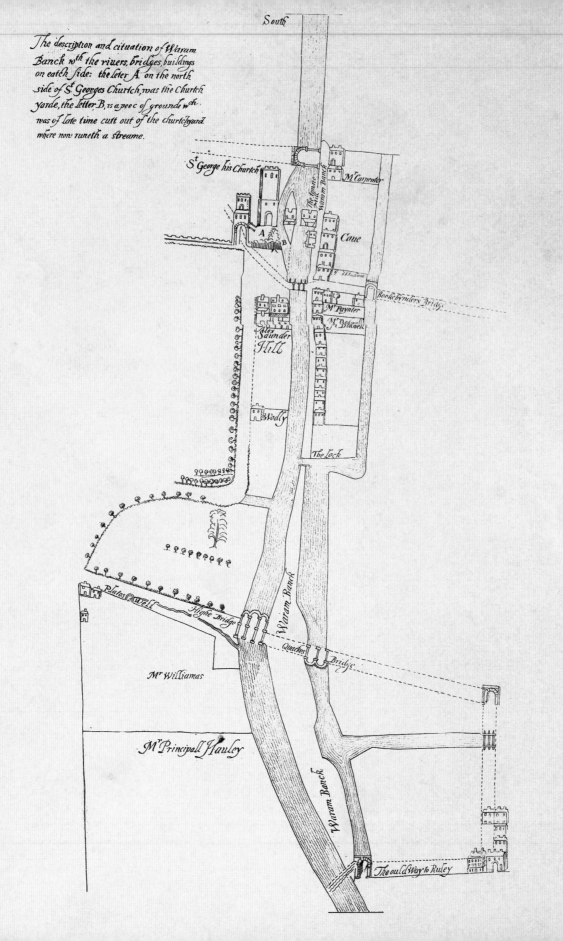

South

The description and cituation of Waram
Banck wth the riuers, bridges, buildings
on eatch side: the leter A on the north
side of St Georges Church, was the Church
yarde, the leter B, is a peec of grounde w^ch
was of late time cutt out of the churchyard
where non runeth a streame.

St George his Church

Mr Carpenter

The Ipnni...
Mill
Waram Banck

Caue

A
B

Bookebynders Bridg

Mr Paynter

Mr Bodenell

Alex Saunder
Hill

Wodly

The Lock

Waram Banck

Plates Well

Highe Bridge

Waram Banck

Quaches Bridge

Mr Williamas

Mr Principall Hauley

Waram Banck

The ould Way to Ruley

c. 1600

Fish, beer and God in the city's watery west

It would be hard to exaggerate the importance of the intricate local river systems to the development of the city of Oxford, not just strategically but economically: by powering mills, providing food in the form of fish and wildfowl, and serving as a highway for heavy goods. The small western suburb of Waram Banck, in the shadow of the city's Norman castle, developed on the Castle Mill Stream in the first half of the twelfth century: not as early as the settlements outside the north and south gates, but perhaps a century before St Clement's in the east. One of several plausible candidates for the original oxen-ford over the Thames that gave Oxford its name was connected to the city proper via an ancient road from Hinksey along much of the present route of Osney Lane, ending at the unnamed topmost/southernmost bridge shown here. Now called the Swan Bridge, after the eighteenth-century Swan's Nest Brewery in Paradise Street (which in turn may

have been named after a much earlier inn or tavern of the same name), this bridge was in the Jacobean period a rickety and unloved structure, almost as old as the castle itself, and known as Castle Mill Bridge.

Certainly dateable to no earlier than 1593, when John Hawley was first named Principal of Gloucester Hall, this wonderfully detailed map is a snapshot of the development of city beyond its walls to the west, complete with details of who owned which buildings and lands at the time – known in cartographic parlance as cadastral information. It is also certainly from before 1617, when a similar map by a less skilful hand was prepared in connection with the sale of Oxford Castle [1605]. Unlike the present map – which shows a long unbuilt-on gap between the two houses owned by Mr Carpenter and four smaller ones nearer the road carried by Bookebynders Bridge – the later map shows Waram Banck Street as a contin-

Anon., *The description and cituation of Waram Banck w[i]th the riuers, bridges, buildings on eatch side . . .* (n.d.)

uous line of nine houses in which Carpenter's two are included. The later map also shows Wodly's place on the east bank as having two neighbouring houses immediately to its north; and at the northeast corner of Highe Bridge, it places an imposing two- or three-storey building that the present map omits altogether. The only detail that might tend to suggest that the present map is later than the Castle-sale map is that the former shows 13 houses in the rectangle bounded by the Bookebynders Bridge road and the Lock, where the Castle-sale map has just six; but this discrepancy could have resulted from a relative lack of interest in this patch of the district on the part of either or both surveyors, or a rebuilding of small wooden cottages as larger, more permanent structures.

Though this map's houses are fairly realistic and given a high degree of individuality as regards both appearance and size, the bridges are more schematic. Certainly, the height and overall appearance of the late fourteenth-century High Bridge, whose name was pedantically re-medievalised to 'Hythe Bridge' only in the nineteenth century, are much more realistically shown in Loggan's magnificent 1:3,265 view of the entire city [1673]. The here-unlabelled Quaking Bridge, marking a route even older than the castle between Oxford and its eastern suburb of St Thomas, is shown correctly as being made of wood, though the specific design again seems implausible. Bookebynders Bridge was named after 'an adjoining tenement . . . occupied by monastic bookbinders' in the fourteenth century (C.J. Day).

Waram was a corruption of *wara*, a medieval Latin term for weir. Confusingly, the name Waram Banck had three overlapping topographical applications: to the long island that divides the Castle Mill Stream into two parts; to a street near the south/top of the map, clearly labelled 'Waram Banck' here, but known as Fisher Row from the middle of the seventeenth century and as Lower Fisher Row today; and to the whole neighbourhood. Interestingly, both branches of the stream are termed 'riuers' by the map's author or owner, perhaps indicating that one or both of them were navigable even to the south of the Hythe Bridge timber-wharf at this date, though there is no positive evidence that this was the case.

The houses shown here on the western side of the future Fisher Row, or at any rate the smaller ones whose owners' names are not given, are thought to have been occupied 'by fishermen fishing for the Oxford market' (J. Cooper), though we can surmise from Chaucer's 'The Miller's Tale' that some craftsmen in the neighbourhood were renting out rooms to students. Apart from fishermen, occupants in the early seventeenth century included 'watermen, boatmen, bargemen, maltsters and brewers' (W.A. Pantin).

The apparently dry land on the west/right side of the map across Bookebynders Bridge and Quackes Bridge (not to be confused with *Quaking* Bridge, the unnamed wooden structure a short way from the castle gateway) is in fact another, much larger island: Osney or Oseney, home to the twelfth-century Augustinian abbey of the same name [1568]. In 1539, at the dissolution of the monasteries, the abbey had been heavily involved in cloth-making, as evidenced by its water-powered fulling-mills and gig-mills, which were leased to a succession of clothiers between the 1540s and the 1580s by the site's new owners, Christ Church. The water for the abbey's first mills was provided by a weir on the other side of Osney Island, and a later arrangement may be shown here: as diagonal dashed lines at the far northern/bottom tip of Waram Banck island.

As opposed to college-owned buildings used merely as a source of rental income, structures actually in use for educational purposes were notable by their absence from the western end of Oxford at this date. The most imposing building in this map, St George's Tower, was built in 1074 immediately to the southwest of the castle's ten-sided keep, and replaced the city's original west gate. It also served as a church, known initially as 'St George's College'. This name did not reflect any educational function, but that it was a live-in facility for multiple priests; and it was this group-residence aspect that led to the same name being applied to higher-education institutions of subsequent centuries.

Following the dashed lines from Bookebynders Bridge to the west/right would shortly bring a traveller to St Thomas's Church: one of the lowest-lying sites in Oxford and very often

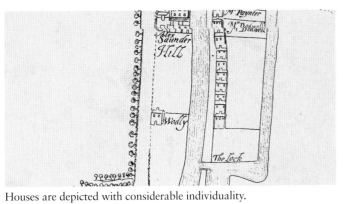

Houses are depicted with considerable individuality.

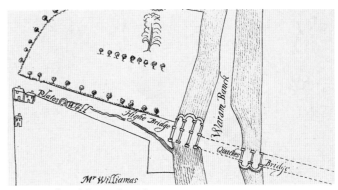

Plato's Well and the High Bridge.

flooded, it was originally co-dedicated to Nicholas of Myra, the patron saint of sailors. Here seemingly devoid of habitations (but compare Aggas [1578]), this route was in fact highly developed and prosperous, to the point that it was called the High Street of St Thomas – one of the city's wealthiest areas by the 1520s, in spite of or perhaps because of its extramural location. It is now simply St Thomas Street, presumably to avoid confusion with the walled city's own High Street a quarter-mile to the east. The 'Ould Way to Ruley' is an allusion to one of the other great monastic houses of the medieval Oxford area, thirteenth-century Rewley Abbey [map, p. xiii]. Like Osney Abbey, it deteriorated with painful slowness for centuries, at first becoming 'malthouses or a brewery' (H. Hurst).

Many of us view the inland waterways of England through Kenneth Grahame-tinted glasses and tend to forget that in the period depicted, 'cluttered up by mills and fish-garths . . . intersected by weirs – sometimes up to ten feet high' or 'infested by river pirates' (H.J. Dyos and D.H. Aldcroft), with dangerous flash-locks, shifting shoals and shifty individuals claiming to be toll-takers and constables, they were difficult and often frightening places. As conflicts between and among watermill-operators, weir-owners and travellers on the river were the subject of frequent and acrimonious Elizabethan and Jacobean lawsuits, it is possible that this map was produced in the context of a legal dispute, presumably involving the new channel of the Castle Mill Stream that is

shown as having been recently cut through St George's churchyard. But the fault was not always on the side of the Castle Mill: Osney and Rewley, as soon as they were turned over to industrial purposes, were both 'often charged with stealing water that should feed the City mill' (Hurst).

Plato's Well was a new, Tudor-era name for the magical healing well that had previously been known as Corn Well, Cornwall, Chough Well and finally Stockwell. North–south-running Stockwell Street, just to the left/east of the three tiny houses on Mr Williamas's land, was named for the well. The street then gradually became known as Worcester Street once Gloucester Hall – just beyond the lower left corner of this map – was re-founded as Worcester College in 1714.

When Fisher Row was all but completely demolished in the mid 1950s, archaeologists found no houses there from earlier than 1658, reflecting the 'very extensive process of rebuilding that was [then] going on . . . at Oxford and indeed throughout the country' (Pantin). The area depicted in this map ceased to be used for navigation once Daniel Harris [1838] built the Isis or 'Louse' Lock in the mid 1790s, after which boats could move directly between the Thames and the Oxford–Coventry Canal [1768] along the Sheepwash Channel. Quackes Bridge later became known as Little Hythe Bridge. The current, iron incarnations of Quaking Bridge and Hythe Bridge were built in 1835 and 1861, respectively, while the most recent of several major reconstructions of the Swan Bridge was in 1895.

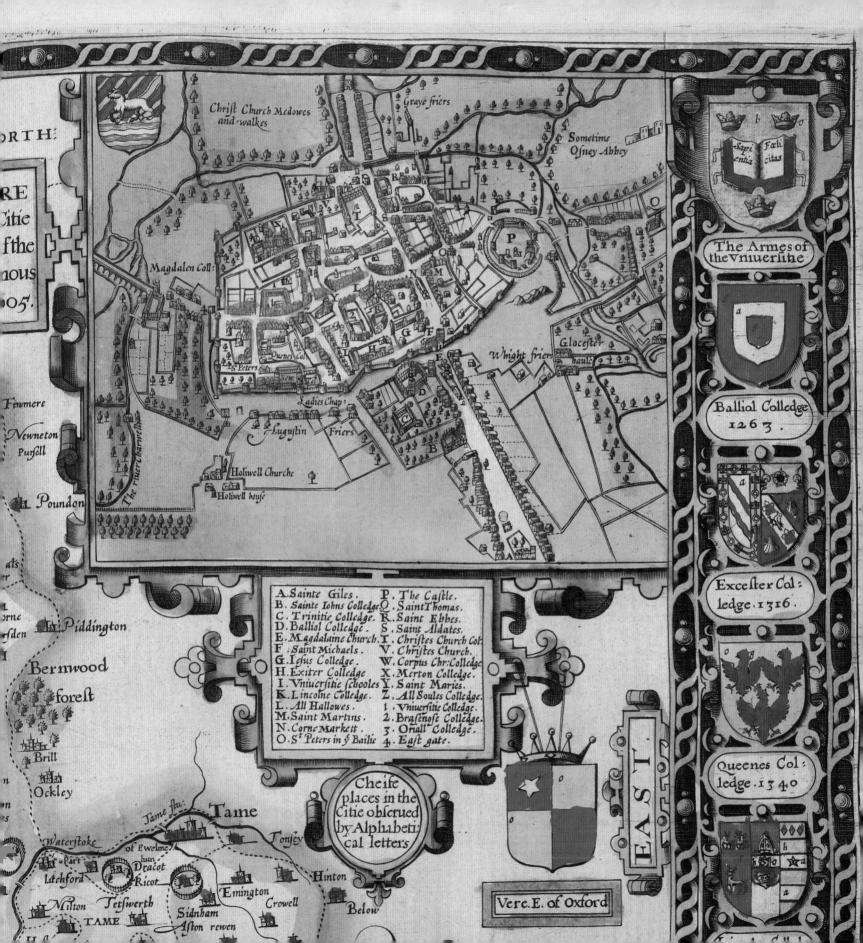

ORTH:

RE
itie
f the
ous
505.

Finmere

Newneton
Purfell

Poundon

Bernwood
forest

Piddington

Brill

Ockley

Tame flu.   Tame

Waterstoke

of Ewelme
hun Dracot
latchford   Ricot

Milton   Tetfwerth
TAME   Sidnham
Afton rewen

Emington   Hinton
Crowell

Below

Christ Church Medowes
and walkes

Graye friers

Sometime
Ofney Abbey

Magdalen Coll:

Glocester
haule

Whight friers

Quenes Col:

S. Peters

Ladies Chap:

Augustin   Friers

Holiwell Churche

Holiwell house

The river Charwell

A. Sainte Giles.   P. The Castle.
B. Sainte Iohns Colledge.   Q. Saint Thomas.
C. Trinitie Colledge.   R. Saint Ebbes.
D. Balliol Colledge.   S. Saint Aldates.
E. Magdalaine Church.   T. Christes Church Col:
F. Saint Michaels.   V. Christes Church.
G. Iesus Colledge.   W. Corpus Chr: Colledge.
H. Exiter Colledge.   X. Merton Colledge.
I. Vniuerfitie fchooles.   Y. Saint Maries.
K. Lincolne Colledge.   Z. All Soules Colledge.
L. All Hallowes.   1. Vniuerfitie Colledge.
M. Saint Martins.   2. Brafenofe Colledge.
N. Corne Markett.   3. Oriall Colledge.
O. St Peters in ye Bailie. 4. East gate.

Cheife
places in the
Citie obferued
by Alphabeti:
cal letters

EAST

Vere. E. of Oxford

The Armes of
the Vniuerfitie

Balliol Colledge
1263.

Excefter Col:
ledge. 1316.

Queenes Col:
ledge. 1340

1605

Shakespeare's Oxford

After 1603, the favour shown by the new royal house of Stuart to Oxford University – as against Cambridge University – was immediate and strong. The feeling was mutual: Oxford's celebration of the publication of King James's *Works* was 'elaborate', and Cambridge's 'perfunctory' (K. Fincham). In August 1605 the king, Queen Anna and their eldest son Prince Henry visited Oxford for four days and attended a series of plays acted by members of several colleges. The theatre set up in Christ Church on this occasion is thought to have made the first use of perspective scenery in the history of English drama. It was only in the following generation that undergraduates were required to obtain special permission before exhibiting 'rope-dancers, actors, [or] shows of gladiators' – and the quality of their performances may have suffered. Following a theatrical performance for the royal family at Christ Church in 1636, one courtier remarked that William Strode's play *The*

Floating Island was the worst he had ever seen, 'except one at Cambridge'.

Clearly, early Stuart Oxford had its fun side. But one of many undercurrents to the clear preference for Oxford on the part of James I and his son Charles I was religious, and the precise nature of the relationship between the broadly western origins of the university's student body and the broadly anti-Puritan outlook of Wales and the West of England remains ripe for further investigation. Brasenose, Oxford's most popular college from 1600 to 1610, was strongly connected to the northwestern counties of Lancashire and Cheshire; Exeter College, which had the largest student body of any college in the 1630s, drew two-thirds of its members from Devon and Cornwall; the personnel of Wadham, newly founded by a lady from Somerset, were almost equally south-western-skewing at the same time; and Jesus College was effec-

---

John Speed, 'Oxfordshire described with the citie . . .', from *The theatre of the empire of Great Britaine: presenting an exact geography of the kingdomes of England, Scotland, Ireland . . .* (1611)

tively a Welsh institution from its foundation in the 1570s down to the outbreak of the Civil War.

William Davenant (1606–1668), the future poet laureate, was the son of the couple who ran the Crown inn in Cornmarket Street. Around the time this map was produced by Cheshire-born John Speed (*c.*1551–1629), Davenant was baptised in St Martin's, Carfax in a ceremony attended by William Shakespeare, his godfather. As well as presumably acting in Oxford during the six visits to the city made by his troupe, the King's Men, between 1604 and 1613, Shakespeare 'was wont to go into Warwickshire once a year, and did

commonly in his journey lie at [the Crown inn] in Oxon, where he was exceedingly respected'. Very near the Crown was the King's Head inn, whose large courtyard stable surrounded by balconies was the frequent site of play performances, with the actors at ground level and the audience watching from above. Courtier and university chancellor William Herbert, 3rd Earl of Pembroke, for whom Pembroke College was named in 1624, was rumoured to have been a patron of Shakespeare's work. The character Shallow in *Henry IV, Part 2* (*c.*1598) mentions that his cousin is a student at Oxford, and an assassination plot hatched in the town features prominently in Shakespeare's *Richard II* (*c*.1595). Life imitated art ten years later, when Robert Catesby, Robert Winter and Thomas Winter met for the initial discussion of their Gunpowder Plot in the Catherine Wheel inn, located in the lane now known as Magdalen Street East between Balliol College and the parish church of St Mary Magdalen. One of Davenant's earliest poems, *In Remembrance of Master Shakespeare*, was produced when he was aged just 12, and concluded with the lines:

> The piteous River wept itself away
> Long since (Alas!) to such a swift decay;
> That reach the Map; and look
> If you a River there can spy;
> And for a River your mock'd Eye,
> Will find a shallow Brook.

Oxford University was not exclusively a place for the training of the clergy, even at this early date. Indeed, it hardly could have been, given that it had 'above two thousand students' in 1613, as compared to only around 9,000 paid clerical positions in the whole country. Davenant attended Lincoln College in the 1620s, with no priestly intentions, and soon afterwards was diagnosed with syphilis. At the time this map was made, the north–south street running south from the High Street to Merton Street beside Oriel College was a haunt of prostitutes, and had been called Gropecunt Lane since the thirteenth century, though the name was already passing out of use by the Elizabethan period, via abbreviation to 'Grope Lane' or even 'Grape Lane'. It acquired its current name, Magpie Lane, later in the seventeenth century from a local tavern – and, perhaps, because the frank use of a certain anatomical word was increasingly seen as improper. Another forthrightly named medieval street called Shitbarn Lane, south of and parallel to Bear Lane, was built over in an earlier period.

Sarah Bendall has described Speed's *Theatre of the Empire of Great Britaine* (1611–12), in which this map appeared, as 'the earliest English attempt at producing an atlas on a grand scale . . . and the first truly comprehensive set of English town plans': 73 in all, of which perhaps two-thirds were surveyed by Speed or his son of the same name. Even if, conceptually, the *Theatre* was an imitation of the work of Abraham Ortelius, Speed's maps and accompanying text were both the products

> of industrious research and reading: from manuscript and printed sources of contemporary topographers such as Christopher Saxton, William Smith, John Norden, Sir Henry Spelman, and others; from Sir Robert Cotton's collection of manuscripts and maps; from records of crown officials in the shires; from field observation; and from illustrations of coins, antiquities, and armorial designs.

Speed's Oxfordshire map in particular would set a fashion for inclusion of the city of Oxford at top right that would be copied regularly for centuries, including by John Rocque [1761]. It was a follower, however, when it came to the decision to keep the 'south-at-top', bird's-flight format originated by Aggas [1578], of whose work the inset seen here is little more than a much-reduced copy. However, it was probably via Speed, and not directly from the small handful of specimens by Aggas and Ryther, that the south-at-top format for Oxford came to be copied by Wenceslaus Hollar 1643 at 1:5,940; and it was probably from Hollar in his turn, not Speed, that Rutger Hermannidae's 1661 version was copied at 1:15,840. Certainly, this was the case with the somewhat later anonymous variant (complete with Hollar's view, greatly expanded and centred) sold 'by Iohn Overton at the whitehorse neere the fountaine tavern without Newgate'.

Ironically, given that Speed's work was intended to glorify the 1603 Union of the Crowns of England and Scotland and the new British polity's status as an empire, Oxford's royal castle had, by the time of the book's publication, developed a prominent and irreparable crack. King James I sold the building to two London speculators, Robert Younglove and Francis James, who sold it on to Christ Church a couple of years later.

Northgate

Castle

Christchurch

Aarts Sconce

Dovers

Est gate

S Teragls

Scale of 70 paces

1646

Royalist capital and salient

In August 1642, hard upon the declaration of the Civil War, Oxford University's 'privileged men', their servants and 'many scholars' were formed into four 'squadrons' for the defence of the town: two armed with muskets, one with pikes and one with halberds. Redoubts – small, probably square, stand-alone forts made of earth, or some combination of earth, stone and wood – were built in a line across the northern part of the city that could not readily be protected by water obstacles. The 'hither end of East bridge, just at the corner of the chaplain's quadrangle of Magdalen College, was blocked up with long timber logs, to keep out horsemen'. A defensive trench was dug at the end of St John's College walk facing the park, South Gate was blocked with chains and Magdalen's tower filled with several cart-loads of stones 'to fling down upon the enemy'. These primitive arrangements were all undone when Parliamentarian troops entered the city the following month. But when the king's army arrived in force in October and

November, the original defensive measures were reinstated and the eastern log-blockade further improved via a two-gun earthwork connecting it to the wall of the Physic Garden [*c.*1834].

The broad-strokes geography of the country's allegiance – with the West and uplands mostly Royalist – was immediately reflected in the strategic position, as John Crofts explains:

[E]very western road leading out of London was either blocked or dominated by a Royalist garrison: the Southampton road at Farnham, or later at Winchester; the Exeter road by the garrison of Basing house; the Bristol road at Reading and subsequently at Newbury, and the Gloucester road, even after the Parliament's forces had taken Abingdon, by the garrison at Wallingford; while the Worcester road through Islip and Woodstock, and the alternative loop by

Bernard de Gomme, *Plane of the Cittie of Oxford* (1646)

Buckingham, were menaced by the King's headquarters at Oxford and the Earl of Northampton's at Banbury.

But as this suggests, the war was still one of movement, and fortification of the city with the latest type of angled earthworks carefully designed to absorb (rather than withstand) artillery fire was not even begun until the spring of 1643. Those in St Clement's parish, on the far side of the Cherwell to the east of the city and therefore deemed most vulnerable, were allegedly mapped out according to 'a mathematical scheme or plot' by Richard Rallingson, recently a student in Queen's College, and completed between April and June 1643. Among the other primary objectives of the amateur builders was to secure the part of Christ Church Meadow nearest the main road to the south, and in the north, to make a continuous line of defences from Holywell via the Wadham College garden and St Giles to Gloucester Hall. This latter work was apparently completed by August 1643, when the artillery was mounted on it. As a general rule, medieval walls were considered useless in the 'modern' artillery warfare of the sixteenth and seventeenth centuries, but written evidence and extant Civil War-era modifications to buildings indicate that the old walls *were* incorporated into Oxford's defensive scheme in some places, at any rate to the south of Merton College and the north of New College – indicated on this map by a thickening of the lines used to depict the medieval fortifications.

Every member of the university aged 16 to 60 was expected to labour on the defences for one day per week from 6 a.m. to 6 p.m. with a two-hour break for lunch, half the colleges turning out on Mondays and the other half on Tuesdays; men who failed to appear were fined a shilling a time. By late May of 1644, the 'works' in St Clement's were in sufficiently good condition, and their gunners sufficiently well trained, that a party of Parliamentarian horsemen was sent packing in 'great confusion and amazement'. The lead roof of Northgate Street's 1536 cornmarket building, shown clearly by Speed [1605], was melted down for ammunition in 1644.

The map reproduced here was a working drawing by Flemish Captain Sir Bernard de Gomme, who had come into England with Prague-born Royalist cavalry general Prince Rupert of the Rhine, Charles I's nephew (and George I's uncle). Carefully drawn to a scale of 1:10,886, it initially appears to date from 1646, since it includes the 'very strong and great Work or Intrenchment of capacity to receive and lodge 3,000 men' that the Parliamentarians built on Headington Hill in preparation for their final attack. But the rendering of this structure – though in de Gomme's handwriting – is in a

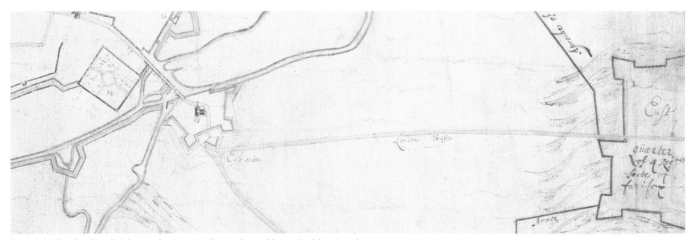

Surprisingly, the drawbridge in the East Bridge indicated by a double triangle was not a wartime expedient, but had been there since at least the fourteenth century.

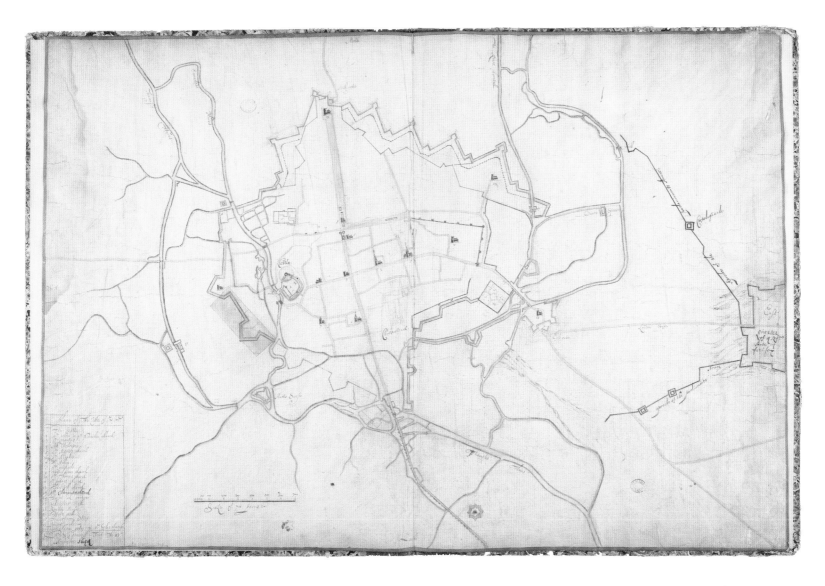

different ink from the rest of the map and was presumably added at a later point. Assessing what the map is meant to depict is further complicated by its original date of 13 November 1645 having been later altered to read 1644.

A crude 1644 'news picture' purporting to be of the same subject, *Oxford As It Now Lyeth*, is so different from de Gomme's careful plan that one wonders if it was actively intended to 'disinform' the enemy. But the degree to which de Gomme was depicting the reality on the ground, versus what he imagined or wished would be built, will probably always be a subject of argument and speculation. Personally, I would suggest that the fainter, dotted lines depicting the city's two southwestern bastions are a clear indication that the engineer followed the standard practice of his profession, and drew built and unbuilt features quite differently from one another, even if the difference was not yet colour-coded. De Gomme had a thriving career after the Restoration, and fortifications he designed at Plymouth and Tilbury can still be seen.

1648

The fortress-city that might have been

In all, the Parliamentarians attempted to seize Oxford three times: once each in 1644, 1645 and 1646. Throughout this period, its defences were being constantly upgraded. The university's and city's working parties were combined from mid 1644, perhaps reflecting a favourable alteration in the latter's enthusiasm, as Royalist refugees continued to flow in to the area and Parliamentarian sympathisers to flow out. In reality, far from a single siege lasting several years – or even three distinct sieges – the so-called Siege of Oxford consisted of a series of opportunistic attempts by the rebels to seize Charles I's person, which in each case ran out of steam when the king slipped out of the city.

Oxford had begun to function as the king's capital quickly and fairly completely. No fewer than 92 royal proclamations were printed in Oxford between the Battle of Edgehill and Christmas 1643, by which time Britain's first true newspaper,

Mercurius Aulicus (the Court Mercury) had been published in the city for a year in editions of unprecedented size – both reflecting and propelling the citizens' 'perpetual discourse of losing and gaining towns and men'. From January 1644, the minority of the members of the House of Commons who remained loyal to the crown held their meetings in the Divinity School, while the loyal majority of the Lords sat in the Convocation House; collectively, they were referred to as the 'Oxford Parliament' to distinguish themselves from the rebel body still meeting in Westminster. The king's court lodged in Christ Church and the queen's at Merton; the Privy Council used Oriel; and New Inn Hall became a mint, producing coins designed by the playwright Thomas Rawlins (d.1670) and struck using equipment sent from the pre-war mint at Aberystwyth. The now-defunct St Mary's College housed a cannon-foundry, and New College and All Souls were used to store arms and explosives.

Anthony à Wood, 'Ichnographia Oxonia una cum Propugnaculis bet Munimentus quibus cungebatur Anno 1648', from *Historia et Antiquitates Universitatis Oxoniensis, duobus Voluminibus comprehensae* (1674)

As well as having a shocking effect on the saltiness of the young scholars' vocabulary, the concentration of soldiery in Oxford led to a vast increase in the sale of tobacco pipes, and a bank of white clay at Shotover was given over entirely for pipe-making. Smoking was said to have played a role in the Great Fire of Oxford in October 1644, which having begun 'at a fiddler's profane taphouse', probably just outside the north wall in Thames Street (present-day George Street), quickly consumed much of the northwest quarter of the old city, destroying more than 300 houses between Cornmarket and New Inn Hall Street and south to 'Bochersrew' (Queen Street). Nevertheless, the city would not acquire its first fire engine for another ten years, or a system of fireplugs until 1702.

In May 1645, a Parliamentary army under Sir Thomas Fairfax constructed formal siege works, including a breast-work on the eastern side of the Cherwell and a bridge over it near Marston. Godstow House was burnt down by its Royalist owner at this time, to prevent it being used as a strong point by the enemy. But Godstow Bridge remained intact, and two Parliamentarian regiments with two cannon crossed by it on their way to (unsuccessfully) storm the city's South Port on 27 May. Six days later, the city's Royalist military governor, Colonel Legge, sallied forth with 1,000 men and inflicted a bruising defeat on the enemy's main base on Headington Hill, effectively ending the siege – though the king's defeat in the pitched battle at Naseby less than two weeks later would render the war unwinnable. In September, the Royalists made a concerted effort to destroy all houses within a 3-mile radius of the city, to prevent any future Parliamentarian besiegers from finding billets.

Ironically, by the time Oxford capitulated in the summer of the following year, it was considered 'impregnable': defended by its rivers on the eastern, western and southern sides, augmented by intentional flooding; giant bastions and ditches on the northern side; a garrison of 5,000 veteran regular troops, not including the university and city regiments; and 38 or 39 cannon supplied by two gunpowder mills (converted from grain mills) at Osney [c.1600]. It had, moreover, enough food to last this army and the civilian population for half a year. It is this zenith of defensibility – tragically achieved only via the 'utter waste' of 'the whole resources of the University and city for three years' – that was long presumed to be commemorated in this map by Anthony à Wood (1632–1695), which was not printed until a quarter of a century later. The defences cost more than £30,000, the equivalent of £68 million in today's money; and a careful examination of this map against other surviving documentary and physical evidence led Captain Gibbs Rigaud of the King's Royal Rifle Corps controversially to conclude in 1851 that it represented not a mere plan or projection, but the defensive works as they actually were, following the final (and most effectual) phase of building in the winter of 1645–46. Historian Anthony Kemp, however, dismisses the possibility that such elaborate works were constructed anywhere but in the north of the city between the two rivers. They 'could never have been built with the slender resources that were available, and within the time', and were in any case unnecessary 'in view of the possibility of inundations' and the relatively low numbers of troops available to man them. At best, for Kemp, Wood's map 'shows what Oxford might have become, had the garrison had twenty years and unlimited funds at their disposal'. Others have claimed that this map is not even Wood's work, but merely a printed version of Richard Rallingson's unexecuted and lost 'mathematical scheme or plot' from 1643 [p. 20]. The best evidence in favour of this is that the only defensive feature that is depicted identically in the de Gomme [1646] and Wood maps is the elaborate 'hornwork' immediately to the southeast of Magdalen Bridge, which was also the only part of Rallingson's 'plot' that his contemporaries positively stated was built.

Though born in Oxford, Wood was a schoolboy in Thame at the time of the siege, and returned to join Merton College as a 15-year-old undergraduate only at the end of 1647. This might explain why this map is dated '1648' rather than 1646. The victorious House of Commons ordered the defensive lines to be 'slighted and dismantled' in early March 1647, making their survival until 1648 unlikely, at least in such a complete form. On the other hand, traces of them could still be seen in

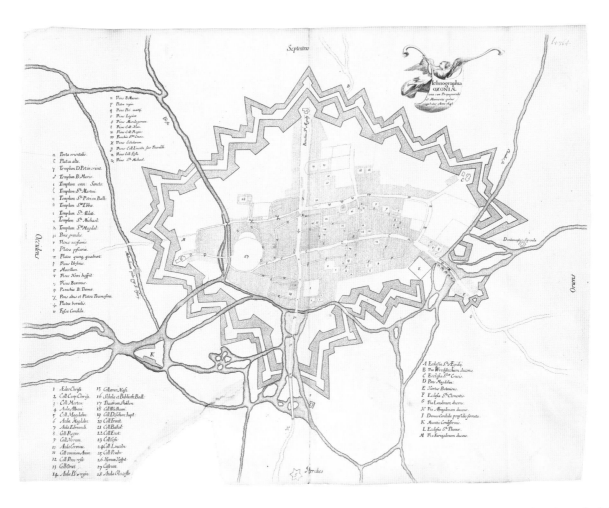

later maps that were certainly based on actual surveys, notably by Loggan [1673] and Williams [1733]; they were also noted by an archaeological survey of 1936, which found that cracks in the walls of Keble College and the Clarendon Laboratory were due to subsidence caused by Civil War entrenchments. But the 'Chinese whispers' character of Wood's map as a whole can be surmised from the small outwork labelled 'Dorobernensis Specula'. Probably originally called 'Dover's Spur', the name of this watch-post on the eastern approaches degenerated over the course of the war first to 'Dover's Spear' and later to 'Dover's Peer'; but in English, Wood's Latin caption would read 'Dover's Mirrors'.

Historical geographers have noted that the western skew

in support for monarchy persisted long after the end of the war and the establishment of the republican regime that named its leading strongman Oliver Cromwell, a Cambridge graduate, as Chancellor of Oxford University in 1650. All of the numerous Royalist insurrections of 1655 erupted to the west of a line that could be drawn from the mouth of the Humber to Poole.

Like so many maps of Oxford, this one had a lengthy but uneven afterlife. A tiny duodecimo version with east at the top was published in the *Viaggi di Coronelli* in Venice in 1697 and included a crude inset view of the 'Teatro Seldoniano', which did not exist yet in the year meant to be depicted; and a reasonably accurate one-quarter size facsimile was printed in June 1817 by J. Skelton of St Aldates.

The Castle

Broken Hays

Beaumont

The white Fryers

Glocester green

1673

A city expanding, mentally and physically

One of the most beautiful maps of Oxford ever produced was the product of an uneasy compromise between a desire to defer to the cartographic and aesthetic decisions taken by Radulph Aggas [1578], and to depict how the city had changed in the century since Aggas's time. The by-now traditional bird's-flight view from the north was adopted, but a wide range of major and minor changes can also be discerned. Taken together, they show the medieval city expanding mentally – as a receiver and transmitter of new ideas, particularly from the Continent – as well as physically, beyond its walls.

Along with a realistic treatment of minor buildings' architectural details that puts Speed [1605] rather to shame, this map exhibits a new interest in gardens: part of a general European movement that included Aberdeen-born Robert Morison (1620–1683), Oxford's professor of botany from 1669. Severely wounded in the Royalist cause, Morison had spent ten years in exile working in the gardens at Blois owned by Gaston, Duc d'Orléans; and it was this experience that laid the foundation of his later success, culminating in the magnificently illustrated *Plantarum Historiae Universalis Oxoniensis*, published in Oxford between 1680 and 1699.

Though it would be used for musical concerts and university ceremonies rather than plays, the magnificent baroque Sheldonian Theatre – completed in 1669 to a design by Christopher Wren at a cost of more than £12,000 (about £23 million today) – represented a 'long bet' that the bad old days of Puritanism, so recently vanquished, were in fact gone for good. Tellingly, the first university oration held there began with a 'satire on Cromwell' and ended 'with invectives against

David Loggan, 'Nova & accuratissima celeberrimae universitatis civitatisque Oxoniensis scenographia', from *Oxonia Illustrata: sive omnium celeberrimae istius Universitatis collegiorum aularum bibliothecae Bodleianae scholarum publicarum theatri Sheldoniani nec non urbis totius scenographia* (1675)

fanatics, conventicles, and . . . Nonconformists'; and William of Orange – in some respects the heir to Cromwellianism – refused to eat a feast that was prepared for him in the Sheldonian in 1695 because he feared it would be poisoned.

Wren, who had been a student at Wadham College in the 1650s, was not yet known as a church architect, but as Oxford's Savilian Professor of Astronomy, and he turned his hand to a host of other non-religious interests including meteorology, optics, navigation and surveying. The Ashmolean Museum, whose eclecticism was also hardly calculated to please the 'Godly' party, opened its doors in 1683; and one of the first events to take place in a 'new dancing school' built against the church of St Michael in the North Gate was the performance of an anti-Puritan comedy play called *The Guardian* by Abraham Cowley (1618–1667), who had been ejected from Cambridge for his Royalism in 1643 and moved to Oxford along with so many others.

Unlike Aggas, who had relied on Augustine Ryther and others to engrave his drawings onto copper for printing, the author of this map boasted considerable skills as both a surveyor and engraver. Born at the height of the Thirty Years' War to Anglo-Scottish Calvinist parents in Gdansk, Poland, David Loggan seems to have had few religious, national or political feelings. By 1658, aged about 24, he had moved first to Amsterdam and then to London, where he achieved fame for the fine quality of his pencil-portrait of Lord Protector Oliver Cromwell. But after the collapse of the English Republic that followed hard upon Cromwell's death, Loggan transitioned smoothly into working for the restored Royalist and Anglican establishment. By 1666 he had produced a picture of Old St Paul's Cathedral, a portrait of King Charles II and a new frontispiece for the Book of Common Prayer. He also collaborated with the antiquarian William Dugdale, a leading light of the wartime Royalist garrison of Oxford and later father-in-law to museum founder Elias Ashmole, whose portrait Loggan also drew.

In March 1669, having moved from London to Holywell Street in Oxford by way of Nuffield, Loggan was appointed engraver to the university at a salary of £1 a year – a sum so

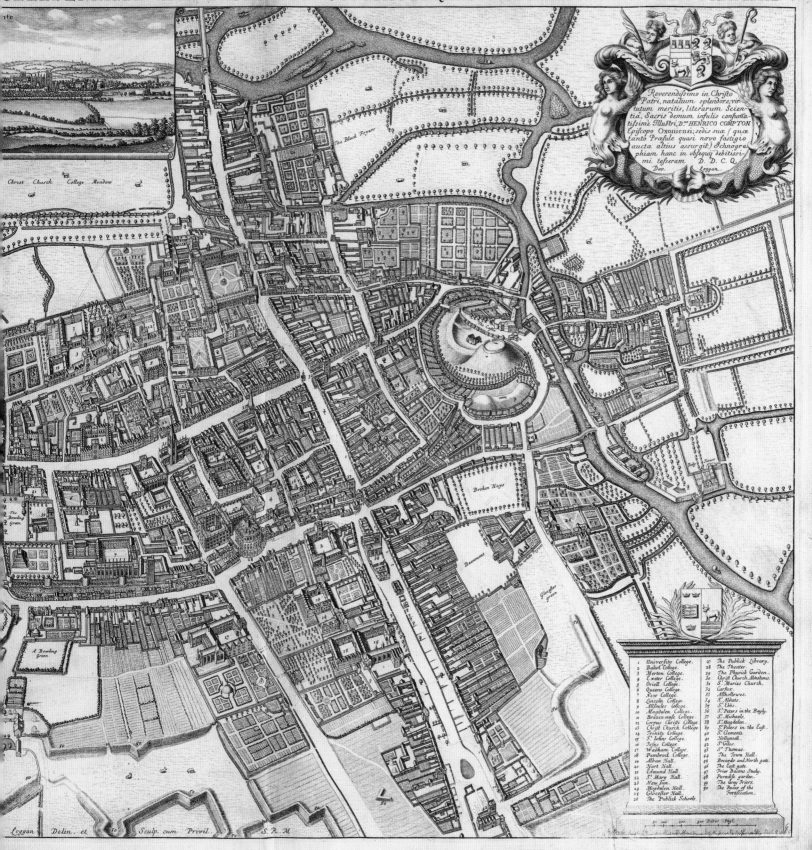

Reverendissimo in Christo Patri, natalium splendore, virtutum meritis, literarum Scientiâ, Sacris demum infulis consumatissimè Illustri, D.no HENRICO COMPTON Episcopo Oxoniensi; sedis suæ (quæ tanto Præsule quasi novo fastigio aucta, altius assurgit) Ichnographiam hanc in obsequij debitissimi tesseram D. D. C. Q. Dav. Loggan.

Christ Church College Meadow

The Black Fryers

The Castle

Broken Hayes

Beaumont

Glocester green

A Bowling Green

The Bowling Green

1	University College.	27	The Publick Library.
2	Baliol College.	28	The Theater.
3	Merton College.	29	The Physick Garden.
4	Exeter College.	30	Christ Church Almshouse.
5	Oriell College.	31	S.t Maries Church.
6	Queens College.	32	Carfax.
7	New College.	33	Allhallowes.
8	Lincoln College.	34	S.t Aldats.
9	Allsoules College.	35	S.t Ebbs.
10	Magdalen College.	36	S.t Peters in the Bayly.
11	Brazen-nose College.	37	S.t Michaels.
12	Corpus Christi College	38	S.t Magdalen.
13	Christ Church College	39	S.t Peters in the East.
14	Trinity College.	40	S.t Clements.
15	S.t Iohns College.	41	Hollywell.
16	Jesus College.	42	S.t Giles.
17	Wadham College.	43	S.t Thomas.
18	Pembrock College.	44	The Town Hall.
19	Alban Hall.	45	Bocardo and North gate.
20	Hart Hall.	46	The East gate.
21	Edmund Hall.	47	Frier Bacons Study.
22	S.t Mary Hall.	48	Paradise garden.
23	New Inn.	49	The Gray Friers.
24	Magdalen Hall.	50	The Ruins of the
25	Glocester Hall.		Fortification.
26	The Publick Schools		

Loggan Delin. et Sculp. cum Privil. S. R. M.

In addition to its main functions, the Sheldonian would house Oxford University Press in its basement for the next 40 years. The coffee-house it displaced, Short's, moved to St Helen's Passage, then known simply as Hell's Passage.

The tiny gate in Turl Street contained the recently installed 'Twirl' or turnstile for which the street, formerly St Mildred's Street, was renamed. City walls and gates served a mostly commercial function by this time.

meagre, even by seventeenth-century standards, that the relationship could only have been a non-exclusive one. (Oxford's volunteer firemen were paid the same sum from 1661 simply for keeping themselves and their engines in readiness, and Humfrey Cole [p. 39] had complained almost a century earlier that his annual pay of £23 plus free lodgings was 'lacking sufficiente maintenance for me and my family'.) Loggan's first task in his effectively voluntary post was to engrave pictures of the newly completed Sheldonian, but the project for which he is now best remembered was the 1675 picture-book *Oxonia Illustrata*: the first depiction of all of the university's buildings and gardens, and which included the 1:3,265 map seen here, surveyed in 1673 with assistance from Anthony à Wood [1648]. Loggan began his sister book about Cambridge, *Cantabrigia Illustrata*, in 1676, but it would not

be completed until 1690, amid rumours that it had ruined the artist's eyesight. He died two years later, in debt by more than a century's worth of his Oxford pay.

In a society that treated homelessness as a crime, the tenants of demolished buildings had to be provided with new places to live rather promptly. Much of the new housing seen here on the south side of Holywell Street was built c.1615 for former inhabitants of Catte Street whose dwellings were eliminated during the building of the Schools Quadrangle. The houses immediately to the west/right of the North Gate were presumably even newer, given that this was the starting point of the Great Fire of 1644 [1648]. At the time this map was surveyed, the inhabitants of Holywell Street included the mapmaker himself, as well as the celebrated clock-maker John Knibb (1650–1722). Refused the freedom of the city, Knibb

Carfax, showing the Conduit House and St Martin's Church.

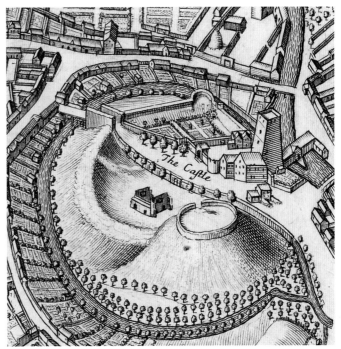

The most immediately obvious change to the city since the pre-Civil War period is the absence of the castle keep, which its Parliamentarian occupiers dismantled in a panic when the Scottish army of the young King Charles II was erroneously thought to be approaching in 1651.

conducted his business under the name of his London-based brother Joseph, who in turn was only allowed to operate in Oxford under a legal fiction that he was one of Trinity College's gardeners. The proliferation of bowling greens reflects that evening lawn-bowling had become a favourite pastime of members of the university by this date. However, it waned in popularity in late Victorian times due to changes in the dinner-hour and a fad for lawn tennis.

Loggan provides us with one of the last views of the original All Saints' Church, a late-Norman house-conversion which collapsed in 1700. One of the many features in this map that post-dates John Speed's *Theatre of the Empire* [1605] is the Carfax Conduit: an elaborate 40-foot-tall neo-Gothic structure to which clean water was piped from a spring above North Hinksey from 1617 until 1787 [1786]. It was made to

emit claret during a visit by King James II in 1687, and allegedly replaced a bull-ring, though nothing of the kind is shown by Aggas or Speed.

Smith Gate, at the north end of Catte Street, was removed shortly before this map was surveyed. Its octagonal chapel of Our Lady was a private house by the seventeenth century, when it was widely supposed 'to have beene a Synagogue of the Jewes'. It became a shop in 1708, and Hertford College's junior common room in 1931.

One of Loggan's sons became Anglican rector of Hanwell, Oxfordshire. Another was an officer in the 1st Foot Guards, arguably the most Royalist regiment in the new British Army, which at this date still comprised an uneasy mixture of units from both sides in the Civil War.

Lane

Comon field

a Hedge

a
7 Short lane

to Gloucester   to London

6   Iſlip

a Comon

Merſh land on both ſides

5 Goſford Stone bridge
Charwell flu.

Lowſe
hall ſo   Enter a lane
Called by
the Scholars
4

Comon   a Gate
to Banbury   a Hedge
3

The way in   a Lane

2

Enter a lane

1   Comon feilds
on both ſides

OXFORD

OXFORD SHIRE

Tingewick
woods

20

Chickwood

a Lane

Newton
purſell   19

a Gate
Paſture
Ground
Enter Bucking-   ham ſhire

a Water Mill   18   a Lane
Incloſures
on both ſides

Comon feilds on   both ſides

17

to Banbury   to London
16

Streton
Audley

Com feilds on both ſides

Enter a lane
Caſfeild   15

Comon feilds
14 both ſides

to Banbury
10. m.

Burceſter
13 Vulgo
Biſceter

to Woodſtock

OXFORD SHIRE

Comon

to Cheſter &   33   the Road to
Holyhead   London
Comon feilds
both ſides

to Leighton
Calverton

32

Paſſingham

Comon feilds
both ſides

a Water
mill   31

Re=   ente r Buckingham
ſhire

Bechampton

a Water mill
30

River Ouſe

Enter North   ampton ſhire
29

Thornton

a Brook   the Way
28   Thro ugh Incloſures

Leckhamſted
Sheep   Downs
Leave the
lane

Foſcot   27   Enter a lane

Com feilds
both ſides   a Water mill

Mades   26

Morton

Com. feilds   Morton

BUCKING HAM SHIRE

Comon

Enter
a lane
42

Large

Lathbury

Newp
Paine

Comon

Linfor

Sta
the
hall

Ha
Vulg
Haſo

Mer
a Br

1675

The city as a hub of communication

Quite apart from containing the first ichnographic plans of Oxford to be created in a non-military context, John Ogilby's *Britannia* was a novelty from head to toe: the first pictorial road-book produced in the modern world, depicting 2,519 miles of roads that had been carefully surveyed using a 'great wheel' – though the preliminary research had covered a distance perhaps nine times greater. As the sharp-eyed reader has no doubt already inferred, British maps were not normally used for route-finding in the first century of their existence, but created as prestige gifts for the 'paper museums' of the well-to-do, or as businesslike tools of attack and defence. And while it is no longer widely believed that owners of Ogilby's magnificent folio cut out the pages that were especially relevant to them and carried them about in their pockets – no positive evidence of this has ever been found, and the book was probably far too expensive to be defaced in this way – its

emphasis on wayfinding in general, and the road network in particular, marked a total departure from what came before. Taken as a whole, moreover, Ogilby's book implies that he saw Oxford as a critical node on the national road network.

To comprehend both the thinking behind such a map and its subsequent popularity, it may first be necessary to shake off two centuries of received opinion, to the effect that the roads of seventeenth-century England were so bad as to not be worth mentioning, except perhaps in jest. It is not necessary here to re-state G.H. Martin's well-documented attack on the idea that journeys in medieval England 'were ordinarily made by water' or 'could only be so made', which at its worst can amount to 'an unwillingness to suppose that the roads were used for anything at all'. Less than 700 miles of inland waterway was still navigable in England in the early seventeenth century (a decline of perhaps two-thirds from the peak

John Ogilby, 'The road from Oxford to Cambridge', in *Britannia . . . or, an illustration of the kingdom of England and dominion of Wales: by a geographical and historical description of the principal roads thereof* (1675)

attained before the Black Death), and this should be measured against uncountable tens of thousands of miles of roads. Including the trying of cases, Elizabethan judges covered the eight counties of the Oxford Circuit in just 28 days. At the time this map was made, the Postmaster of Oxford was concurrently the landlord of the Cross Keys (modern 36–37 Queen Street), presumably because of his inn's situation on the major east–west road through the city. Coupled with gossip, the road network ensured that any type of news could spread over the entire country within a week or two. For an individual on horseback, or leading a string of packhorses in single file, the network was as good as it needed to be. As Martin put it, '[i]t was the road, wet, rough, and uncertain as it sometimes was, that made the land a kingdom.'

Long before the 1670s, Oxford was renowned as a centre for printing, papermaking and publishing – with Britain's first newspaper, *Mercurius Aulicus*, appearing in the city on 1 January 1643, and the oldest still in print, the *London Gazette*, beginning life as the *Oxford Gazette* in 1665. Unsurprisingly, given the subsequent close association between news-reading and coffee-drinking, Britain's first coffee-house opened in Oxford's High Street in 1651, on the site of the present-day Grand Café; and the Queen's Lane Coffee House, dating from 1654, is said to be the oldest extant in Europe. In the plague year 1665, Parliament returned to Oxford, the Commons meeting in the Convocation House and the Lords in the Geometry School (now a part of the Bodleian Library's Lower Reading Room). The same arrangements would be repeated, albeit for purely political reasons, in 1681. The number of coffee-houses of the original, seventeenth-century type – lavishly equipped with 'books suited to every taste' – may have reached a peak in 1740, when there were 13; in the early 1860s there were still 11, but by 1900 there was just one.

One of cartography's oddest figures, Forfarshire-born Londoner John Ogilby (1600–1676) was first touched by fame when he won the Virginia Company's lottery in 1612. By the 1630s he had worked mostly in the theatre in England and Ireland, and probably served as a soldier in the Duke of Buckingham's ill-fated expedition to the Île de Rhe. The outbreak of the Civil War found him in the Earl of Strafford's guards in Dublin and teaching Strafford's daughters to dance – a service he had previously performed in Somerset for the sisters of Ralph Hopton, the future Royalist general. Ogilby made his way back to London after being nearly 'blow'n-up' while fighting in the Irish Royalist army of the Earl of Ormonde (who would go on to serve as Chancellor of Oxford University from 1669 to 1688).

Despite having spent a decade and a half working in Parliamentarian-controlled territory, mostly as a translator, Ogilby quickly gained the approval of King Charles II and befriended other towering figures of the age, including Robert Hooke, Robert Boyle and Christopher Wren. Funded by lotteries, advertisements and subscriptions, Ogilby's atlases began to appear in 1670, and like his previous translations of Virgil, Homer and Aesop were beautifully presented, though fundamentally unoriginal. The *Britannia* road atlas, the final major project of the elderly Ogilby's odd 'demand-led' career, is today recognised as 'the first major advance in cartography in England since the Tudor period' (C.W.J. Withers). Among other things, it helped cement the length of the English mile as 1,760 yards; this had been fixed by statute in 1593 (hence the term 'statute mile'), but in practice the distance called a 'mile' varied from county to county, and three different lengths of mile were in simultaneous use in some counties of England during Ogilby's lifetime. As well as being reissued three times within 50 years, and many times since, Ogilby's *Britannia* was directly imitated by a number of other authors, notably including John Owen and Emanuel Bowen, whose version of 1720 – expanded in scope, but greatly reduced in size – would sell even better than the original, going through four editions by 1736.

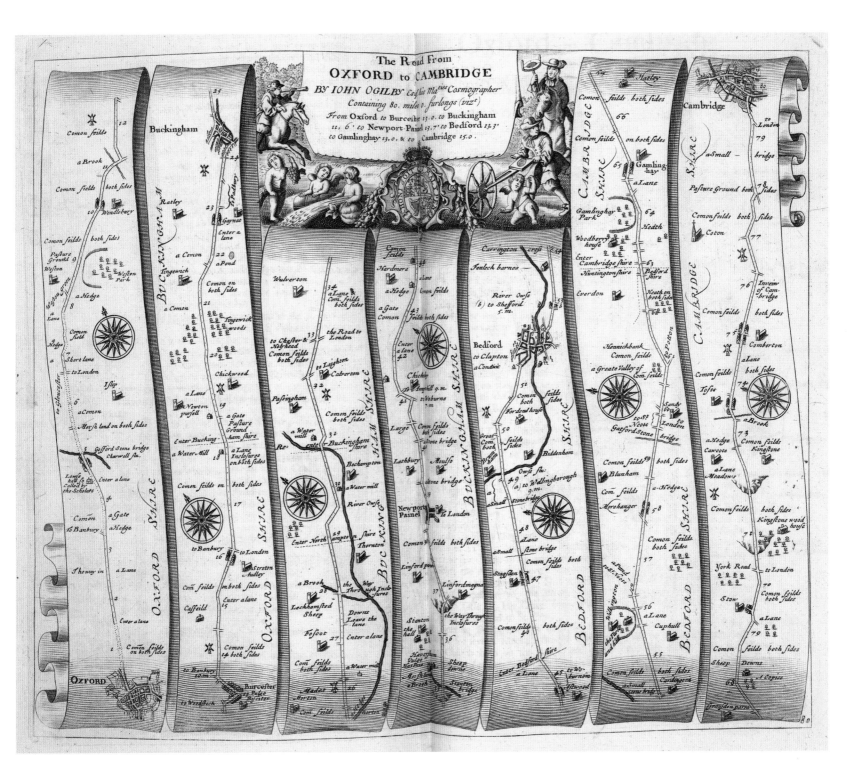

The Road From
OXFORD to CAMBRIDGE

BY IOHN OGILBY Esq. his Ma.ties Cosmographer
Containing 80. miles 2 furlongs (viz.t)
From Oxford to Burcester 13.0. to Buckingham
11. 6. to Newport-Painel 13.7. to Bedford 13.3.
to Gamlinghay 13.0, & to Cambridge 15.0.

1	Magdalen College.
2	New College.
3	St. Giles's Church.
4	The Schooles.
5	The Theatre.
6	St. Maries Church.
7	Trinity new Chappel.
8	Merton College.
9	All Sts. Church.
10	St. M. Mag: Church.
11	St. Michaels Church.
12	Christ Church Cath:
13	St. Martins als Carfax.
14	Christ Church new Tower.
15	St. Aldates Church.
16	St. Peters in the Baily.
17	The Castle Hill.
18	The Castle Tower.
19	Glocester Hall.
20	St. Thomas par: Church.

Godstow Abby

The RIVER ISIS

M E A D O W

The Round Hill

Woolvercot Lake

A Scale of Perches.

10 20 30 40 50 60 70 80 90 100

Upper

1695

Pasturage and recreation

Before estate maps came into existence in the later sixteenth century, their role had been filled for some 700 years by non-pictorial written descriptions, which following the Norman Conquest came to be known as 'terriers' (from *terre*, the French word for land, ground and earth). Depending on the size of the properties concerned, and the purposes for which these records were made, they might consist of anything from a single page to a weighty tome. Many terriers were in effect written versions of the traditional community ceremonies of 'ridings of the marches' or 'beating the bounds' on Holy Thursday that began in Saxon times and still occur regularly in some places, notably the Oxford city parishes of St Mary the Virgin and St Michael at the North Gate, as well as in Cornwall, southern Scotland, and New Hampshire in the United States.

Some scholars have plausibly argued that the mapping of small parcels of rural land was necessitated by enclosure, the long-term replacement of common landholding by formal ownership [1819, 1830]. As geographer David Fletcher puts it, mapping 'was important in furthering the fundamental transition of the definition of property from the feudal notion of bundles of assorted rights to the capitalist conception as absolute ownership of definable pieces of soil'. Nevertheless, the emergence of estate maps in Elizabethan times did not supplant terriers quickly. Rather, the two types of survey would continue to exist side by side for another 250 years. As well as wealthy families and individuals, major institutional landowners sponsored and utilised both types of document. An excellent example was Christ Church, which for centuries had the most extensive landholdings of any Oxford college: at one point consisting of 11,000 acres in Oxfordshire alone, plus an even larger territory in 18 other counties the length

Benjamin Cole, *A Map of Port-Meadow, With a Prospect of all the Adjacent Places &c. Containing 439 Acres 1 Rood and 30 Perches of Land* (1695)

it; in the Christ Church case, written surveys of a given property outnumbered maps of the same property by better than six to one in the period from 1600 to 1840. Nevertheless, in the eighteenth century, the surveyors gained the upper hand and succeeded in convincing English society that estate maps – like the previous two centuries' maps of cities and countries – were objects of prestige, worthy of possessing for their own sake. Evidently produced with great care, the present map can be seen as a key moment in that process of transition, even though the land it depicts belonged to the city rather than a college or individual, and has been preserved as a common from pre-Norman times down to the present day. By the time of its formal registration as a common, in 1970, it had shrunk from 439 acres to 342, but this may merely reflect ambiguities about what originally constituted Port Meadow as distinct from Wolvercote Common, Wolvercote Green and Binsey Green. In addition to its extensive and ongoing use for pasturage – albeit never for sheep – Port Meadow was frequently laid out as a racecourse by this date, and a number of small stone bridges over its rivulets have been traced to this horse-racing use. In September 1710, the German traveller and collector Zacharias von Uffenbach (1683–1734) attended the Port Meadow races and reported that there were

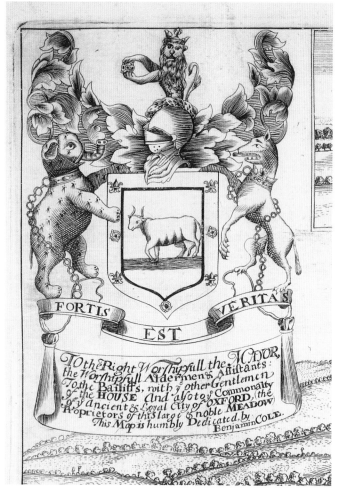

While the shield of the city of Oxford is well known around the world, its supporters – a white-speckled black elephant and a green beaver – are less so.

> many booths set up, where beer was sold, and each one had its sign, a hat, or glove or some such. . . . Nearly everyone from the City was there and many visitors, some on horseback, some in coaches, some in boats.

and breadth of England and in Montgomeryshire in Wales. It was vital for the college to have up-to-date information on this land's productivity, as well as the specific uses to which it was being put by its numerous tenants, if rents were to keep pace with changes on the ground.

Because mapping was considerably more expensive than terrier-writing, surveyors had a vested interest in promoting it, and their clients an equally strong motivation for avoiding

On that occasion, six horses and their jockeys made two circuits of the meadow, a total distance of 5 miles, at an average speed in excess of 30 miles per hour.

We have little definite information about the Benjamin Cole who surveyed and engraved this map, except that his son and grandson – both also named Benjamin Cole – went on to greatness as engravers in London, both working for the masonic Grand Lodge of England, and the youngest collaborating with cartographer John Rocque [1761]. Historian

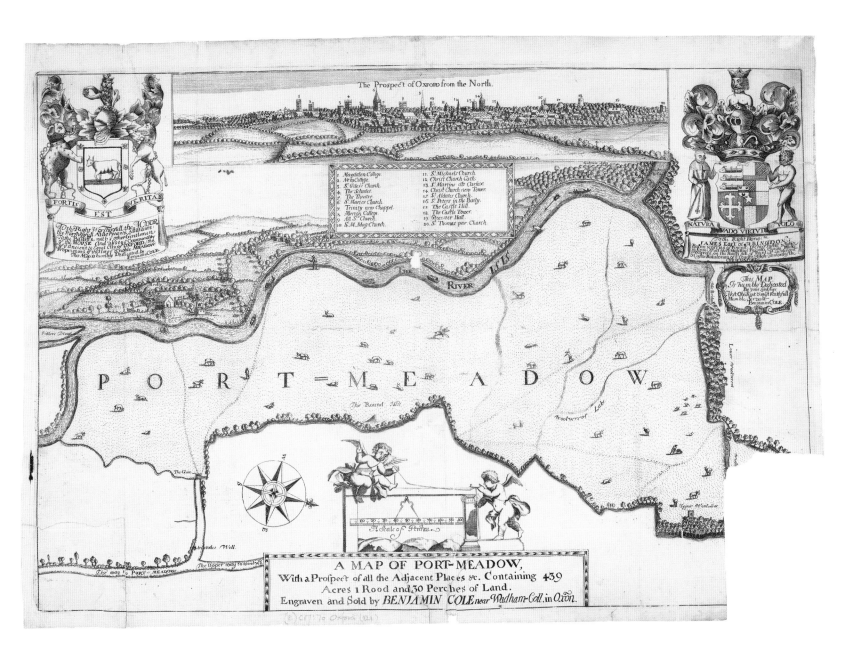

Willem Hackmann speculates that the first, Oxford-based Benjamin Cole was related to Humfrey Cole (d.1591): a northern English die-sinker who was inspired to begin making surveying instruments by Leonard Digges's *A Geometrical Practise Called Pantometria* (1571), the first surveying handbook in English to mention mapmaking. Humfrey Cole's change of profession was timely, as he is now remembered as the co-inventor of the theodolite and 'the father of the English instrument-making trade', which went from nonexistence to world dominance over the course of his career.

1724

'The Jacobite capital of England'

Almost nothing is known of the private life of the engraver of this view, Sutton Nicholls (1668–1729), other than that he was probably born at Eltham in Kent and married a woman from Oxford in 1702. In spite of his 'crude and hasty draughtsmanship . . . [the] frequent inaccuracy of his views, and an apparently shaky grasp of perspective' (L. Peltz), Nicholls would be steadily employed over a period of more than 40 years beginning in the early 1680s. Modern critics may underestimate the charm of his work, strangely distorted and compressed though it may be. Nor is this the only depiction of Oxford that bends the part of the picture plane upwards or downwards by as much as 90 degrees, to render some of the scene in 'top view' and some in 'side view': a better-known and arguably odder such example being Jan de Wyck's late-seventeenth-century *Siege of Oxford*. Towards the end of a lengthy and prolific career that focused disproportionately on the new discipline of road-mapping [1675] alongside subjects of military significance from Gibraltar to Namur to Londonderry, Nicholls here captures Oxford on the verge of its transformation from a bastion of the Establishment to the more porous and multifaceted creature that it has since remained.

Early modern Oxford and Cambridge were nowhere near as similar to each other as one would gather from the now prevalent term 'Oxbridge' – a term coined by William Makepeace Thackeray as recently as 1849 – or, indeed, from their shared status as virtual suburbs of a present-day London that appears to be metastasising. While some historians have claimed that the two universities represented a uniform system of higher education as early as the 1630s, it is hard to agree that this was the case before Thackeray's time. Around 400 of the university's students and fellows were expelled by the Parliamentarian regime for refusing to 'submit' after the town's

---

Leonard Knyff/Sutton Nicholls, 'Oxoniensis Universitas. The south prospect of the City of Oxford', from Joseph Smith, *Britannia illustrata . . .* , vol. 3 (1724)

41

surrender in 1646, and this probably represented the tip of an iceberg of strong Royalist feeling in the university (which was not nearly so strong in Cambridge); and unabashed Oxford Royalists including the young Christopher Wren [1673, 1675] continued to meet and scheme through the years of the English Republic – and beyond – at Arthur Tillyard's coffee-house near All Souls. When Richard Cromwell was proclaimed head of the Republic in succession to his father Oliver at the church door of Mary the Virgin in 1658, the city officials making the announcement 'were pelted with carret and turnip tops by young scholars and others', despite the presence of a body of soldiers protecting them. Over the half-century following the restoration of the monarchy in 1660, moreover, the observable correlation between Protestant Nonconformity and a rebel stance in the 1640s hardened into a belief among many Anglicans that Nonconformity itself was politically suspect. Such fears were expressed clearly in the Five Mile Act or so-called 'Oxford Act', passed in the 1665 Oxford session of Parliament [1675], which targeted

> persons not ordained according to the Forme of the Church of England . . . [who] preach in unlawfull Assemblyes Conventicles or Meeteings under colour or pretence of Exercise of Religion contrary to the Lawes and Statutes of this Kingdome [and] have setled themselves in diverse Corporations in England . . . thereby takeing an oportunity to distill the poysonous Principles of Schisme and Rebellion into the hearts of His Majestyes Subjects to the great danger of Church and Kingdome.

Any of these non-Anglican ministers who refused to 'sweare That it is not lawfull upon any pretence whatsoever to take Armes against the King' – and thousands *did* refuse – were banned from coming within 5 miles of any towns or cities that sent members to Parliament, on pain of a £40 fine and six months' imprisonment. Among those immediately banished were a group of five Presbyterian and Congregationalist college fellows who had prospered under Cromwell, but were turfed out of their jobs in 1662 and had taken to preaching in private houses in the city. Whatever the dreaming spires were dreaming of, it was not another revolution.

But revolution did come, in 1688, and the victorious Whig party proved no more tolerant of Roman Catholics than the cock-a-hoop Tories had been of the Baptists, Presbyterians and Quakers a quarter of a century earlier. Charles II's Catholic brother James II was ousted and disappeared into a highly militarised exile with thousands of his most extreme followers, known as Jacobites – though many others remained at home across Britain and Ireland. Oxford's High Street was bedecked with orange ribbons in support of the revolution, and all its parish clergy swore allegiance to the new regime, but the city soon became a magnet for those who would not so swear, much as it had been a magnet for unemployable church musicians in Cromwell's time.

The doomed Catholic king's younger daughter, a staunch Anglican, was greeted with great enthusiasm in Oxford just nine days after her father's defeat at the Battle of Reading, and allowed to ascend the throne as Queen Anne in 1702. Incidentally, her maternal grandfather had been the politician and historian Edward Hyde, 1st Lord Clarendon, whose book royalties paid for Oxford's magnificent Clarendon Building during her reign. Scuffles broke out during the queen's visit to Oxford in the year of her accession; these were not political, but over the issue of whether the city or the university should take precedence in the procession. The city council in Anne's reign was 'predominantly Jacobite' (A. Crossley), and '[t]he Oxford mob was now managed with Jacobite money' (C.W. Boase).

The well-liked queen had 17 pregnancies but was tragically predeceased by all of her children. When she died at the age of 49, possibly of exhaustion, the crown was required by recent parliamentary legislation to pass, not to her nearest relative, but to her nearest *Protestant* relative. The lucky winner of this peculiar religio-genetic lottery was Georg Ludwig, Elector of Hanover, whose maternal grandmother had been Charles I's sister. Nationwide rioting against the obscure and non-Anglican new king, who dismissed Anne's

Magdalen Bridge was at all times much longer than it appears here, with Aggas [1578] showing between 20 and 22 arches and Loggan [1673] 19 or 20.

Tory administration and replaced it with a Whig one, began in London in early 1715: with mobs burning Oliver Cromwell in effigy, shouting in favour of high-church Anglicanism and a 'new Restoration' of the Stuarts, and denouncing Presbyterians. (The people were not ignorant of the fact that King George was a Lutheran; rather, 'Presbyterian' seems to have been used as a derogatory term for anyone who placed the needs of the Church above those of the state.)

The disturbances spread first to Oxford on 28–29 May, with mixed groups of townspeople and undergraduates shouting 'No Roundheads!' and attacking Nonconformist chapels that had operated intermittently since the Roundhead occupation. A pulpit used by the (actual) Presbyterians was burnt at Carfax, along with an effigy of their minister; a meeting-house of the Quakers and at least one Quaker's home were attacked the following day, along with a Baptist chapel in St Ebbe's. Troops were sent to Oxford and martial law declared there, but on the violence spread. Townspeople in Manchester, and villagers in Norton St Philip, Somerset, went so far as to proclaim James II's exiled son 'King James III'.

It is curious indeed that, despite it having been repeated across whole swathes of western England – as well as in the

eastern cities of London, Cambridge and Leeds – the Jacobite agitation of the early eighteenth century now tends to be misremembered as an exclusively Scottish phenomenon. The Oxford Jacobite club known as the High Borlace met regularly from 1715 to 1752 in the King's Head tavern (10–12 High Street), and continued in existence for a further 14 years after the tavern closed. Other Jacobites frequented the Antiquity Hall tavern, which was shown in Loggan's view [1673] a short way to the west of Hythe Bridge. One of them sniffed in 1733 that 'one Handel, a foreigner . . . born at *Hanover*' – in fact he was from Saxony – had been allowed to perform his *Athalia* in the Sheldonian and sell tickets priced at 5 shillings.

Born in Lichfield, son of a high-church Anglican bookseller who was strongly suspected of Jacobitism, Samuel Johnson of *Dictionary* fame was taken to St James's Palace at the age of two and a half to be touched by Queen Anne as a treatment for his scrofula (lymphadenitis), a disfiguring disease of the neck. It had been believed since at least the thirteenth century that any sovereign of England or France could effect this magical cure; many sufferers probably improved due to a placebo effect, though the disease is seldom deadly and often simply goes away. James II had performed the ceremony in Christ Church Cathedral in September 1687. Along with a number of other aspects of the monarchy that had hitherto linked it to the populace in a more or less immediate way, the twice-yearly scrofula ceremony would be cancelled permanently by the new Hanoverian regime.

The teenaged Johnson enrolled at Pembroke College in October 1728, apparently under the mistaken impression that his well-to-do school friend Andrew Corbet would defray his costs; in the end he survived less than 14 months, and his fees were a full term in arrears when he quit the scene. Neverthe-less, Johnson apparently retained a lifelong affection and respect for Pembroke and its other members, and accepted an honorary MA in his mid forties. He was also keenly aware of the riots of May 1715, and quoted the following lines of poetry about them:

Our royal master saw, with heedful eyes
The wants of his two universities
Troops he to Oxford sent, as knowing why
That learned body wanted loyalty
But books to Cambridge gave, as well discerning
How that right loyal body wanted learning.

The mob had effectively broken the Baptist and Quaker presence in Oxford for generations to come, though the Presbyterians were paid £109 in government compensation for the loss of their chapel, and used it in 1719 to acquire the site of a new one – later to become known as the New Road Baptist Chapel. But Jacobitism, by now degenerating into a sort of totem for Highland hatred of the Lowlands, Lowland hatred of the English and English hatred of Germans, could never be welded into a single harmonious movement. When George I's impeccably English and Anglican great-grandson ascended the throne as George III in 1760, Jacobitism in the city, and around the world, rapidly dwindled into insignificance. Former fellow-travellers of Oxford Jacobitism as different as Dr Johnson and John Wesley, co-founder of Methodism [1883], were united in their vociferous opposition to the American Revolution.

Among the important newer buildings shown here is Christ Church's Tom Tower, completed in 1682 to a design by Christopher Wren, who said it 'ought to be Gothick to agree with the Founders worke'. The copy of this structure that adorns Dunster House at Harvard has had the unexpected Gothic touches removed, and therefore looks more plausibly like a building of the Tom Tower's age than the Tom Tower does itself. The college chapels of Wadham, Lincoln and Jesus were also important ultra-early examples of the Gothic revival in architecture.

The Gothic/baroque twin towers of All Souls College, built beginning in 1716, were designed by Nicholas Hawksmoor (1661–1736), as was the 1718 replacement steeple for All Saints parish church. However, Hawksmoor's 1713 plan for a complete rebuilding of the city around a new 'university temple' and two 'forums' never really got off the ground.

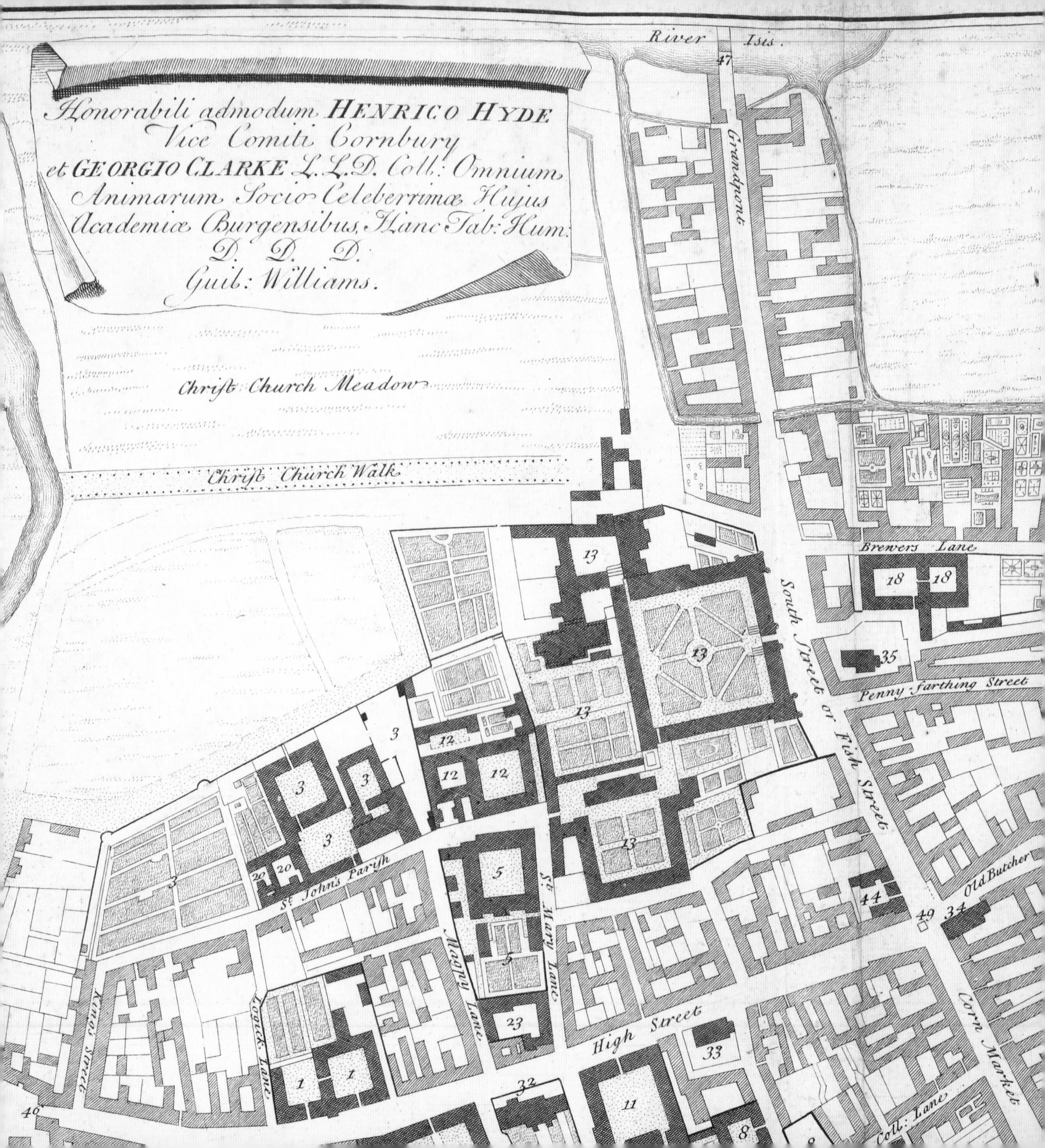
Honorabili admodum HENRICO HYDE
Vice Comiti Cornbury
et GEORGIO CLARKE L.L.D. Coll: Omnium
Animarum Socio Celeberrimæ Hujus
Academiæ Burgensibus, Hanc Tab: Hum:
D. D. D.
Guil: Williams.
River Isis.
47
Grandpont
Christ Church Meadow
Christ Church Walk
Brewers Lane
18
18
13
13
13
13
35
South Street or Fish Street
Penny-farthing Street
3
3
3
3
3
12
12
12
5
5
20
20
St. Johns Parish
St. Mary Lane
Magpy Lane
44
Old Butcher
49
34
Kings Street
Logick Lane
23
High Street
33
Corn Market
1
1
32
11
8
Coll: Lane
46

1733

Meandering into modernity

Despite the prominence of many persons of Welsh origin or descent in the field of cartography, including Oxford graduates Humphrey Lhuyd and Robert Hues in the sixteenth century, there has been 'no comprehensive history' of the mapping of Wales itself (R. Davies). One milestone in that history, were it to be written, would be William Williams's large-scale county mapping of Denbighshire and Flintshire in 1720, which would stand as the first and only thing of its kind for nearly 80 years. This achievement was all the more remarkable, in that the heyday of large-scale estate mapping had not yet begun in the Principality.

The map now before us was included in *Oxonia Depicta* (1733), whose magnificence may be conveyed by the fact that a copy once owned by the 10th Duke of Hamilton, bound in gilt red morocco leather, was sold for more than £8,000 in 2009. Aside from the inclusion of an ichnographic town plan, the *Depicta* was effectively a new version of Loggan's *Oxonia Illustrata* [1673] of 58 years earlier: a royal-folio-sized book consisting mostly of architectural elevations, again complete with a south-at-top bird's-flight view in imitation of Aggas [1578], relatively minimal captions engraved directly into the plates, and no typeset text at all. Apart from their other similarities, the two books appear to have been the only ones printed by Oxford University Press in this all-engraving format prior to 1780. In all, Williams's work, begun in 1726, would contain 63 engraved double-page plates. The architectural pictures of ten colleges – Brasenose, Corpus, Magdalen, New, Oriel, Pembroke, Queen's, St John's, Trinity and Wadham – are the primary or only detailed records of how these buildings looked in the first third of the eighteenth century. Perspectively,

William Williams/William Henry Toms, 'Nova & accuratissima celeberrimae Universitatis Civitatisque Oxoniensis ichnographia', from William Williams, *Oxonia depicta, sive Collegiorum et aularum in inclyta Academia oxoniensi ichnographica, orthographica et scenographica delineatio . . .* (1733)

the treatment is fairly miscellaneous, with Trinity rating a bird's-eye view, Magdalen an inset plan, the Clarendon Building a so-called bird's-flight, and so forth.

This was the last hurrah of the south-at-top format that had been elevated by Speed [1605] from an idiosyncrasy into a norm, but Williams did make the important leap to what we would now consider a 'normal' ichnographic depiction, previously used only by specialists like de Gomme [1646] and Ogilby [1675]. This shift in perspective, coupled with an increase in scale, allows us to see clearly– for the first time – the southern road out of the city, Folly Bridge, and the three-storey bridge tower known since the time of Charles I as 'Friar Bacon's Study' (see also Nicholls [1724]), here marked '47'. In fact dating from some 80 years after the death of the scientific pioneer Friar Roger Bacon in the late thirteenth century, and known for most of its existence as New Gate, the South Bridge Tower, or Bachelor's Tower, it would be demolished in 1779 amid a series of improvement drives [1771, 1786].

Williams was not overly ambitious in terms of the proportion of the city's streets that were given any name at all, but he helpfully gives us alternatives for some of the larger ones, including the rarely heard 'South Street' for Fish Street (now St Aldates). Of 'George Lane or Thames Street', the latter name was considerably older. In this case, the use of 'lane' – a term which, unlike 'street', clearly implied a route with buildings, walls or other obstacles *on both sides* – was only justified by the building of houses on its northern side, a new development since the days of Hollar and de Gomme.

We can also see that intensive building has taken place in the northern parts of the western suburb of St Thomas's, along both the east side of present-day Hollybush Row and the western side of the west branch of the Castle Mill Stream. The laying of the cornerstone for the Radcliffe Library was still four years in the future, so it may seem odd that there are no houses or college outbuildings shown in the middle of 'Ratclif Square'. However, arranging for the clearance of this site was a monumental legal and business task in itself, lasting more than a decade, while the stipulations of Dr John Radcliffe's will prevented building from commencing until after the death of both his sisters, so the square did simply stand empty for a considerable period.

So little is known of Williams's life that we cannot even say whether the idea for *Oxonia Depicta* was his or something brought to his door by the university. A great deal more is known about William Henry Toms (d.1765), who engraved this map along with seven of the book's other plates. Born to a London naval family, Toms made his first engraving in 1723, and three years later was named in a list of the top practitioners of this art compiled by Samuel Sympson. By 1728, Toms was hard at work as an illustrator, for books on subjects as diverse as agricultural improvement, house-building and hydraulics. The present 1:3,168 map of Oxford may have been his first foray into cartographic subjects, but it would not be his last; within two years, he would collaborate with Henry Popple on 'the largest printed map of North America published during the colonial period' (E. Potten) and with Francis Blomefield on a *Topographical History of the County of Norfolk*. Then, between 1735 and 1739, Toms and the painter Robert West created a book of *Perspective Views of all the Ancient Churches, and Other Buildings, in the Cities of London, and Westminster*, for a list of subscribers that included pictorial satirist William Hogarth and the architect James Gibbs, who designed Oxford's Radcliffe Camera as well as St Martin-in-the-Fields. In the 1740s, Toms lived up to his early promise, developing 'a particular expertise in engraving maps and plans, many clearly intended for naval instruction and aimed at naval buyers. . . . His output in this field was prolific and his naval connections allowed him to respond rapidly to contemporary events' (Potten).

Toms's political views are suggested by the fact that he named one of his four children Henrietta Maria, after the wife of King Charles I. The map's two dedicatees were Oxford University's two Tory MPs: Viscount Cornbury, a crypto-Jacobite who offered the Old Pretender his support at a meeting in Rome in 1731, and spent most of his time in France after 1748; and George Clarke, a non-Jacobite and notable amateur architect. Between 1706, when he designed a warden's lodging at All Souls, and his death 30 years later,

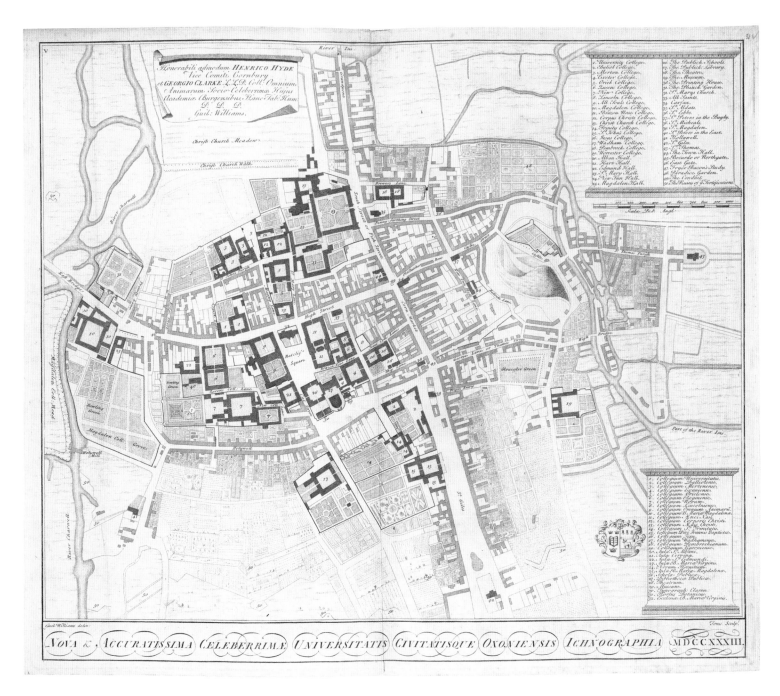

Clarke worked with Nicholas Hawksmoor [1724] on the Clarendon Building, Queen's College, Worcester College and the Codrington Library, and he modified Henry Aldrich's plans for Christ Church Library. Clarke 'left the bulk of his fortune' for the completion of the chapel block of Worcester that he and Hawksmoor had co-designed (T. Clayton).

1750

The most detailed mapping since Aggas

The son of a Worcester brass-founder, Isaac Taylor's childhood work included engraving customers' initials on silverware. According to legend, he walked to London after a fight with his father, 'fired with the ambition of distinguishing himself' as an oil painter. This fire, however, did not manifest itself as what might be called artistic temperament, and Taylor was noted for his strict morality and 'austere reserve' (J. Gilbert). It is widely believed that his first cartography-related work was as an apprentice to the great Thomas Jefferys, not yet geographer to the king; certainly, he married Jefferys's niece in 1754. It was around the same time that Taylor tried, and failed, to establish himself as a land surveyor in Essex.

The *Dictionary of National Biography* dates Taylor's move from his parental home in Worcester to Jefferys's employ to early 1752, but this seems unlikely on several grounds. Circumstantially, Taylor was by that date quite old to become an apprentice in any discipline, being already 21; but more significantly, we know that before the end of 1750 he had already surveyed not only the map of Oxford now before us, which was published in October 1751, but a map of Wolverhampton that Jefferys engraved. One wonders if, between his time in Worcester and London, Taylor worked in Birmingham for George Anderton, the engraver of this map, who had been in a position to take on multiple apprentices in 1745 and 1746.

Moreover, at 1:2,376, this was the largest-scale map of the whole city of Oxford that had been produced since Radulph Aggas's deeply flawed 1:1,800 effort at the dawn of English town mapping nearly two centuries earlier [1578]. This fact by itself hardly suggests that it was the work of a rank novice who definitively failed as a surveyor just four years later. Indeed, in terms of the naming of streets and parishes, and the demarcation of the latter using dotted lines,

---

Isaac Taylor/William Jackson and George Anderton, *To the Chancellor, Vice Chancellor, & Heads of Colleges, And to the High Steward, Mayor Aldermen &c. Of the University & City of Oxford; This Plan is humbly inscribed . . .* (1751)

A vision of Oxford's place in a society that was polite, prosperous and harmonious, but ultimately rural.

it was the most systematic map of Oxford produced up to its time, even if this made it look rather busy in comparison to Williams and Toms's splendidly clear plan of a few years before [1733]. Taylor's decision to orient his map with north at the top suggests that he was *au courant* with the latest European conventions and unafraid to step on a few toes in Oxford; and the human figures in the inset views at top left and top right imply an idealised audience drawn from 'polite society'. Likewise, the insets at the two bottom corners highlight the city's most fashionable new buildings, the James Gibbs-designed Radcliffe Library – completed as recently as 1749 – and Magdalen College's severely neo-classical New Building (it is still known by this name), begun in 1733 to a design tidied up by the Scottish Catholic Tory Gibbs but originated by the Hampshire-born Jacobite poet Edward Holdsworth (1684–1746). Taylor also chose Nicholls's [1724] neologistic 'Magdalen Bridge' over Williams's 'East Bridge': a name so traditional that it pre-dated the founding of Magdalen College and, as 'Estbrugge', modern English itself.

Taylor's inclusion of what we would now think of as census data in a rococo panel in the right margin also seems part and parcel of an ever-improving world in which gentlemen in knee-breeches point out the important features of the landscape with their walking-sticks, as ladies in side-hoops nod in agreement. The mapmaker's concerted attempt to project the qualities of 'politeness' and 'advancement' is partially undercut by his own naked eagerness to do so. In the same vein, it is worth noting his use of the vernacular rather than Williams's Latin and his (or Anderton's) partial abandonment of the ichnographic perspective: with houses of worship – but little else – depicted in side view, after the manner of Sir Bernard de Gomme [1646] a century before. In short, the map *is* plausibly the work of a lower-middle-class boy in his late teens, desperate for metropolitan and aristocratic approbation but still casting about for exactly how to achieve it.

Thomas Jefferys's son, also Thomas, was a business partner of William Faden's in the 1770s. It may have been through Taylor's web of Jefferys connections that Faden obtained the plates to this map, which became the basis of his own map of the city [1789]. As a general matter, the plates Taylor engraved 'were said to wear better at the press than those of any other engraver of his time' (R.T. Gilbert), and the longevity of these particular ones may further suggest Anderton's formative influence on Taylor.

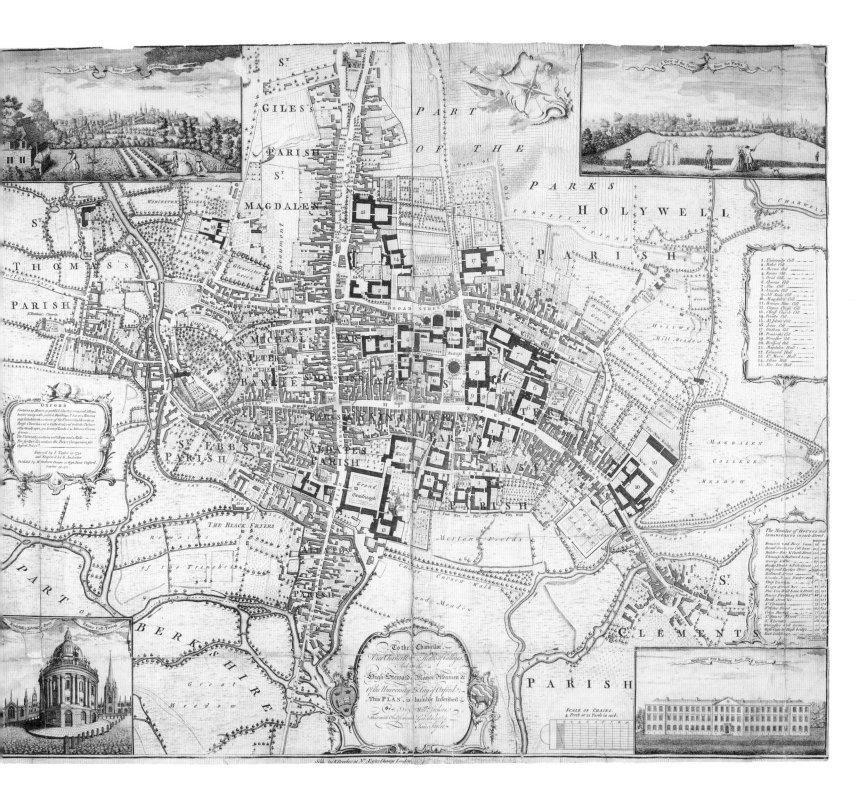

OXFORD
a 52 miles.
Ouest de Londres.

1759

Planning for a French descent on the British Isles

Jacobite plots, riots and rebellions aside [1724], the 1688 overthrow of King James II by his nephew/son-in-law William of Orange would have a host of long-term socioeconomic and cultural consequences. Not the least of these was that the peoples of Britain – who within living memory had focused their hostility on their Dutch colonial rivals, or on one another – inherited and rapidly internalised their pugnacious Dutch ruler's justifiable fear and suspicion of the authoritarian France of Louis XIV. Whereas the immediate pre-William era had been marked by a series of wars between Britain and the Netherlands, the 'long eighteenth century' from the Revolution to Waterloo would be a nearly continuous struggle between Britain and France.

Arguably, the apogee of this century of strife was its fourth major conflict, the world war known as the Seven Years' War – which actually lasted nine years, 1754–1763, if its critical North American theatre of operations is taken into account. To make a long story short, Britain and her allies (not including the Dutch Republic, for a change) humiliated France and all but ruined her financially, with Britain acquiring the bulk of the French colonial possessions in both India and Canada. The decisiveness of our final victory, however, can obscure just how dangerous and close-run this strategy had been.

After a string of setbacks, King Louis XV appointed Étienne-François, Duc de Choiseul, as his foreign minister and chief strategist. Choiseul aimed to end the war in 1759 by invading the British mainland with an army of up to 100,000 men, carried on a host of flat-bottomed barges specially constructed for the purpose. In an odd prefiguration of the Allies' successful 1944 disinformation campaign, a fake invasion would be launched from the Pas de Calais, while the real thrust came from Normandy. But amid a string of other lucky breaks (including 32-year-old Major-General James Wolfe's capture of Quebec City) that would go down in history as Britain's *annus mirabilis* of 1759, the Royal Navy first destroyed part of the invasion fleet in harbour at Le Havre in July, then crippled the French Mediterranean fleet off the coast of Portugal and finally, on 20 November, decimated the French Channel fleet at the Battle of Quiberon Bay. Incredibly, the French decoy force based at Dunkirk then actually captured Carrickfergus in the north of Ireland. They were soon rooted out; but if even 60 per cent of the main enemy force had been able to land in Hampshire, they would have outnumbered the British regular army forces then at home by more than three to one.

This crude 1:25,000 map comes from a 1759 addendum to Nicholas Bellin's lavishly illustrated *Essai Geographique sur les Isles Britanniques . . . Pour la Service des Vaisseaux du Roy* (Paris, 1757). In the original volume, the only maps were of Berwick, Caernarvon, London, Newcastle, Dublin, Galway, Kinsale, Kinsale Harbour, the 'Gulf of Edinburgh', Leith, the Bay of 'Locknouer' and the Isle of 'Pomona', also spelled 'Pomana' (Orkney Mainland), though the more numerous views included both Oxford and Cambridge. In the year of the planned invasion, however, a 'Recueil des Villes Portes d'Angleterre' containing many more town plans – including this page with Waterford and Oxford – was added to the book as an appendix. Bellin would have been well aware that the Thames was not navigable as far as Oxford by ocean-going warships. Rather, like York, it was probably included due to its historic status as an alternative capital city where British forces might rally if the French plan worked and London

quickly fell to the invaders. Nor did the British authorities entirely ignore this possibility themselves, as evidenced by a 1756 military report that Oxford's inns had sufficient beds for 270 soldiers and stabling for 550 horses, and by the 1759 formation of the Oxfordshire Militia.

That the French approach to the city was expected to come from the east is suggested by the undue prominence, strength and integrity assigned to the eastern face of the city wall, which had been labelled 'Ruins' by Taylor [1750]. Given that military mapping was, on the whole, still superior to civilian mapping at this time in scope if not always in quality, it should not surprise us that this French naval book of ichnographic town plans of Britain appeared several years earlier than its first civilian equivalent: Andrew Dury's *A Collection of Plans of the Principal Cities of Great Britain and Ireland with maps of the Coast . . .* (1764).

Bellin (1703–1772) was a child prodigy, appointed chief cartographer to the French navy at the age of 18. Over the next half a century, his output of maps, plans and charts was both enormous and renowned for its accuracy, and he was concurrently made Hydrographer to King Louis XV in 1741. In perhaps the ultimate vindication of the old saying, 'If you want something done quickly, ask a busy man,' Bellin also contributed nearly 1,000 articles to the *Encyclopédie* of Denis Diderot.

French support for the rebelled Thirteen Colonies was, in part, intended as retribution for her own Seven Years' War colonial losses – though the financial cost of this intervention, and of another failed descent on the British mainland planned for 1779, undoubtedly hastened the French Revolution. A further French invasion of Ireland took place in August 1798.

Opposite. Basic though they were, Bellin's maps of British and Irish towns would have been invaluable to French officers who found themselves in unfamiliar enemy territory.

WATERFORD
Près la Côte Meridionale de l'Irlande.

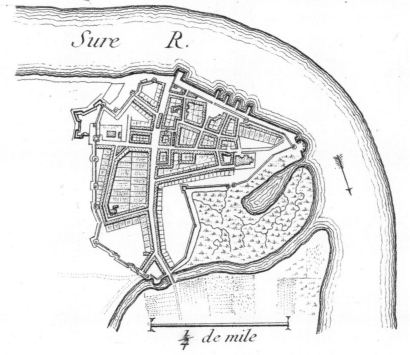

Sure R.

¼ *de mile*

OXFORD
a 52 mile.
Ouest de Londres.

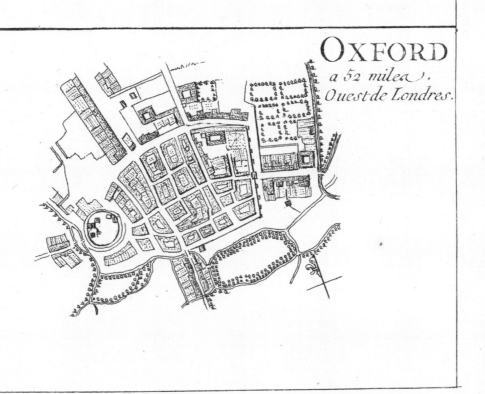

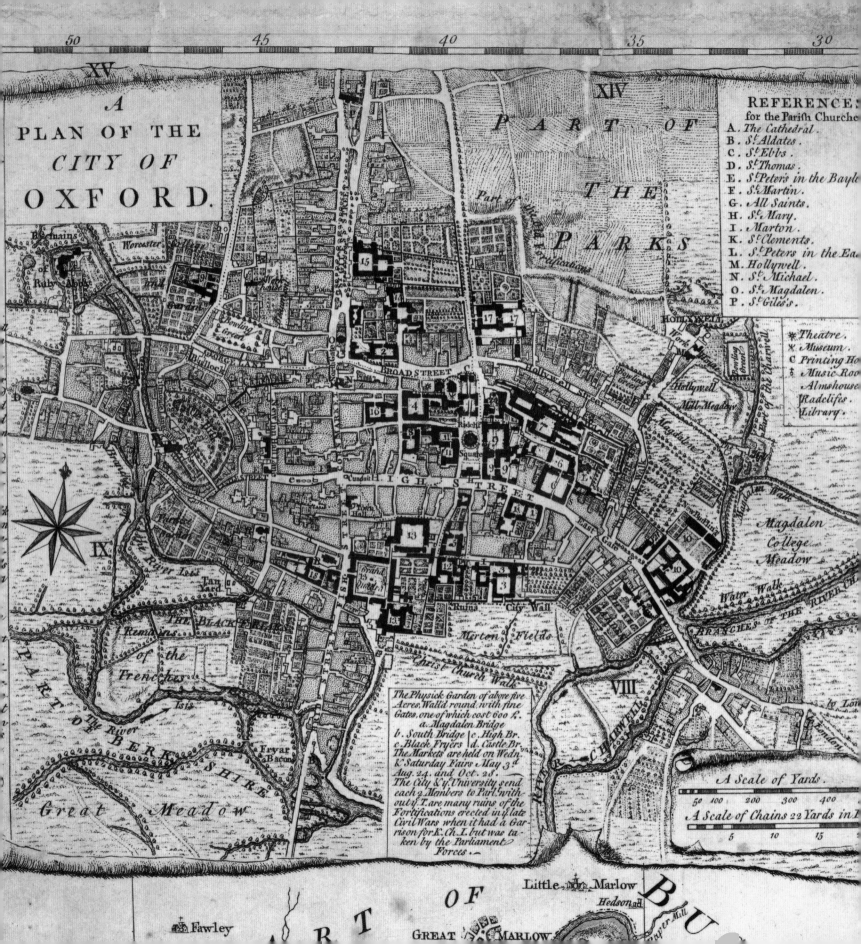

A PLAN OF THE CITY OF OXFORD.

50   45   40   35   30

XV

XIV

PART OF THE PARKS

Part of the old Fortifications

REFERENCES
for the Parish Churches
A. The Cathedral.
B. St Aldates.
C. St Ebbs.
D. St Thomas.
E. St Peter's in the Bayle
F. St Martin.
G. All Saints.
H. St Mary.
I. Marton.
K. St Clements.
L. St Peters in the Ea...
M. Hollywell.
N. St Michael.
O. St Magdalen.
P. St Giles's.

Theatre.
Museum.
Printing Ho...
Music Roo...
Almshouse...
Radclifes.
Library.

Worcester

B. chains of Ruly Abbey

Bowling Green

Bullock

BROAD STREET

HOLLYWELL

Hollywell
Mill-Meadow

Radcliff Square

HIGH STREET

East Gate

Magdalen College Meadow

Watr. Walk

BRANCHES OF THE RIVER CH...

Town Hall

Grand Quadr.

Ruins   City Wall

Mirton Fields

Christ Church Walk

THE BLACK FRIER

Remains of the Trenches

PART OF BERKSHIRE

The River Isis

Fryar Bacon

Great Meadow

IX

VIII

RIVER CHARWELL

to Lon...

to London

A Scale of Yards.
50 100   200   300   400
A Scale of Chains 22 Yards in...
5   10   15

The Physick Garden of above five Acres, Wall'd round, with fine Gates, one of which cost 600 £.
a. Magdalen Bridge
b. South Bridge   c. High Br...
c. Black Fryers   d. Castle Br...
The Markets are held on Wedn... & Saturday Fairs May 3d Aug. 24. and Oct. 28. The City & ye University send each 2 Members to Parl. with out ye T. are many ruins of the Fortifications erected in ye late Civil Wars when it had a Garrison for K. Ch. I. but was taken by the Parliament Forces.

Little Marlow
Hedson...
Fawley

PART OF BU...

GREAT MARLOW.

1761

John Rocque and the re-mapping of England

One of the acts that earned Louis XIV the mistrust of the rest of the world was the forcible conversion or expulsion of his country's entire Protestant population, who had been granted toleration since 1598 by an act of King Henri IV, Protestant convert to Catholicism and, incidentally, the maternal grandfather of Kings Charles II and James II of Great Britain. France's loss was, in large measure, England's gain. Despite homegrown English dissenters being still subject to major legal disabilities, their French equivalents – known as Huguenots – suffered little discrimination, especially within the British Army. Whole Huguenot regiments were raised for William III's war against the Irish Jacobites in the 1690s, and an act of Queen Anne briefly enabled the group's mass naturalisation, regardless of which Protestant denomination they associated themselves with. Appointed commander-in-chief in 1757 and tasked with defending Britain from invasion [1759], John

Ligonier (1680–1770) had been born to a Protestant family in Castres, Languedoc; his military career was almost as astonishing for its sheer length as for the fire-breathing bravado of his exploits on the battlefield. The noted cartographer Captain John Montresor (1736–1799), appointed chief engineer of the British forces in North America in 1775 largely on the strength of his survey work in Quebec, Nova Scotia and Maine stretching back into the early 1760s, was the grandson of another French-born British officer, who had been entrusted with the command of Fort William in Scotland in the 1720s. In all, some half a million Huguenots fled France and the French territories in present-day Belgium, and a high proportion of them settled in England and Ireland, in what the *Economist* newspaper has called 'the biggest influx in British history . . . relative to the population at the time'.

One of the newcomers – whose family seems to have been

John Rocque/Mary-Ann Rocque, *Map of the County of Berks reduced from an actual survey in 18 sheets by the late John Rocque* (1762)

drawn in specifically by Queen Anne's abovementioned Foreign Protestants Naturalisation Act – would be instrumental in what I have elsewhere called the 'civil-isation' of cartography in the middle years of the eighteenth century: the gradual process by which mapping, and engineering disciplines more generally, ceased to be subordinated to military requirements, though often still executed by military officers. Having arrived in the French Quarter of London's Soho via Geneva, John Rocque (c.1704–1762) rapidly made a name for himself as a 'dessinateur des jardins' and estate surveyor, beginning with the royal park at Richmond. His assiduous and successful cultivation of royal and aristocratic patrons throughout his career meant that he would be one of the few cartographers of his era who both undertook major new survey work and was never declared bankrupt. His estate planning enabled him to travel widely, which in turn both inspired and facilitated his production of improved county maps and town plans. He also kept up his connections on the Continent, particularly with an engraver nephew who had fled to Mannheim. An advertisement from June 1751 mentioned that Rocque's shop sold 'a great choice of foreign maps, plans, battles, sieges, &c. newly imported, likewise plans of Nimes and Montpelier', and he eventually published atlases that included plans of larger foreign cities; '[i]t is this breadth of output which established his reputation as one of the most prolific and innovative map makers of the eighteenth century' (P. Laxton). Rocque's masterpiece was arguably the survey of London he commenced in 1738 and which was printed in 1746 from 24 plates engraved by John Pine.

Over the course of the rest of his life, Rocque produced stand-alone plans of three more English and three Irish towns, beginning with Bristol in 1743; from the early 1750s, this work overlapped in time – if rarely in space – with his large-scale mapping of four English and two Irish counties, starting with Shropshire. A leader of this period's trend for mapping multiple counties at a large scale and in a similar style, Rocque also broke from county-mapping tradition by showing even quite small towns in plan view, rather than side view or as mere icons – though for settlements below a certain population threshold, he still employed icons of an essentially medieval type, as seen here. That his county maps were intended for wayfinding is suggested by the inclusion of individual farm names and the positions of windmills, and whether or not each road was unenclosed (dotted lines) or hedged/fenced (continuous fuzzy lines). Printed on 18 sheets at an impressively large scale of 2 inches to the mile, Rocque's atlas of Berkshire – co-surveyed by Josiah Ballard and engraved by L.F. Deharme and Richard Benning – was originally conceived in 1751 as a part of a 1-inch mapping that would include Oxfordshire and Buckinghamshire, but in the event, Rocque's organisation never published atlases or maps of the other two counties. Work on Berkshire was slow and intermittent, apparently due to Rocque's frequent absences in Ireland, with only the first six sheets being produced in the first six years of the project. This map, itself a healthy size, was published as a key: covered with a grid numbered in Roman numerals, 'to shew in what manner the large Map is Divided, and the Number of Sheets it Contains'.

In a nod to Speed [1605], an inset street plan of the city of Oxford is placed at the upper right of the county map. This plan is quite problematic in terms of its scale, which is given as 1:10,440 in yards, but 1:9,900 in chains. In content, it is beholden to Taylor [1750] in terms of the use of dotted lines for parish boundaries, but steadfastly rejects his non-ichnographic visual touches, as well as his focus on modernity in the captions: instead discussing the twelfth- and seventeenth-century civil wars, town-and-gown violence in the reign of King John, the 1630s cost of the Physic Garden's gate, the ancientness of the colleges and so forth.

Though the engraver and cartographer Thomas Jefferys (d.1771) is often described as a mere follower of Rocque, the present map's emphasis on market and fair days indicates that the influence might have operated in the other direction as well, for such information had been a priority for *The Small English Atlas* Jefferys had produced with Thomas Kitchin in the late 1740s. Moreover, Jefferys had been working for the successful Ogilby-imitator Emanuel Bowen [1675] as early as the mid 1730s, when Rocque had yet to enter the printed-map business at all.

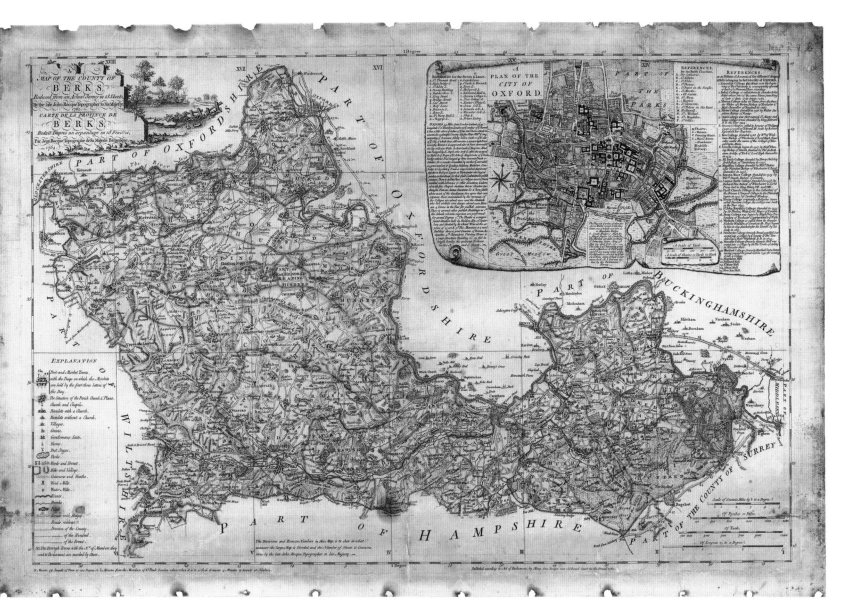

Rocque was appointed Topographer to the Prince of Wales in 1751, and his 1756 plan of Dublin 'so impressed George II that he had it hung on the walls of his apartment' (Laxton). As indicated here in the cartouche, Rocque's title was then upgraded to Topographer to His Majesty upon the prince becoming George III in 1760 – though Jefferys was concurrently made the king's *geographer*, probably due to his direct contribution to military mapping in the ongoing war against France. Rocque's Surrey appeared posthumously, and an Essex project that he had planned was commenced by his widow, Mary-Ann (Bew) Rocque, in partnership with their colleague Pierre André. Mrs Rocque is also identified as the publisher of this map, in its lower margin.

1762

The first street map of a British town in a tourist guidebook

This small, unassuming 1:21,120 plan, which was engraved by B. Green and printed in the *Pocket Companion for Oxford* (1762) published by Daniel Prince, John Rivington and Richard Baldwin, holds a remarkable place in the history of tourism: as the first, or at any rate oldest surviving, street map in a guidebook to a British town. The next-oldest equivalent, published a year later, was of Cambridge, followed by Bath after a gap of a decade; and only four other towns are known to have received the same treatment by the end of the eighteenth century. As this might tend to suggest, tourism itself was a fairly new concept – though it should be noted that an earlier, map-less edition of the *Pocket Companion* was advertised in the left-hand cartouche of Isaac Taylor's much larger map from the previous decade [1750]. On an international level, it is only after the seventeenth-century 'push factors' of

political and religious exile are largely supplanted by the 'pull factors' of foreign cultures – especially Italian and ancient Roman – that we can speak of tourists rather than travellers. Nevertheless, Oxford's Physic Garden [*c.*1834], today called the Botanical Garden, drew in a fair share of visitors from other parts of England and abroad almost from its first formation in the early seventeenth century. One of these was Celia Fiennes, whose extraordinary horseback journeys around England and Scotland, undertaken for their own sake over two decades beginning in 1684, could be classified more as 'exploration' than tourism in the modern sense (D. Hey). She wrote, but did not publish, a 2,000-word description of her trip to Oxford, including that the church of Mary the Virgin, though 'very large and Lofty', had 'Nothing very Curious in it'. The Physic Garden was 'great diversion and

---

B. Green, 'A Plan of the University and City of Oxford', from Daniel Prince, John Rivington and Richard Baldwin,
*A Pocket Companion for Oxford: or, guide through the University. Containing an accurate description of the public edifices,
the buildings in each of the colleges; the gardens . . . Adorned with a plan and other copper-plates* (1762)

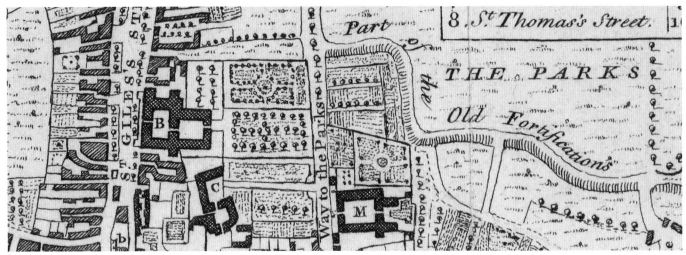

The gardens to the north and east of St John's, Trinity and Wadham colleges are rendered in surprising detail, given the map's small scale.

pleasure [. . . which] would have entertained one a week', but Fiennes seems to have been even more impressed by the Sheldonian: both as a building, and for the printing house it contained, where she was allowed to print her own name 'Severall tymes' in the basement and see 'the Drying [of] the Printed Sheetes of bookes' in the attic.

For the most part, however, people's itineraries within Britain at the beginning of the eighteenth century were determined by business and family considerations and the attractions of a handful of important spa towns. The turning point in the rise of English domestic tourism can probably be traced to the runaway success of Daniel Defoe's non-fiction *A Tour thro' the Whole Island of Great Britain, Divided into Circuits or Journies* (3 volumes, 1724–27). Conceptually unprecedented, it would be his most lucrative project apart from *Robinson Crusoe* (1719). As expanded by the noted novelist and printer Samuel Richardson, the *Tour* was republished five times between 1738 and 1762.

As one might have gathered from Shakespeare's regular itinerary alone [1605], Oxford was an important way station for travellers between London and the Midlands from a very early date. It was this, rather than any academic or military considerations, that led to the development of immense

courtyard inns, including the Mitre, that took up 'much of the available space in the central streets' (A. Crossley). The number of temporary visitors of the middling and upper ranks of society is suggested by the statistics on the number of horses that could be accommodated by the inns: 504 in 1686, and 550 60 years later.

The *Pocket Companion* itself was not the first thing of its kind, and a number of other guidebook publishers were quick to include maps in their own rival volumes. One of the first, in 1763, was a 1:19,800 plan in the third edition of *A Gentleman of Oxford, The New Oxford Guide*, published in Oxford by James Fletcher and Sackville Parker. Since the appearance of *A Gentleman*'s first edition in 1759, when James Rivington – presumably a relative of John Rivington – had acted as a third partner, Fletcher's shop had been located in the Turl, and Parker's in the High Street. Daniel Prince's was 'near the Clarendon Printing-House', but both of his partners were based in London.

The man sometimes controversially referred to as the first travel agent in British history, Richard Cox (1718–1803), had been made private secretary and personal banker to General the Lord Ligonier [1761] in 1758, and began his agenting career as a broker for army commissions, uniforms and

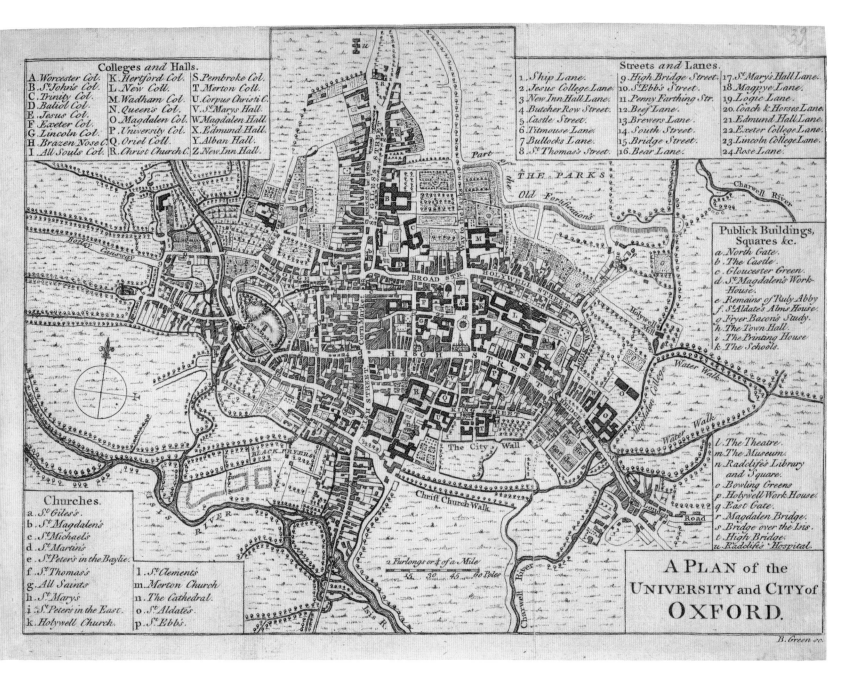

Colleges *and* Halls.

A. *Worcester Col.*
B. *St John's Col.*
C. *Trinity Col.*
D. *Baliol Col.*
E. *Jesus Col.*
F. *Exeter Col.*
G. *Lincoln Col.*
H. *Brazen Nose C.*
I. *All Souls Col.*
K. *Hertford Col.*
L. *New Col.*
M. *Wadham Col.*
N. *Queen's Col.*
O. *Magdalen Col.*
P. *University Col.*
Q. *Oriel Coll.*
R. *Christ Church C.*
S. *Pembroke Col.*
T. *Merton Coll.*
U. *Corpus Christi C.*
V. *St Marys Hall.*
W. *Magdalen Hall.*
X. *Edmund Hall.*
Y. *Alban Hall.*
Z. *New Inn Hall.*

Streets *and* Lanes.

1. *Ship Lane.*
2. *Jesus College Lane.*
3. *New Inn Hall Lane.*
4. *Butcher Row Street.*
5. *Castle Street.*
6. *Titmouse Lane.*
7. *Bullocks Lane.*
8. *St Thomas's Street.*
9. *High Bridge Street.*
10. *St Ebb's Street.*
11. *Penny Farthing Str.*
12. *Beef Lane.*
13. *Brewers Lane.*
14. *South Street.*
15. *Bridge Street.*
16. *Bear Lane.*
17. *St Mary's Hall Lane.*
18. *Magpye Lane.*
19. *Logic Lane.*
20. *Coach & Horses Lane.*
21. *Edmund Hall Lane.*
22. *Exeter College Lane.*
23. *Lincoln College Lane.*
24. *Rose Lane.*

Publick Buildings, Squares &c.

a. *North Gate.*
b. *The Castle.*
c. *Gloucester Green.*
d. *St Magdalen's Work-House.*
e. *Remains of Ruly Abby*
f. *St Aldate's Alms House.*
g. *Fryer Bacon's Study.*
h. *The Town Hall.*
i. *The Printing House*
k. *The Schools.*
l. *The Theatre.*
m. *The Museum.*
n. *Radclife's Library and Square.*
o. *Bowling Greens*
p. *Holywell Work House.*
q. *East Gate.*
r. *Magdalen Bridge.*
s. *Bridge over the Isis.*
t. *High Bridge.*
u. *Radclife's Hospital.*

Churches.

a. *St Giles's.*
b. *St Magdalen's*
c. *St Michaels*
d. *St Martin's*
e. *St Peter's in the Baylie.*
f. *St Thomas's*
g. *All Saints*
h. *St Mary's*
i. *St Peter's in the East.*
k. *Holywell Church.*
l. *St Clements*
m. *Merton Church*
n. *The Cathedral.*
o. *St Aldate's.*
p. *St Ebbs.*

A PLAN of the
UNIVERSITY and CITY of
OXFORD.

B. Green sc.

supplies. Concurrently Secretary to the Board of Ordnance from 1759, Cox was married to a great-granddaughter of Christopher Codrington, benefactor of All Souls College's Codrington Library. Now based in India, the rather astonish- ingly miscellaneous agency Cox established as Cox & Drummond in London in 1765 remains prominent in the travel business under the name Cox & Kings, and is still in private hands.

...vigable CANAL,
...near the City
of Oxford.
...S.

			M.F.	Ch.	F.I.		
From	Gosford Green near Coventry, to Bindley		1 6	9 48	64 0	Fall
	Bindley, to Brinklow		4 7	5 33	64 0	Rise
	The Coventry Canal near Bedworth, to Brinklow		10 7	2 35		Level
	Brinklow, to Hill Morton		9 1	2 60		Level
	Hill Morton, to N.º 106 near the top of Napton field		17 1	4 78	88 0	Rise
	N.º 106 to N.º 123, near Claydon		8 5	0 97		Level
	Claydon, to Banbury		6 4	8 40	88 0	Fall
	Banbury, to the River Isis near Oxford		29 3	8 72	116 0	Fall

PART OF

OXFORD

to London

OXFORDSHIRE

Svell Bridge *Aynho*
Souldern
Sommerton
Upper Heyford
Lower Heyford
North Brook
Kirtlington
Blechington
Clifton
Deddington
North Aston
Middle Aston
Steple Aston
Rousham
Tackley
Whitehill
Enslow Bridge
Shipton
Hampton Gay
R. Charwell
Kidlington
Thrap Begbrook
Hillhetton
Water-Eaton
Price House
Price Brook
Wolvercott
Hayfields
Hutt
River Isis
Medley House
R.Isis
Begbrook
Woodstock
Blenheim
Hooknorton Lodge
Sibberts
Temple Mill
Brails Mill
River Stour
Whichford Mill

S H I R E

J. Cole, sculp. Oxon.

1768

Planning the Oxford Canal

One of the more interesting figures in the immediate prehistory of the industrial revolution, James Brindley (1716–1772) – nicknamed 'The Schemer' – was born to a Derbyshire farming family and apprenticed to a millwright. By the 1740s he was involved in the mechanisation of the silk- and papermaking trades in various parts of the Midlands and Northwest of England, and in the following decade received English patent no. 730 for a steam-engine boiler design. But what really made his name was his ambitious and successful effort to drain Manchester's Wet Earth Colliery via a water-powered pumping system fed by an 800-yard-long underground tunnel connecting the mine to the River Irwell.

In 1758, Brindley was hired to survey a 93-mile canal linking Liverpool to the Staffordshire potteries – built as the Trent–Mersey Canal from 1766–77 – and in 1759 was brought into an existing project for the 41-mile Bridgewater Canal, by which coal from the Duke of Bridgewater's mines at Worsley would be transported into Manchester. Brindley's radical reimagining of the original route led to the canal being carried over the Irwell on an aqueduct high enough to allow sailing vessels to pass underneath; it was this tour de force element that led to the canal as whole being hyperbolically described as the most remarkable thing in Europe. Previously, coal on the same route was carried largely by packhorses, which could only haul a few hundred pounds each; now, a single horse could tow a 30-tonne, 7-foot-wide canal boat. The maximum width of a boat was initially constrained to 7 feet by the width of the Brindley-designed Harecastle boat tunnel on the Trent and Mersey Canal, but this quickly emerged as a de facto national standard, prefiguring the railway gauges of the following century. Unsurprisingly, the price of coal in Manchester fell by half, but the canal's owners still made sizeable profits by

Robert Whitworth/J. Cole, *A Plan of the intended Navigable Canal, from the Coventry Canal near the City of Coventry, to the City of Oxford* (1768)

charging tolls. Because the cost of digging tunnels by hand increased drastically with their diameter, early canal tunnels mostly lacked towpaths. The crewmen (or locally hired specialists) therefore had to power the boats through by pushing off the tunnel walls or ceilings with their feet, a technique known as 'legging'. As the speed of a fully laden 'legged' boat might be less than 1 mile per hour, there was ample time for the horse to be walked round to meet its boat at the other end.

Though surveyed a year later than the Trent and Mersey, the Bridgewater Canal opened first, in 1761, and was so successful that it ushered in a national period of 'canal mania'; Brindley himself was involved in no fewer than 23 canal schemes, of which 18 came to fruition, in just 14 years. One of his few failures, the Stockton and Darlington Canal, famously succeeded as a railway instead, from 1825. The fever of largely justified excitement regarding the economic potential of 'wholly artificial' canals culminated in a major speculative bubble, with nearly £3 million in canal shares issued as of 1793.

Immensely talented surveyor and engineer though he was, Brindley's claim to 'visionary' status rests on the fact that he correctly foresaw the possibility of the world's first holistic national canal system, linking England's four major rivers: the Mersey, Trent, Severn and Thames. Specifically, this would take the form of a cross, with the northern and eastern arms formed by the Trent and Mersey Canal, and the western arm by the Staffordshire and Worcestershire Canal, authorised in 1766. This left the southern arm, to the Thames, to be completed; and the city of Oxford stood on the verge of becoming the midpoint of the shortest and most economical transport route between London and the new factories of the Midlands. The people of Oxford bought £30,000 worth of shares in the scheme and contributed a further £70,000 in loans.

Brindley began the 78-mile Oxford Canal at its southern end, with a canal basin excavated just south of Hythe Bridge [1838]. Though corrupted to 'High Bridge' by Jacobean times, the original name of the place, spelled *hýð*, was Old English for a 'port or haven, *esp.* a small haven or landing-place on a river' (*OED*), correctly reflecting the use of this point on the Castle Mill Stream as a commercial landing-place since before

the Norman Conquest. But in the event, the main part of the precariously financed project would proceed southwards from Coventry. When Brindley died of a chill caught while surveying a canal near Wedgwood's Etruria factory in Staffordshire at the age of 56, the duty of completing the 'Grand Cross' fell in part to his Bridgewater Canal colleague and brother-in-law Samuel Simcock (*fl.* 1766–92), and in part to the author of this map, the Yorkshireman Robert Whitworth Sr (1734–1799). Brindley's most able assistant, not only as a surveyor and draughtsman but as political lobbyist for the canal-building

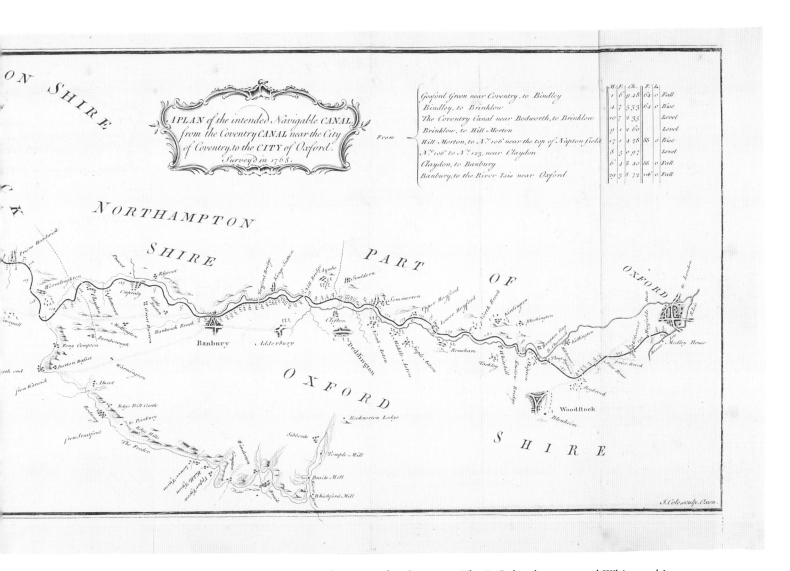

A PLAN of the intended Navigable CANAL from the Coventry CANAL near the City of Coventry, to the CITY of Oxford. Survey'd in 1768.

From	M.	F.	Ch.	P.	L.	
Gosford Green near Coventry, to Bindley	1	6	9	48	61	o	Fall
Bindley, to Brinklow	4	7	5	33	61	o	Rise
The Coventry Canal near Bedworth, to Brinklow	10	7	2	35			Level
Brinklow, to Hill Morton	9	1	2	60			Level
Hill Morton, to No. 106 near the top of Napton field	17	1	4	78	88	o	Rise
No. 106 to No. 123, near Claydon	8	5	o	97			Level
Claydon, to Banbury	6	4	8	40	88	o	Fall
Banbury, to the River Isis near Oxford	29	3	8	72	116	o	Fall

interest, Whitworth went on to become chief engineer for the extension of the Forth and Clyde Canal in the later 1780s; and it is conceivable that the notorious cheapness and corner-cutting of the Oxford Canal's final stretch from Banbury to Oxford, built between 1786 and 1789, may have been due in part to rival claims on Whitworth's attention. Nevertheless, the Oxford Canal would become one of the most successful in Britain, and especially so until the 1805 completion of the rival Grand Junction Canal, which provided an easier and more direct route between the West Midlands and London.

The J. Cole who engraved Whitworth's map may or may not have been Benjamin Cole I's grandson, John [1695]. Whitworth's sons Robert Jr and William carried on after their father in the canal-building business, arguably extending Brindley's influence on British civil engineering far into the nineteenth century. Debates still simmer over whether the Bridgewater Canal or the Sankey Brook Navigation (from St Helens to the Mersey) was the first modern canal in Britain, though the Newry Canal in Northern Ireland is quite a bit older than either.

RWELL.

BRIDGE

S.T CLEMENTS
CHURCH

Church
Yard

idge as at present w.th the parts Adjacent.

1771

John Gwynn and the making of modern Oxford

Oxford's constraint by swampy ground on three sides – the very feature that had made it an ideal site for settlement from Saxon times down to the end of the Civil War [1646, 1648] – rapidly became a disadvantage with the coming of internal peace and a growing population and economy in the eighteenth century. Certainly, the city would not experience comprehensive re-planning of the sort seen in Bath, Edinburgh and elsewhere, but this is not to say that the services of an important town planner were not sought, or obtained. Shrewsbury-born John Gwynn (1713–1786), like his contemporary James Brindley [1768], was from lower-middle-class origins and largely self-taught; contemporaries remarked his 'integrity', 'industry' and 'perseverance' as much as the accuracy of his drawing and measurement. Having begun his career as a carpenter, he gained considerable attention for his *An Essay on Design* (1749) and un-adopted 1759 plans for the rebuilding of London's Blackfriars Bridge, and became a

lifelong friend of the celebrated Dr Samuel Johnson [1724]. Long before King George III named him as one of the 34 founding members of the Royal Academy of Arts in 1768, Gwynn had attained – though it is difficult to say 'earned' – a reputation as one of the foremost architects in Britain.

The medieval East Bridge over the Cherwell, just outside Oxford's East Gate, was surveyed in late 1770 or early 1771 and deemed irreparable by local mason John Townsend. No one was especially surprised when it collapsed at its western end during floods in 1772, but plans to remake it had already been afoot for some time, due to its manifestly poor condition and the fact that it was too narrow for the amount and type of vehicular traffic the city was now receiving. The triangular projections at its sides, shown clearly by Nicholls [1724], allowed pedestrians a refuge from passing carts, waggons and carriages. The replacement bridge was built by John Randall beginning in 1772, to a design by Gwynn in his guise as

---

John Gwynn, *Plan of Magdalen Bridge as at present w[i]th the parts Adjacent* (1771)

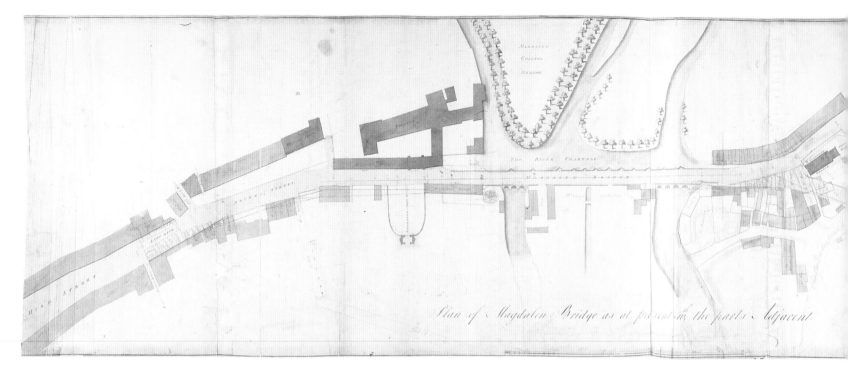

Plan of Magdalen Bridge as at present in the parts adjacent

Surveyor to the Commissioners of the Oxford Paving Act, for which he was paid £150 per annum 'for three years certain and . . . one year more if necessary'. Gwynn's architectural commissions had been so few, up to this time, that this salary may have represented the bulk of his income during the years in question.

Milham Bridge, consisting of two stone arches over the west branch of the Cherwell at the southwest corner of the Physic Garden [*c*.1834] joined by a causeway to a wooden bridge over the eastern branch, had been destroyed during the Civil War; however, it was now re-created on a temporary basis to facilitate traffic flow during the lengthy rebuilding process. The new Magdalen Bridge had just over half as many arches as its predecessor, but was considerably wider, at 27 feet. Plagued by budgetary problems, it did not open to traffic until 1778. Its balustrade was completed only in 1782 – and without the imposing stone sphinxes by Anglo-Swiss sculptor Henry Webber (1754–1826) that Gwynn had wanted – while work on various other aspects would continue intermittently for a further eight years, four of them after its architect had died of old age.

Oxford's medieval city wall had four main gates, named for the cardinal compass directions, and four subsidiary gates. The High Street ended at the East Gate: two squat three-storey crenellated towers joined by an arch, immediately to the east of Coach and Horses Lane, one of the then-prevailing names for the north–south-running part of Merton Street (the east–west-running portion was called King Street). Beyond the gate, the roadway narrowed drastically and was called Bridge Street or Briggeshythe, running across the East Bridge and then via St Clement's to the top of Headington Hill. The gate was ordered removed by an Act of Parliament in May 1770, specifically so that Bridge Street could be made as wide as the High Street proper. As shown, this scheme involved the partial or complete demolition of around a dozen houses and shops.

The gate-removal and bridge were not Gwynn's only commissions in Oxford, however. The city's workhouses, which had long been organised on a parish-by-parish basis, had begun consolidating half a century before this date: with Mary the Virgin, St Martin's and All Saints jointly leasing the Flying Horse inn (now called the Eastgate Hotel, 73 High Street) to use for this purpose in 1726. In the same year, a workhouse serving seven or eight parishes was established in part of the Whitefriars building on Gloucester Green by a

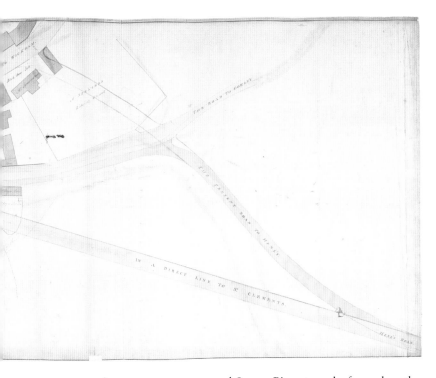

private contractor named James Piggot, and after a lengthy period of disorganisation resulting from Piggot's retirement, was taken over by a new contractor named Solomon Cross. When Cross in his turn quit the scene, in 1767, a less volatile solution was sought. Authorised by another Act of Parliament in 1771, a large committee called the Guardians of the Poor was established and voted to erect a 'General House of Industry . . . to contain at least 300 Poor' on a 5-acre site in the parish of St Mary Magdalen called Rats and Mice Hill, previously part of Beaumont Palace [1831b] and subsequently known as Wellington Square. (Converted into a Carmelite friary in the fourteenth century and closed at the Reformation, much of the palace was 'recycled' into seventeenth-century extensions to nearby St John's College.) Advertisements seeking an architect were placed in the newspapers in September of the same year. Gwynn won the contract, with the stipulations that the workhouse be finished within two years at a cost of less than £4,030 – around £6.2 million at today's values. Apart from the basic functions that would have been necessary in any small self-contained community, such as baking, brewing and burying the dead, the inmates were involved in carding and spinning wool, making sacks and

sweeping the city streets. Though the building itself was praised by contemporaries as having a 'good plan' and 'airy situation', it soon became 'exceedingly dirty', a state that was blamed largely on bad management.

The initial, 1771 design for Oxford's famed Covered Market was also Gwynn's. Rather precisely, it marked a moment of transition between the medieval mode of internal trade, in which merchants hauled their goods to public market-places and fairs – sometimes at a great distance from their homes and warehouses, but only on certain set days – and the modern form of retail shopkeeping that is fixed in space but virtually unrestricted in time. As an attempt to marry the advantages of the medieval marketplace with those of enclosed buildings, it succeeded admirably, though it came somewhat too late to have more than a local impact on retailing trends. Gwynn's greatest contribution to architecture, however, was not a building at all, but another publication, *London and Westminster Improved* (1776), a proto-Keynesian argument in favour of magnificent public-works projects as a means of spreading prosperity via the workmen's wages while simultaneously boosting public morale. The blame, or credit, for no such programme having been adopted in Oxford should not be laid at Gwynn's door, however. A 1773 proposal by recent Queen's College graduate Edward Tatham (1749–1834) for the complete re-planning of the city was roundly ignored, much as Hawksmoor's had been 60 years earlier [1724], though this did not stop Tatham from expanding and republishing it in 1777.

The Covered Market was never completed to Gwynn's design, which at just under £4,000 was deemed far too expensive; rather, it continued to be developed, altered and improved almost continuously into the late Victorian period, which explains its present appearance. The workhouse population was relocated to Cowley in the 1860s, and Gwynn's building demolished. Magdalen Bridge today generally preserves its Gwynn-era appearance, but only when seen from the sides, having been widened by 20 feet to the southward in 1882 to make room for a tramway down the centre [1930].

1 St Giles's Church
2 House of Industry
3 St John's College
4 St Magdalen's Church
5 Baliol College
6 Trinity College
7 Wadham College
8 Music Room
9 Printing House
10 Theatre
11 Musæum
12 St Michael's Church
13 Jesus College
14 Market
15 Exeter College
16 The Schools
17 Hertford College
18 New College
19 Radclife Library
20 St Mary's Church
21 All Souls College
22 Bowling Greens

WORCESTER COLLEGE

LAND

and

GARDENS

Gloucester Green

Beaumont

St GILES'S STREET

BOTLEY
ROAD
High Bridge
Street
High Bridge

St THOMAS'S STREET

George Lane
GEORGE LANE

Castle Upton
Fismouse Lane

Castle Hill

New Inn Hall Lane

Ship

CORN MARKET

Butcher Row Street

49
50
48
52
45
46
47
4

1773

Improvement in full cry

The 'modern' history of the city of Oxford is widely held to have begun with the formation in 1771 of the Paving Commission, who were certainly conscientious in their pursuit of something akin to city planning. Though this map owes a great deal to Isaac Taylor's [1750], of which it is effectively a reduction and simplification, many changes since Taylor's time are accurately reflected. For instance, the North Gate and its small attached prison known as the Bocardo were taken down in 1771, to 'general approbation' (C.J. Day), and the four butchers' buildings down the centre of what is now called Queen Street were dismantled two years later. Headline-grabbing one-off demolitions were only part of the story, however. From 1773, the Commissioners oversaw the installation of streetlights at regular intervals in the main streets and all other streets that had been newly paved, and ensured

that they were lit for eight hours nightly between October and March. This was a major improvement on the frequently evaded seventeenth-century rule that freemen mount lanterns on their houses and keep them lit from 6 p.m. to 9 p.m. during the months of November, December and January. Arguably the most complex aspect of the Commission's work, however, was road-widening and the clearance of permanent obstacles to traffic [1771, 1786], alongside its titular function – paving the city streets using 'large squared blocks with side gutters ... equal to the best-paved streets in London'. This would not be completed until 1779; and the Commissioners' war against illegal parking by 'postchaises, carts, or waggons' would go on indefinitely, and in a sense continues still.

This *c.*1:5,000 plan by Barak Longmate II (d.1793), who is now remembered almost exclusively as an illustrator of

Barak Longmate II, 'New Map of the City of Oxford', from Anthony à Wood,
The antient and present state of the city of Oxford . . . ed. J. Peshall (1773)

books about heraldry, appeared at the beginning of the 1773 edition of Anthony à Wood's *The Antient and Present State of the City of Oxford* . . . edited and expanded by Revd Sir J. Peshall, Bt, JP, antiquary. Given such a provenance, and that Longmate decided to re-create the side views of churches that were already old-fashioned when Taylor and Anderton deployed them a generation earlier, it might be tempting to see this map as a kind of final punctuation mark on the old city of towering, ramshackle half-timbered houses, overburdened carriers' waggons, stinking open-air butchers' and fishmongers' shops, Jacobite plotters and streets paved with gravel, if at all. This would be quite unfair, however, not least because Peshall himself was 'among the most active' of the Paving Commission's members during its first four years of existence (R.H. Sweet); and in his separate capacity as first governor of the Board of Guardians of the Poor, he personally laid the foundation stone of John Gwynn's new workhouse [1771]. Moreover, the Commission's formation – though partly a reaction to improvements that were occurring outside the city's boundaries, particularly to the national road-transport network – was in some sense merely an intensification and integration of improvement drives within the city that dated back a century or more.

At the time this map was surveyed, the centre of Oxford had recently been connected to the nascent turnpike system via Park End Street and the New Road – both still unnamed here. It had had a waterworks at Folly Bridge since 1694, connected by wooden pipes to a network of fireplugs since 1702. The Radcliffe Infirmary, the city's first hospital in the modern sense, had been planned as long ago as 1758 for a site running from Woodstock Road to Walton Street, and completed (according to Peshall's addenda to Wood's text) at a cost of £7,000 in 1771, not counting the value of 10 acres of land donated by the Duke of Marlborough in 1772; Peshall himself contributed money to the cause.

Even paving per se was hardly a novelty. As early as 1517, it was recorded that Corpus Christi College was responsible '[f]or paving half the street from the woodyard gate by the wall of Merton College to the corner of the wall next to Canterbury College' with 'stone and sand', and it appears that similar arrangements were normal for all the colleges in those days. (Established in 1362, Canterbury College was dissolved at the Reformation and its buildings acquired by Christ Church.) When Merton leased inner-suburban land for house-building in the late Elizabethan period, they stipulated that the tenants/builders pave the street to the whole width of each new house, and as far as the gutter that ran down the middle. City-owned building plots carried similar requirements; and given that many or most of Oxford's private houses in the early modern period were built on leased land, this must have had some effect, even if quite a few lessees and their numerous sub-tenants evaded their responsibilities. In 1682, the street connecting the end of the Marston road to the parish church in the eastern suburb of St Clement's was paved with cobbles rammed into pebbles, a process known as 'pitching', and flanked with 'hard white stones' for pedestrian use. The High Street in the immediate vicinity of St Mary the Virgin had been 'pitched' a few years earlier, and some of the less salubrious city lanes were derisively described as 'unpitched'. That being said, it is not clear that any similar improvements had been made to the main north–south route through the city by 1687, when (on the occasion of a royal visit) the whole way from the North Gate to Christ Church was 'laid thick with gravel, that no horses or coaches could be heard tread or go'. This was evidently not 'gravel' as we know it, not least because 'abundance of rain . . . turned it all to dirt' just one day later. In the early 1690s, however, Celia Fiennes described the major streets within the walls as all 'very Cleane and well Pitched'.

Longmate went on to edit the nine-volume fifth edition of *Collins's Peerage* that appeared beginning in 1779. In the following decade he produced *Longmate's Pocket Peerage*, which went through seven editions in 25 years, the last four of them appearing posthumously under the supervision of his son, Barak Longmate III (1768–1836). The elder Longmate's success as a publisher is further indicated by the fact that upon his death, he left books worth £235 and £1,500 in cash.

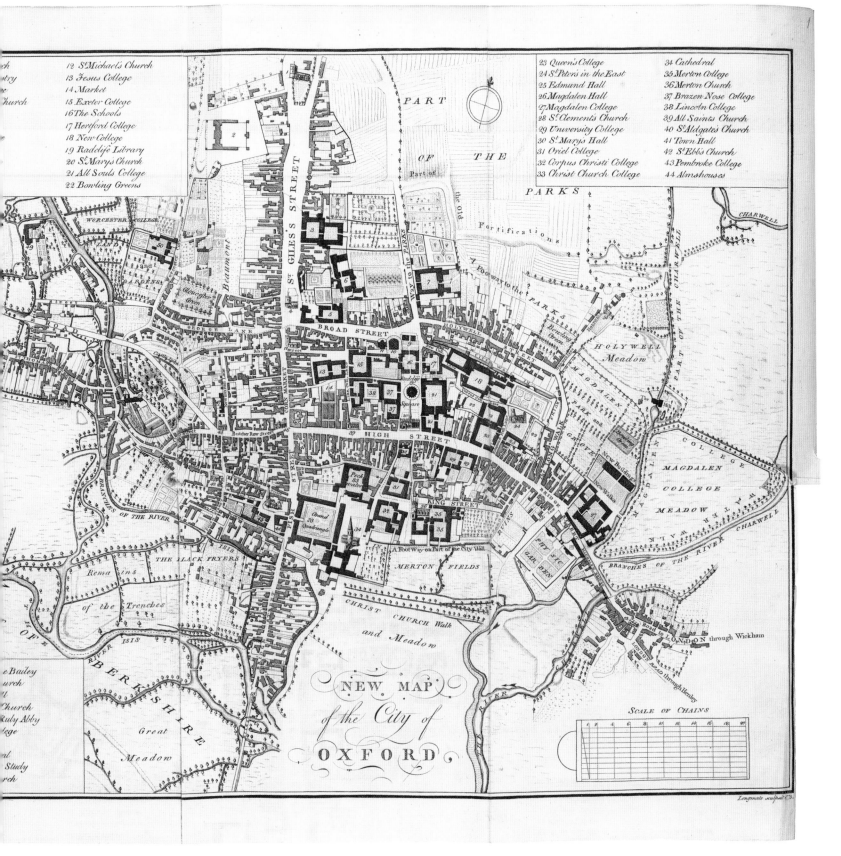

12 St Michael's Church
13 Jesus College
14 Market
15 Exeter College
16 The Schools
17 Hertford College
18 New College
19 Radcliffe Library
20 St Mary's Church
21 All Souls College
22 Bowling Greens

23 Queen's College
24 St Peter's in the East
25 Edmund Hall
26 Magdalen Hall
27 Magdalen College
28 St Clement's Church
29 University College
30 St Mary's Hall
31 Oriel College
32 Corpus Christi College
33 Christ Church College

34 Cathedral
35 Merton College
36 Merton Church
37 Brazen Nose College
38 Lincoln College
39 All Saints Church
40 St Aldgate's Church
41 Town Hall
42 St Ebb's Church
43 Pembroke College
44 Almshouses

PART OF THE PARKS

CHARWELL

Part of the old Fortifications

A Foot way to the PARKS

HOLYWELL Meadow

WORCESTER COLLEGE

Beaumont

St GILES'S STREET

BROAD STREET

HOLYWELL STREET

MARKET STREET

Radcliffe Square

HIGH STREET

KING STREET

MERTON FIELDS

A Foot Way on Part of the City Wall

PHYSIC GARDEN

MAGDALEN PARK and WALK

New Buildings

New Walks

MAGDALEN COLLEGE MEADOW

VIA FLUMINIS WITH CHARWELL

BRANCHES OF THE RIVER CHARWELL

PART OF THE CHARWELL

THE BLACK FRYERS

Remains of the Trenches

BRANCHES OF THE RIVER

ISIS

CHRIST CHURCH Walk and Meadow

BERKSHIRE

Great Meadow

Road to LONDON through Wickham

LONDON ROAD through Henley

NEW MAP
of the City of
OXFORD

SCALE OF CHAINS

Longmate sculpsit

CONDUIT.

CORN MARKET.

MIDWINTER.

SMITH

MOORE.

BAYLIS.

Mr DEWE.

MASON.

HORN.

to the West end of Mr Smith house approved

Jos: Chapman

1786

Widening the High Street at Carfax

In the many centuries before planning offices were even dreamt of, encroachment onto the city streets by houses, shops and other structures – to say nothing of teetering piles of merchandise and rubbish of all kinds – was a perennial problem. Payments to the sheriff by people whose buildings had permanently narrowed the streets were recorded as early as 1175. These may have been in the nature of fines; but by the end of the sixteenth century, the city government had adopted a 'policy of allowing encroachments under licence for a small annual fee called a landgable', and the resulting riot of 'protruding inn- and shop-signs . . . myriad stalls, pumps, porches, penthouses, spouts and projections' (A. Crossley) became yet another source of long-term conflict between the city and the university. In the 1630s, chancellor William Laud saw to it that cottages erected in the town ditch, on the wall, 'and in the middle of the street by Trinity College gate, and near . . . Smithgate' were demolished. These structures had been so numerous that Smithgate had become impassable to coaches. At around the same time, houses that had been illegally built on the East Bridge were removed, as was an extension to the Shambles in Butcher Row so tall that it blocked sunlight from entering the neighbouring houses. Over the ensuing century, however, such victories were rare. One, in the reign of Queen Anne, was the removal of the four- or five-century-old Mermaid tavern from the southwest corner of Carfax, specifically for road-widening purposes. Previously known as the Swyndlestock – a Middle English word for a type of agricultural flail – this tavern had been the epicentre of the notoriously bloody town-and-gown riot on St Scholastica's Day in 1355.

The clearance of free-standing street obstacles, along with road-widening per se, became major priorities for the city only with the passage of the Oxford Mileways Act 1771, which led directly to the establishment of the city's Paving Commis-

James Chapman, Plan for widening the High Street at Carfax (1786)

sion, and of which the improvement of Bridge Street [1771] was just one of many consequences [1773, 1789]. There was precedent for such actions even in the Middle Ages, however, with archaeologist Colin Platt reporting 'evidence for cellars partially underlying lanes . . . suggesting that house-fronts had actually been pushed back at some later date' than that of their initial construction. It should also be remembered that, despite its overwhelmingly stone-built appearance today, central Oxford was until relatively recent times characterised by a very high proportion of half-timbered houses, which we should not assume were *destroyed* simply because the records say they were 'removed'. Herbert Hurst, for instance, remembered a Jacobean wooden house on the south side of Broad Street being taken round the corner into Turl Street and re-erected there (albeit 'altered in its dimensions') in about 1850.

The most elaborate street obstacle of all was sited in what was almost literally the crossroads of England: for, almost from its very first appearance in Jacobean times, the size and placement of the Carfax Conduit House led to fears of market-day visitors being 'thronged to death'. Finally, in 1786, the Commission decided that 'the northern side of High Street next to [. . . the Conduit be] opened by setting back the projecting houses, and building in a right line with the front of the new market' (Boase), as an integral part of the scheme for the removal of the Conduit House and its replacement by a smaller one, which took place early the next year. It is precisely the attempt to determine that 'right line' that led to the drawing of this 1:110 plan by James Chapman. It presents three possible options, of which the red 'Middle Line' had been approved by 27 October 1786, but only as far as the boundary wall between the properties occupied by Smith and Moore.

In Scotland and Ireland at this date, the honorific 'Mr' was still generally reserved to those with university degrees, and if Chapman grew up in one of those places, it might explain why he applied it to only two of the 15 tenants' names. Of the three occupants only mildly affected by the scheme – at least in terms of sheer space lost – Slatter's was a bookshop that became increasingly involved in map publishing over the course of the nineteenth century [1805], latterly under the

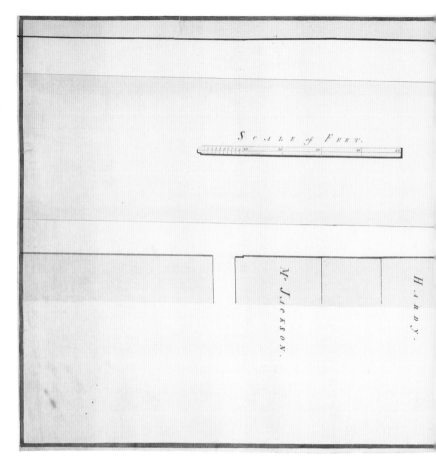

name Slatter & Rose. By 1839, it had moved westward to nos. 2 and 3 High Street, where it remained until 1900, when nos. 1–3 were cleared for the construction of the current neo-baroque Lloyds Bank building. Among the eight tenants who were severely impacted by the 1786 scheme, Dewe's also became locally prominent in map publishing [1855]. An Edward Midwinter, presumably of the same family (and conceivably the same person) as the 'Midwinter' connected with the fifth shop from the right, operated a tiny beer-house on this corner in the early nineteenth century; it was inherited by his brother-in-law, a tailor, who was running it as a combined pub and tailor's shop in 1851, by which time it was known as the Jolly Farmer. None of the other tenants of nos.

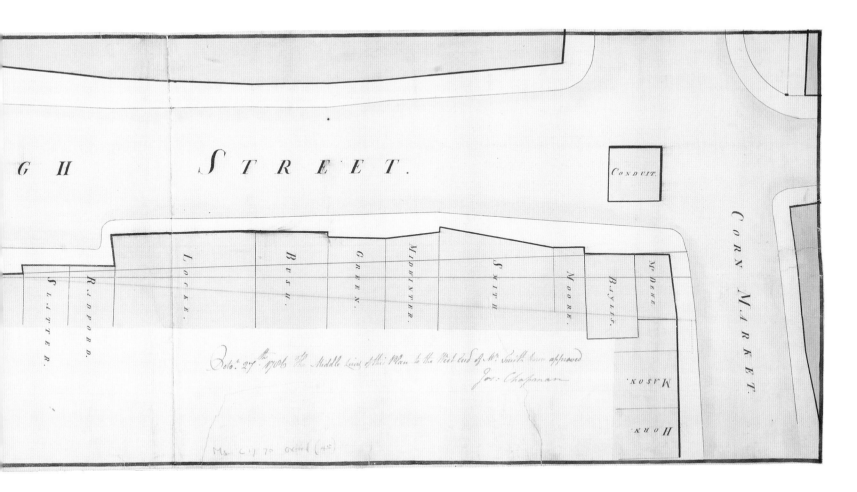

1–5 as shown in this map were still in the immediate vicinity at the end of the 1830s, when in addition to Henry Slatter this row included a draper, a hatter and an ironmonger.

The loss of the original Conduit House had few if any negative practical implications, for it was essentially a figure-head for an elaborate water-distribution system that was mostly unseen. Multiple springs fed a 2,000-gallon tank on a hill by North Hinksey, whose water flowed into the city via elm-clad lead pipes. These divided into a main branch to the Conduit House, and a subsidiary branch to Pembroke College. From the upper of the Conduit House's two cisterns, further branches carried water to seven more colleges, and to a cistern by All Saints Church that served three more colleges and some private residences. The general water supply for the city came out of the lower of the two cisterns at Carfax, though as we shall see [1848, 1872], not quite 8 per cent of the city's houses took the city supply even in 1851, with the overwhelming majority continuing to use well-water as they had since medieval times. The original Conduit House, far too fine a baroque thing to be destroyed even at the height of the Age of Reason, was re-erected in 1789 in the 2nd Earl Harcourt's Capability Brown-designed park at Nuneham House in Nuneham Courtenay, Oxfordshire, and it remains there to this day. The Jolly Farmer was renamed the Original Jolly Farmer in 1872 to distinguish it from a newer pub in Paradise Street, and closed in 1887.

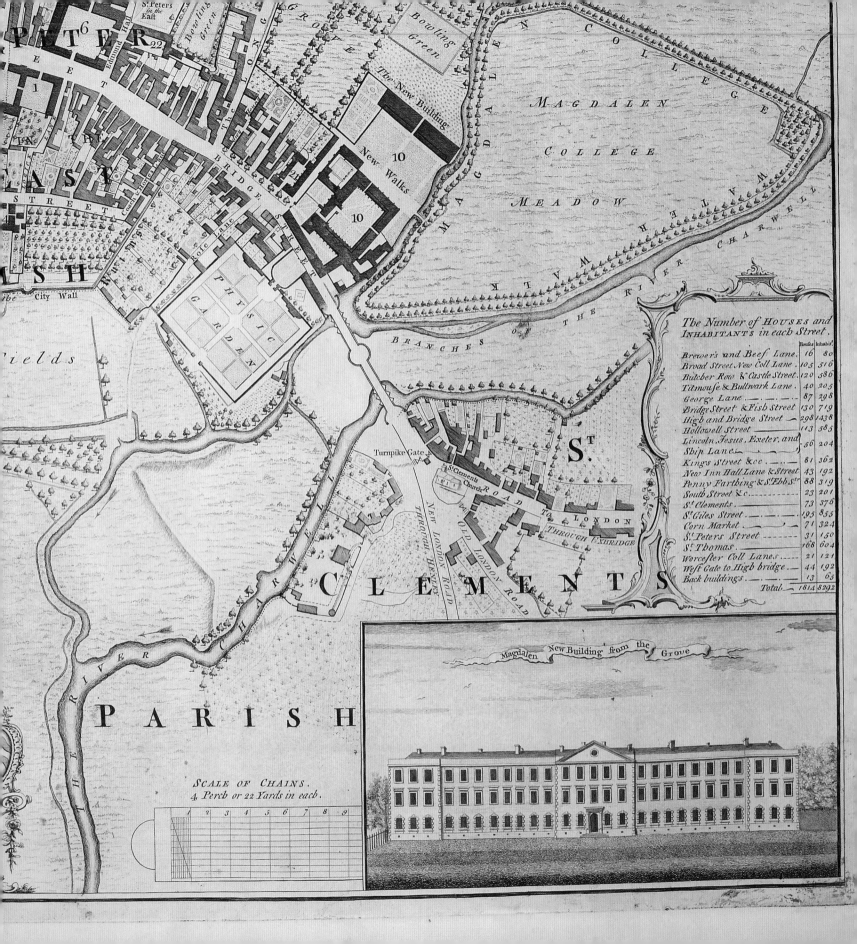

PITER 6 22

S.t Peters in the East

MASY

STREET

City Wall

Fields

GROVE

Bowling Green

Bowling Green

The New Building

New Walks

10

10

MAGDALEN COLLEGE

MAGDALEN COLLEGE

MEADOW

MVLVM HVLM

OF THE RIVER CHARWELL

BRANCHES

PHYSIC GARDEN

Rose Lane

Turnpike Gate

St Clements Church

S.t

CLEMENTS

ROAD TO LONDON THROUGH UXBRIDGE

NEW LONDON ROAD THROUGH HEADLEY

OLD LONDON ROAD

PARISH

RIVER CHARWELL

The Number of HOUSES and INHABITANTS in each Street.

	Houses	Inhabit.t
Brewers and Beef Lane.	16	80
Broad Street New Coll Lane.	105	516
Butcher Row & Castle Street.	120	586
Titmouse & Bullwark Lane.	40	205
George Lane	87	298
Bridge Street & Fish Street	130	719
High and Bridge Street	298	1438
Hollowell Street	113	585
Lincoln Jesus Exeter and Ship Lane	56	204
Kings Street &c.	81	362
New Inn Hall Lane & Street	43	192
Penny Farthing & St Ebb St.t	88	319
South Street &c.	23	201
St Clements	73	376
St Giles Street	195	855
Corn Market	71	324
St Peters Street	31	150
St Thomas	168	604
Worcester Coll Lanes	21	121
West Gate to High bridge	44	192
Back buildings	13	65
Total	1814	8292

Magdalen New Building from the Grove

SCALE OF CHAINS.
4 Perch or 22 Yards in each.

1 2 3 4 5 6 7 8 9

1789

A *missing link between amateur and professional cartography*

Like the bird's-flight views of Oxford that remained popular for a century and a half from the 1570s, the large-scale ichnographic plans of the city that were produced beginning in the 1730s had a long shelf-life and many imitators. The map now before us is recognisably the one surveyed by Isaac Taylor in 1750 and engraved by George Anderton in 1751, but it has been partially re-engraved to reflect changes on the ground. In addition to the demolition of the Bocardo, the making of the New Road to the west, the removal of trees from the south front of Balliol College as part of the widening of Broad Street there and other major alterations that were already captured by Longmate [1773], we see a number of features here for the first time. Foremost among these is the new city gaol which has been constructed in the centre of Gloucester Green (as Broken Hayes had been renamed since Loggan's time [1673]). The many subtler changes include the widening of Turl Street

to almost the same width as Lincoln College Lane immediately to its south, via the removal of some private buildings on its eastern side. The long, narrow garden immediately to the east of Balliol and south of Trinity has also been widened by the same method. In both these cases, interestingly, the buildings that were removed either post-dated Williams's survey of 1733, or were deemed unworthy of inclusion in it.

Not far beyond the east end of John Gwynn's nearly completed Magdalen Bridge, in a reminder of the critical importance of toll income to the modernisation of Oxford's roads, bridges and streets in the post-1771 period, we can see a tiny toll-taker's house and two turnpike gates: one for the old road to London via Uxbridge and the other for the new approach to the road to London via Henley, now called Iffley Road, which had required substantial demolitions (compare [1773]). The removal from the South Bridge of the picturesque

---

Isaac Taylor/William Faden, *To the Chancellor, Vice Chancellor, & Heads of Colleges, And to the High Steward,*
Mayor Aldermen &c. Of the University & City of Oxford; This Plan of the City of Oxford is humbly inscribed . . . (1789)

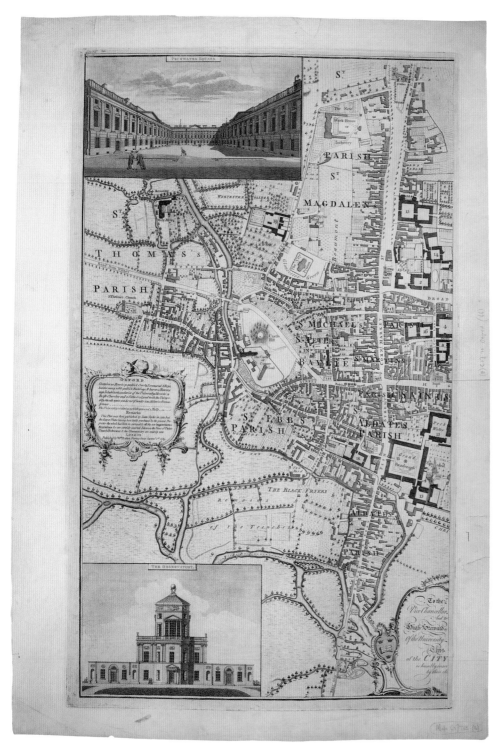

gate-tower called Friar Bacon's Study – one of just two non-ecclesiastical buildings that both Taylor and Longmate showed in '3-D' – has led here to the hopeful renaming 'Friar Bacon's Bridge', though in the event, this would not catch on. Publisher William Faden's claim that 'the whole has been re-surveyed and all the new *Improvements Alterations* &c . . . carefully inserted' is not fully supportable, however, in that Taylor's butchers' shops partially obstructing what is now Queen Street were correctly shown as removed by Longmate, but are now back again: a violation of both the letter of the law and the spirit of the 'New Market' on the north side of the High Street.

There have also been major revisions to the map's peripheral content, reflecting new tastes on the part of Faden or his clients. The scenic vignettes mark a sharp change of tone. Where Taylor and Anderton's rather generic 'polite society' had at least included women and agricultural workers, albeit deferential ones, we now see a city completely dominated by the university and university men. At lower left, the quasi-baroque of James Gibbs's Radcliffe Library has given way to the far more severe lines of the south front of James Wyatt's Radcliffe Observatory, which in fact would not be completed for another five years. At upper left, Taylor and Anderton's traditionalist view of the city from Headington Hill has been supplanted by a severe and claustrophobia-inducing scene of the not-yet-grassed 1711 Peckwater Quad at Christ Church, looking not at all unlike a cavalry barracks, with two men in mortarboards seemingly having an angry argument in the foreground.

No such minor criticisms, however, should detract from what William Faden achieved in his wider career. Son of the prominent Fleet Street printer William Mackfaden, who shortened his surname on the occasion of the final Jacobite Rebellion, Faden served an apprenticeship with engraver James Wigley from the usual age of 15 before going into partnership with the Jefferys family [1750, 1761]. Having joined the recently founded Society of Civil Engineers in 1776, Faden pounced on the task of revising and publishing maps relevant to the conduct of the war against the rebelled colonies in North America, including many news-maps of battles in scales ranging from 1:7,320 to 1:85,000 and the magnificent *North American Atlas* of 1777. He was made Geographer in Ordinary to King George III in 1783, and thereafter went from strength to strength, developing 'the most competent cartographic service of the period', which supplied various needs of the British government, including Admiralty charts, and 'foreshadowed the emergence of national cartographic agencies' (L. Worms). This activity overlapped in both time and content with the birth of the Ordnance Survey, whose first map to be published, *An Entirely New & Accurate Survey of the County of Kent* (1801), was distributed by Faden. Derivative and hastily prepared, the present map is a reminder that post-Rocque aspirations to total coverage came at a steep price.

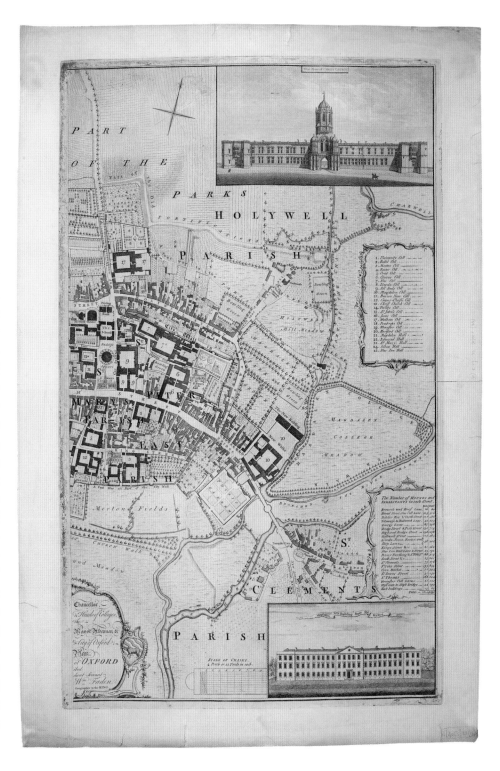

New and accurate MAP of the Country for
Twenty five Miles round the University of
OXFORD,
Exhibiting all the direct and cross Roads the Hills,
Vales, Woods, Rivers, Canals, Towns, Villages, Hamlets,
Parks and Seats of the Nobility & Gentry,
from the latest Surveys and Observations.

WARWICKSHIRE

GLOUCESTERSHIRE

OX

Bath House
Horley
Part of Alkerton
Gloucester Sh.
Wroxton
Balscot
Wroxton Abbey
Compton Winyate
Epwell
Shutford
Winderton
Broughton Castle
Swalcliff
Tadmarton
Swalclif Grange
Lower Tadmarton
Sutton
Part of Gloucester
Stour River
Brails
Tibford Gore
Pt. of Gloucester
Stour Well
Hook Norton Lodge
Tadmarton Heath
Mileomb
Cherrington
Weston
Whichford
Scotland
Hook Norton
Wiggington
Som Newin
Biall
Little Wolford
Wolford
Barton on the Heath
Long Compton
Great Rolright
Lumpiss
Worcester Sh.
Grove Ash
Glocester Sh.
Little Compton
Little Rolright
Shalford Hill
Swarford Heath
Swarford
Funnington
Chastleton
Shalford
Over Norton
Pumphery tas
Great Tew Park
Nether Worto
Broadwell
Addlestrop
Chapel House
Duntrop
Priory
Heythrop
Little Tew
Cornwell
Over Norton Heath
Broad Stone
STOW on the Wold
Oddington
Dalesford
CHIPPING NORTON
Cling Well
Church Enstone
Lower Swell
Hangersbury
King ham
Churchill Hill House
Lidston
Spilsbury Downs
Neat Enstone
Gagingwell
Radford
Lower Slaughter
Iccombe
Churchill
Knollberry Banks
Bean
Over Kiddington
Wick
Barrow Beacon
Bleddington
Marsden
Chadington
Kiddington
Rifsington Wick
Wick Hill
Westcote
Bold Gate
Merry Court
Spilsbury
Taston
Ditchley House
Clmpton Park
Bourton on the Water
Little Rifsington
Idbury
Lynham
Ditchley
Clapton
Bruern Abbey
Lower End
Ascot
Shorthampton Chilson
Walcot
Charlbury
Wood
New Bridge
Great Rifsington
Warren
Fifield
Milton
Shipton under Whichwo
Upper End
Blandford Park
Limbeck
Littleworth
Stonesfield
Old Park
Tangley
Crows Castle
Barrington Park
Barrow Hill
Finstock
Fawley
Combe
Farmington
Hemps Hill
BlackHeath
Langley
Leafield
Ramsden
Wilcot
Sutton Park
Sherborne
Tainton
WHICHWOOD FOREST
North Leigh
Windrush
Eastington
Lit Barrington
Fulbrook
WITNEY CHACE
Long Hanbo
Sherborne Lodge
New Inn
Upton
Swinbrook
Astally
Kelley Chapel
Newgate
Enshe

1805

A constellation of gentlemen's houses

Rarely has a map pointed so clearly as this one does to the central importance of the horse in European life in the pre-industrial age. Backed with cloth and clearly intended to be carried in the coat pocket, it is centred on Oxford University as a starting point for journeys on horseback by fox-hunters, and has much to tell us about British society in the last generation before the coming of the railways. Justified fears of invasion during Britain's long war against Napoleonic France had recently inspired the formation of mounted local-defence units known as yeomanry. This naming reflected the idea that their soldiers – in sharp contrast to the impoverished wretches swept into the foot regiments by promises of free food and clothing – would mostly be from prosperous farming families who owned their own land. But this was just one of many ways in which the armed forces reflected a wider social structure in which greater involvement with horses was associated with higher social status. This operated even between officers of the same rank; in 1800, daily pay for a cavalry captain was 14s 7d, or 55 per cent higher than that of an infantry captain. In 1798, a year in which the French actually landed in Ireland [1759], the Oxfordshire Fencible Cavalry was formed, although the plan for doing this had been hatched four years earlier at the Star Inn in Oxford by a meeting of 'Nobility, Gentry, Freeholders and Yeomen'.

Hunting from horseback, especially for wild boar, had been popular among the wealthy since the Middle Ages, when a European nation's cavalry corps and its male nobility were virtually interchangeable concepts. Hunts were valued as training in vital battlefield horsemanship skills as much as they were for the entertainment, and food, they provided. The 1st

George Pawley/Samuel Neele, *Gentleman hunter's and sportsman's pocket companion: in a circle of twenty-five miles round Oxford* (1805)

Duke of Wellington, a keen fox-hunter, owed several of his victories to his own remarkable horsemanship, which allowed him to appear in multiple parts of long battle lines in quick succession, assessing the situation at the 'micro' and 'macro' levels more or less simultaneously and offering direct encouragement to his troops, verbally or just by showing his face at the right moment. And it is unlikely to be a coincidence that the style of fox-hunting's most iconic clothing – red tailcoats and brown-topped black boots – can be dated rather precisely to Wellington's lifetime. With its prominent reference to 'parks, and seats of the nobility & gentry', this engraved map by Samuel Neele (based on a drawing by George Pawley) reflects the fact that, even as factories sprang up in the northwest and railways in the northeast, the young gentlemen of Oxford University still saw – or at any rate were expected to see – their country as a federation of country houses and a patchwork quilt of quasi-martial sporting opportunities.

The fairly enormous radius around the university depicted by this map, of 25 miles, also reflects the fact that travel in the Georgian and earlier eras was not half as difficult as most modern historians would have us believe [1675]. The maximum range of an individual rider without changing horses was considered to be 56 miles per day in medieval times, and the wardens of Merton College travelled at a rate of 25 miles a day or faster on all of their journeys in the early fourteenth century, often covering 50 miles. But information could travel even faster than the fastest individual rider, due to a 'Pony Express'-style system of relays established in the fifteenth-century reign of King Edward IV. This changing of riders and horses at regular intervals allowed news to travel at 100 miles per day and to reach every part of the kingdom, usually within a week to ten days. Originally, 'post' was the term for one of these riders, not the messages he carried, and the phrase 'post haste' derives from a standard sixteenth-century exhortation: 'Haste, post, haste for life.'

Probably best known for his contributions

to *Pawley's General Atlas* of 1825, Neele collaborated with William Faden [1789] on a magnificent map of Dublin in 1797. He also produced another map similar to this one, though not circular, covering the 24 miles of country around Bath in or by 1820, at the same scale of 3 miles to the inch (1:190,080); and this Oxford radius map was reissued in 1831, several years after his death, under the doubly misleading title *Slatter's New Map of the Country Twenty-five Miles Round Oxford*. Based in London, Neele was also a heraldic engraver, and evidently quite successful: in 1817 he was able to finance the publication of the first book by his son Henry Neele, who went on to considerable success as a poet and critic before tragically dying by his own hand shortly after his thirtieth birthday.

Albeit in a crude way, this odd and rather beautiful map anticipates by several decades maps overlaid with circles or hexagons for the rapid calculation of distance without using tools: for example, J. Friedrichs's 1847 'Circuiteer' map of London, and Llewellyn Syers's 1860s hex-maps of Liverpool and Manchester. Hexagon-gridded maps, in particular, are still widely used in war-gaming. The fox-hunting angle aside, however, it was not especially novel: the ladies' sewing-pattern section of the 1795 Bowles & Carver map catalogue advertised paper patterns for maps of 'Twenty Miles round London', 'Twenty Miles round Cambridge' and 'Twenty Miles round Oxford'. Sadly, whether due to their popularity or lack thereof, no such patterns have survived. Conceptually, all seem to have been based on a circular *Map of the Country Round the City of Oxford* that was produced earlier in the eighteenth century by B. Donne Jr, who in turn may have been copying an oval 1:190,080 map of the same area by Benjamin Cole or his son of the same name [1695], which can be seen in the Bodleian Library. Before 1700, the elder Cole also published a broadside titled *Proposals for delineating and engraving a map of Oxford-shire, and the adjacent counties, as far as 20 miles round Oxford*, a lone copy of which survives in the library of University College.

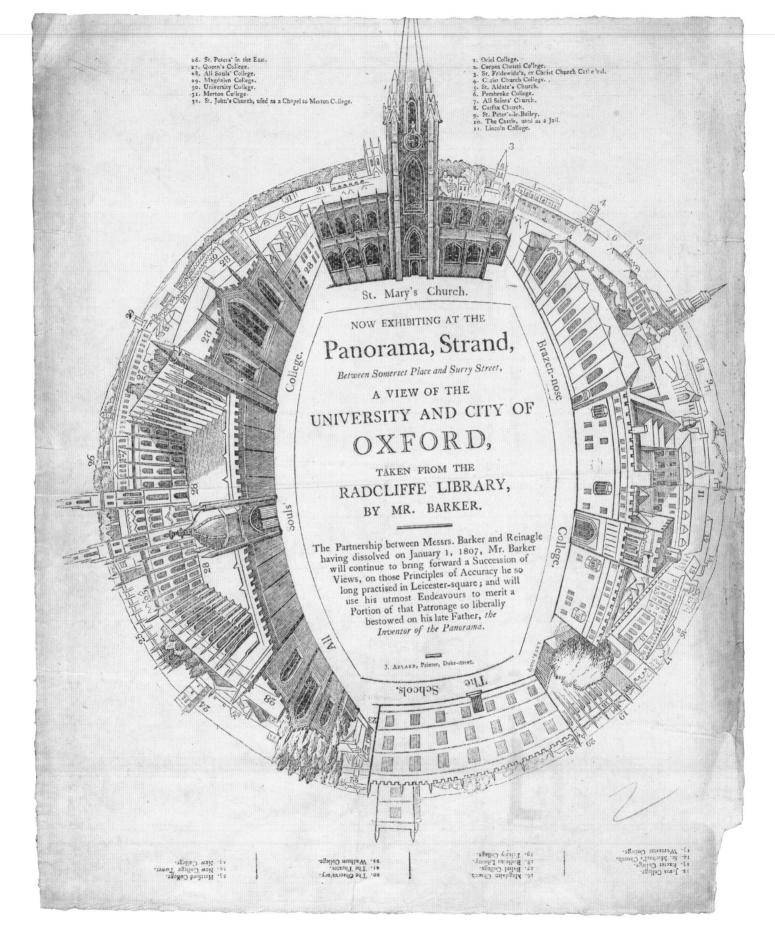

St. Mary's Church.

NOW EXHIBITING AT THE

Panorama, Strand,

Between Somerset Place and Surry Street,

A VIEW OF THE

UNIVERSITY AND CITY OF

OXFORD,

TAKEN FROM THE

RADCLIFFE LIBRARY,

BY MR. BARKER.

The Partnership between Messrs. Barker and Reinagle
having dissolved on January 1, 1807, Mr. Barker
will continue to bring forward a Succession of
Views, on those Principles of Accuracy he so
long practised in Leicester-square; and will
use his utmost Endeavours to merit a
Portion of that Patronage so liberally
bestowed on his late Father, *the
Inventor of the Panorama.*

J. ADLARD, Printer, Duke-street.

26. St. Peters' in the East.
27. Queen's College.
28. All Souls' College.
29. Magdalen College.
30. University College.
31. Merton College.
32. St. John's Church, used as a Chapel to Merton College.

1. Oriel College.
2. Corpus Christi College.
3. St. Fridewide's, or Christ Church Cathedral.
4. Christ Church College.
5. St. Aldate's Church.
6. Pembroke College.
7. All Saints' Church.
8. Carfax Church.
9. St. Peter's-le-Bailey.
10. The Castle, used as a Jail.
11. Lincoln College.

12. Jesus College.
13. Exeter College.
14. St. Michael's Church.
15. Worcester College.

16. Magdalen Church.
17. Baliol College.
18. Bodleian Library.
19. Trinity College.

20. The Observatory.
21. The Theatre.
22. Wadham College.

23. Hertford College.
24. New College Tower.
25. New College.

1807

Mapping an immersive 360-degree view

The Napoleonic era was the heyday of panoramas: immense semi-circular or circular paintings, ideally exhibited on the interior walls of purpose-built round buildings and lit from above by natural daylight diffused through translucent oilcloth. These paintings' curvature and sheer size gave the people looking at them an IMAX-like sensation of immersion within the scene. Queen Charlotte complained of seasickness when viewing a panorama of the Grand Fleet at Spithead, and one viewer, himself an artist, wrote after seeing a panorama landscape: 'I actually put on my hat imagining myself to be in the open air'. The very first panorama was a townscape of Edinburgh, painted from life by Robert Barker, who was born in 1739 in County Meath, Ireland. Barker patented the idea of the panorama in 1787 and made some money from touring and temporary exhibitions, but problems persisted, as Kathryn Kane explains:

[P]anorama painting . . . was best viewed from a narrow location within the circle, from a precise height and distance, and under specific lighting conditions. None of this could be controlled when a very long and tall painting was simply hung on the walls around a large square room. People entered the opening between the two ends and simply wandered around the space, looking at the painting from any number of angles and at various distances, in essentially uncontrolled light.

Fortunately, in the early 1790s, Barker was able to build a brick rotunda, known simply as the Panorama, in Cranbourne Street, Leicester Fields, London, specifically for the exhibition of these works under ideal conditions. As scenes from the war joined cityscapes, sales of 1- and 2-shilling tickets were brisk enough

---

Thomas Barker/J. Adlard, *Now exhibiting at the Panorama, Strand, Between Somerset Place and Surry Street, a view of the University and City of Oxford, taken from the Radcliffe Library, by Mr. Barker* (1807)

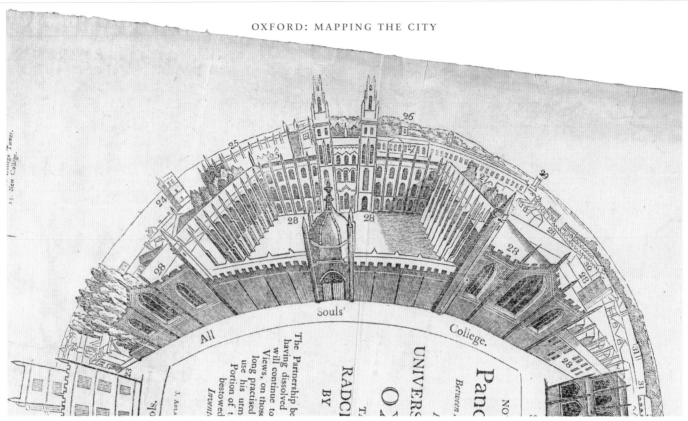

Panorama painters generally chose to depict their subjects from a single, high vantage point.

to make Barker a multimillionaire in modern terms. Moreover, his unique building helped secure an insurmountable advantage over the many rivals, foreign and domestic, who emerged after his exclusive patent lapsed in 1801. But this was not to last, for Barker's estranged non-artist son, Thomas, completed a nearly identical rival rotunda in the Strand just three years later, in partnership with a young artist named Ramsay Reinagle.

The elder Barker died in 1806, loudly denying to the end that Thomas Barker had ever had anything to do with the original Panorama, or that he himself had ever had any part in the Strand operation. The Leicester Fields building was taken over by his favourite son, Henry (1774–1856), a Royal Academy-trained artist who had assisted him since the age of 12, and the business carried on with few changes. Married to a daughter of Captain William Bligh of *Bounty*-mutiny fame, but evidently fascinated by the enemy, Henry Barker travelled to France during a brief window of peace in 1802, and while there was granted an audience with the Emperor Napoleon,

who remained on friendly terms with Barker for the rest of his life. Lord Nelson was also a fan of Henry Barker's work and met him twice. Unsurprisingly, Henry chose the Battle of Trafalgar as his initial solo offering at the Panorama. It was evidently very successful, 'running' (for it is nearly impossible to avoid comparisons to the cinema) from May 1806 to May 1807 – about five months longer than average. Like most of the paintings exhibited in the larger ground-floor spaces of either the Leicester Fields or Strand operations, the Trafalgar painting was approximately 36 feet in height and 280 in circumference, yielding a much-boasted-about surface area of 10,000 square feet.

It is the measure of Oxford's enduring hold on the English imagination that Thomas Barker's answer to his brother's Trafalgar was a panorama of the city of dreaming spires. The painting itself seems not to have survived. Most did not; and in any case, reproducing one – even in a much larger book – would hardly do it justice. But we are fortunate indeed to have

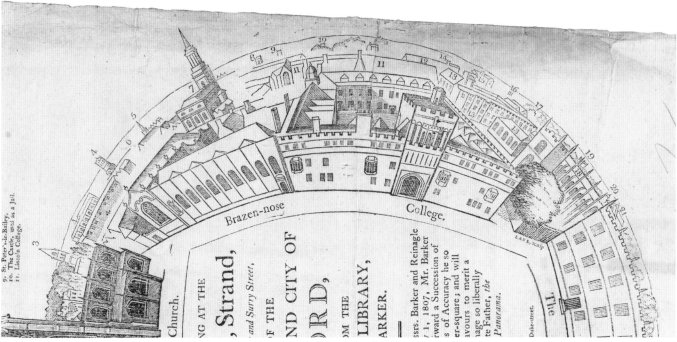

It is easy to imagine why some contemporary viewers of panoramas felt confused and overwhelmed.

one of the small maps issued to its viewers to help them orient themselves during what must have been, for some at least, a confusing or even overwhelming experience.

Panorama painters' choice of a single, high vantage point such as the Radcliffe Library was typical. Interestingly, and in sharp contrast to Faden [1789], the artists employed by Thomas Barker were prevented by this perspectival necessity from focusing primarily or exclusively on Oxford's newest, most fashionable buildings. Indeed, only seven of the 35 locations identified by name in this map – the parish churches of All Saints ('7') and Peter-le-Bailey ('9'), Worcester College ('15'), the Observatory ('20'), Hertford College ('23'), All Souls College ('28') and the Radcliffe Library itself – had been built or substantially rebuilt within the previous 100 years. The map also makes reference to Thomas Barker's recent split with Reinagle. Though the precise reason for their falling-out is unclear, the painter John Constable is known to have remarked that Reinagle had 'lost a great deal of money' through the Strand venture.

Henry Barker retired at the age of 48, having made the modern-day equivalent of £7 to £11 million from his Battle of Waterloo panorama alone. The business outlived him, but not by long, closing its doors for the last time in 1863. Its remarkable building, however, survives in modified form as the Roman Catholic Church of Notre Dame de France, Leicester Square. The rival Strand rotunda, which Henry Barker bought out in 1816 or 1817, closed in 1831 and was torn down in the 1850s. Moving panoramas mounted on vertical rollers – and therefore displayable in ordinary proscenium theatres – had been invented in 1809 and grew steadily more popular from the 1820s onward; and it was this alternative form of entertainment, often equipped with sound effects and a narrator, that led to the static panorama's demise in Europe in the 1860s. It is now widely accepted that, far from being a sudden technological explosion, the early cinema was part of a slow evolutionary process in which the Barker family's invention played a critical 'platform' role.

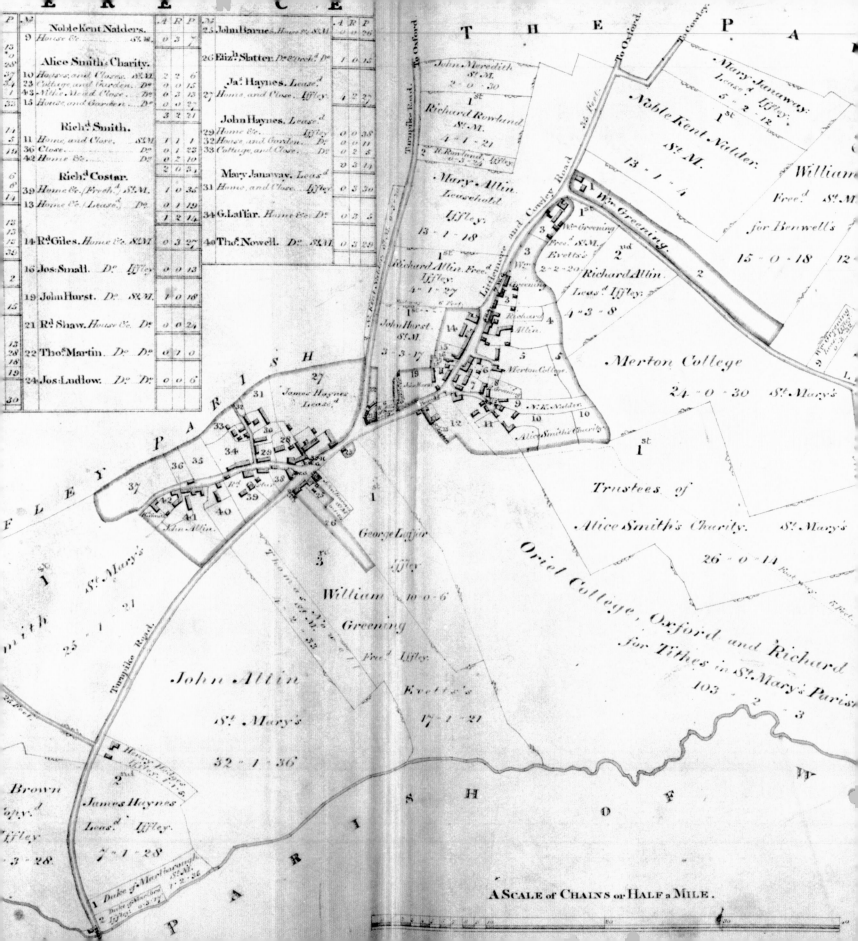

1819

Enclosure and charity in Littlemore

Between 1760 and 1800, the countryside around Oxford – previously worked on an open-field system – was the subject of 67 Enclosure Acts: local Acts of Parliament that transferred specific areas of land previously designated 'common' or 'waste' into private ownership. This was around 1.3 per cent of such acts that were passed in the whole country from the accession of King James I in 1603 to the outbreak of the First World War. Writing in 1809, Arthur Young plausibly suggested that a greater acreage of land had been enclosed in Oxfordshire than in any other county in England over the preceding 40 years.

The ostensible purpose of this frenzy of activity was the improvement of the land according to the latest agricultural techniques, including crop rotation, fertilisation and the introduction of new plant species. In addition to having profoundly positive effects on local and national food supplies, this would roughly double a given piece of land's monetary value. As a statute of 1773 put it, many wastes, commons and open fields 'by reason of the different interests [of] the several land owners and occupiers, or persons having right of common . . . cannot be improved, cultivated or enjoyed to such great advantage for the owners and occupiers thereof.' For radicals, enclosure in England was a pivotal moment in the transition from feudalism to capitalism, not least because it created a pool of suddenly landless rural poor who could be counted on to gravitate towards factory work. Others, however, have pointed out that Georgian-era subsistence farming was in many ways no better than factory work and in some ways worse; that many small agriculturalists welcomed enclosure as a chance to escape lives that were by turns very boring and terribly precarious; and that under the law (though abuses were frequent), moves towards any particular enclosure in England had to be publicly revealed and discussed, and agreed to by a majority of the people affected, who then received compensation.

William Church, *A map of Littlemore as referred to by the annexed award* (1819)

Down to 1525, when it was dissolved by the (still-Catholic) Church due to a grotesque litany of sexual misconduct, assault and theft, there had been a Benedictine nunnery in Littlemore on the later site of Minchery Farm. Since then, as this map makes clear, a sizeable village had grown up along both sides of the major road that ran from London to Oxford via Cowley. Though it would not become part of the contiguous built-up area of the city of Oxford until the inter-war years, Littlemore had always been part of the city, in the sense that the majority of its inhabited area was an 'exclave' (i.e. a detached part, the opposite of 'enclave') of the urban parish of St Mary the Virgin. This detailed cadastral plan reveals that, as in urban St Giles's [1832] but in sharp contrast to neighbouring rural Iffley [1830], Littlemore was the site of a complex patchwork of ownership that included Oxford-based institutions, including Merton and Oriel colleges, and the aristocracy (as represented by George Spencer-Churchill, 5th Duke of Marlborough), as well as a range of relatively obscure individuals. Uniquely, however, significant tracts of Littlemore were controlled by the Trustees of Alice Smith's Charity.

Born in Iffley, Alice Smith left all her 'lands, tenements and hereditaments in Littlemore' to the poor of her native village in November 1678; but perhaps realising how odd this must have seemed to the poor of Littlemore itself, she later modified her will, allowing the latter 'from time to time . . . [to] have their proportionable share'. In practice, Littlemore's slice of the cake was established in the Court of Chancery in 1718 to be five-sixteenths of the total, which in addition to rents involved the interest on a fairly significant sum of money. As their names would suggest, Smith's holdings called Nye-mead Close, Down-lane Close and Down-land Close had already been fenced at that date. As of 1802, the seven trustees of the charity comprised the local curate, three doctors of divinity, a medical doctor and two other gentlemen. Among other matters, they had 'the right of appointing and removing' the mistress of a school in neighbouring Iffley that had been established in 1805 to teach ten poor children reading, spinning and knitting, and provide them with suitable clothing.

The teacher was required to be already a resident of Iffley and 'discreet, prudent and religious'.

In all, the charity's land in 1823 consisted of a little under 60 acres, divided between the Haynes family and James Boswell, who between them paid rent of £92 per year: 'the full value . . . fixed by the valuation of a surveyor'. The charity's non-land investments yielded a further £11 per year; but in 1817 the trustees had been forced to borrow £200 at 5 per cent interest 'towards defraying the expenses of the

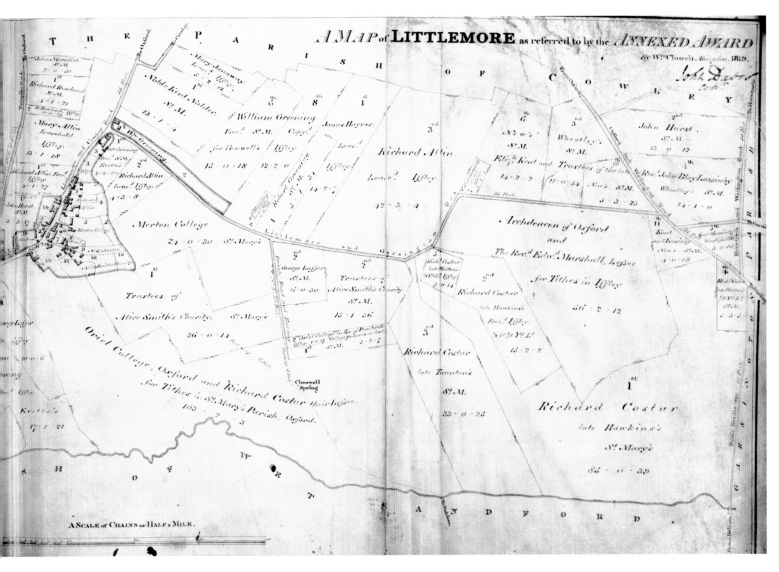

A MAP of LITTLEMORE as referred to by the ANNEXED AWARD

By Wm. Church, Abingdon, 1819.

A SCALE of CHAINS or HALF a MILE.

inclosure'. They were also reeling from a scandal. A number of £10 bounties had been paid by Alice Smith's Charity to tradesmen for taking on poor boys from Littlemore and Iffley as apprentices, but in fact the money was merely split between the supposed employers and the boys' parents, 'a considerable grievance', not least because the boys remained unemployed. Records of a small annual dole of money from the charity reveal that 86 families were deemed poor in Iffley and 55 in Littlemore in the early 1820s.

Fatefully, John Henry Newman (1801–1890) would be appointed vicar of St Mary the Virgin in 1828, and take an interest in his detached charge of Littlemore almost immediately. As his rift with Protestantism deepened in the 1840s, he moved with some friends to a converted stables – a short distance off the northern edge of this map – where they lived more or less as monks until Newman's formal conversion to Roman Catholicism in 1845.

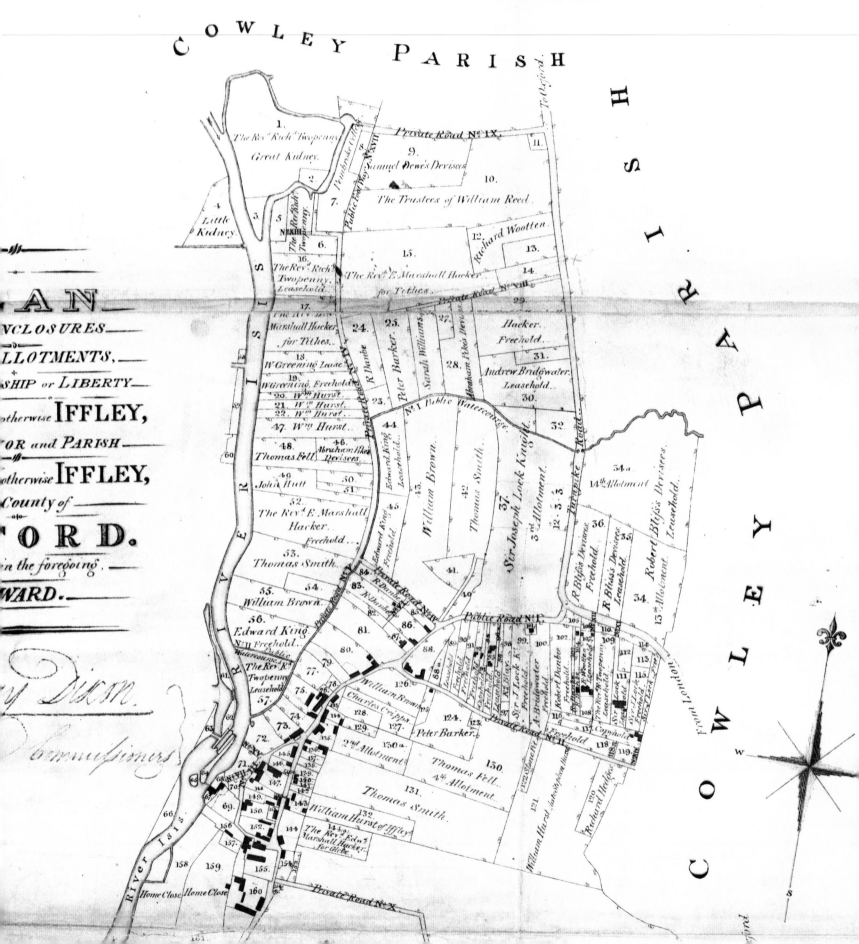

COWLEY PARISH

COWLEY PARISH

PLAN
ENCLOSURES
ALLOTMENTS,
SHIP or LIBERTY
otherwise IFFLEY,
OR and PARISH
otherwise IFFLEY,
County of
FORD.
in the foregoing
WARD.

1.
The Rev.ᵈ Rich.ᵈ Twopenny
Great Kidney.

Private Road Nº IX.

9.
Samuel Dewe's Devisees

10.
The Trustees of William Reed.

12. Richard Wootten

13.

14.

4
Little Kidney

16.
The Rev.ᵈ Rich.ᵈ
Twopenny.
Leasehold.

15.

The Rev.ᵈ E. Marshall Hacker.
for Tithes.

Private Road Nº VIII.

17.
The Rev.ᵈ E.
Marshall Hacker.
for Tithes.

24.

25.

27.

Hacker.
Freehold.

31.

18.
W. Greening Lease

28.

Andrew Bridgwater.
Leasehold.

19.
W. Greening, Freehold.

30.

20. W.ᵐ Hurst.
21. W.ᵐ Hurst.
22. W.ᵐ Hurst.

47. W.ᵐ Hurst.

23.

44.

Nº 1 Public Watercourse

34.a
14.ᵗʰ Allotment

32.

48.
Thomas Fell.

46.
Abraham Pikes
Devisees.

45.

43.

William Brown.

42.
Thomas Smith.

37.

Sir Joseph Lock Knight.

3.ᵈ Allotment

12.3.3

36.
R. Bliss's Devisees
Freehold.

35.
R. Bliss's Devisees
Leasehold.

Robert Bliss's Devisees.
Leasehold.

49.
John Hutt

50.

51.

52.
The Rev.ᵈ E. Marshall
Hacker.
Freehold.

53.
Thomas Smith.

55.
William Brown.

54.

56.
Edward King.
Nꞷ Freehold.

57.
The Rev.ᵈ R.
Twopenny
Leasehold.

Public Watercourse

41.

40.

84.
83.

82.

81.

80.

79.

77.

78.

75.

74.

73.

72.

85.

86.

87.

88.

88.a

90.
91.

89.

99.

100.

102.

Public Road Nº I.

126.

Charles Cripps.

128.

129.

127.

124.

123.

Peter Barker.

130.

Thomas Fell.
4.ᵗʰ Allotment

2.ⁿᵈ Allotment

131.
Thomas Smith.

132.

William Hurst of Iffley.

144.
The Rev.ᵈ E.ᵈ.
Marshall Hacker.
for Glebe.

Private Road Nº X.

Home Close. Home Close.

River ISIS

34.
15.ᵗʰ Allotment

From London

W

S

1830

Connecting Iffley

Iffley, first recorded under the name Gifteleia, has been inhabited since at least the tenth century due to its combination of relatively high elevation and close proximity to the river, making it reasonably 'flood proof'. It became a parish in the late twelfth century and its church is of about that age. The village was clearly shown by Rocque [1761] as unconnected to the main road system. As this map makes clear, its main artery and inhabited area in 1830 was along the north–south stretch of Church Way, as well as to the west of it along Mill Lane, here called 'No. III'. This modest street system was in the process of being connected to the turnpike via a new 'enclosure road', marked 'Public Road No. I', running along the southern edge of the large parcel of land recently granted to the banker and goldsmith Sir Joseph Lock (1760–1844). Mayor of Oxford in 1813 and 1829, Lock had lived at Denton House in Iffley ('111') from 1794 to 1805, but since decamped

to Bury Knowle House in Headington, where he was roundly hated. The area directly south from Public Road No. I to present-day Tree Lane, here marked 'Private Road No. II', appears to consist of tiny, unenclosed farms, as the surveyor Henry Dixon has helpfully added semi-circular lobes along property boundaries to indicate those that are fenced. The term 'Close' applied to certain fields, more prevalent in the south of the mapped area, specifically implies that they had been fenced during some earlier time period [1819].

The present map shows only five structures to the south of 'Private Road No. X' – today known as Eastchurch at its western end and Lenthall Road in the east – and none at all to the north of 'Private Road No. IV', now Meadow Lane. The key to the future development of the area as a contiguous part of the city of Oxford was the turnpike road, which is now referred to as the Iffley Road to the north of the bridge

Henry Dixon, *Plan of the old inclosures and new allotments, within the township or liberty of Yeftley otherwise Iffley, within the manor and parish of Yeftley otherwise Iffley, in the County of Oxford. Referred to in the foregoing award* (1830)

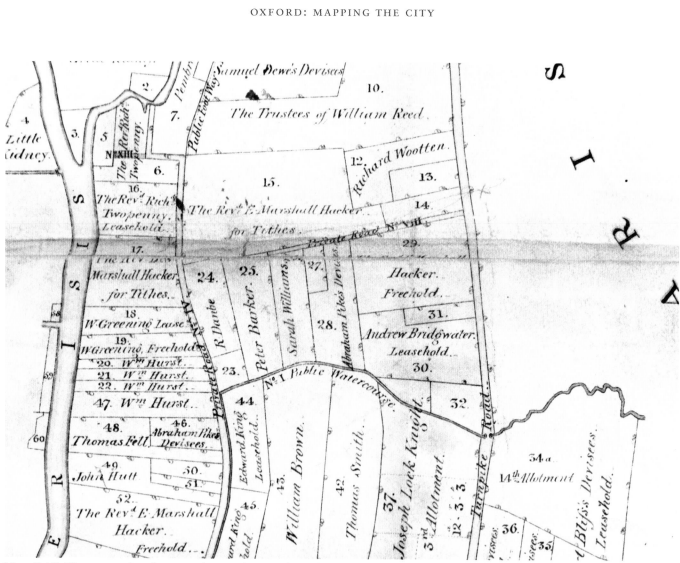

No. 1 Public Watercourse, later known as the Boundary Brook, marks the present-day transition between Iffley Road and Iffley Turn.

over 'No. I Public Watercourse', and as Iffley Turn immediately to the south of it. This watercourse was chosen as the southern boundary of the Oxford parliamentary constituency in 1867, but somewhat confusingly, it runs more than 200 yards to the south of the modern Boundary Brook Road.

Turnpike and new public road notwithstanding, the main focus of housing development in the area over the half-century following the creation of this map would be along both sides of Private Road No. II. In the almost entirely undeveloped area to the North of No. I Public Watercourse, meanwhile, Victorian building activity would consist almost entirely of mansions: Fairacres, at the eastern edge of plot '9', and Donnington Lodge and Fleetlands House on the northern and southern sides of Private Road No. VIII, which would eventually become the B4495 Donnington Bridge Road. As of the end of the nineteenth century, the southward expansion of the Oxford conurbation stopped at the Donnington Lodge nursery.

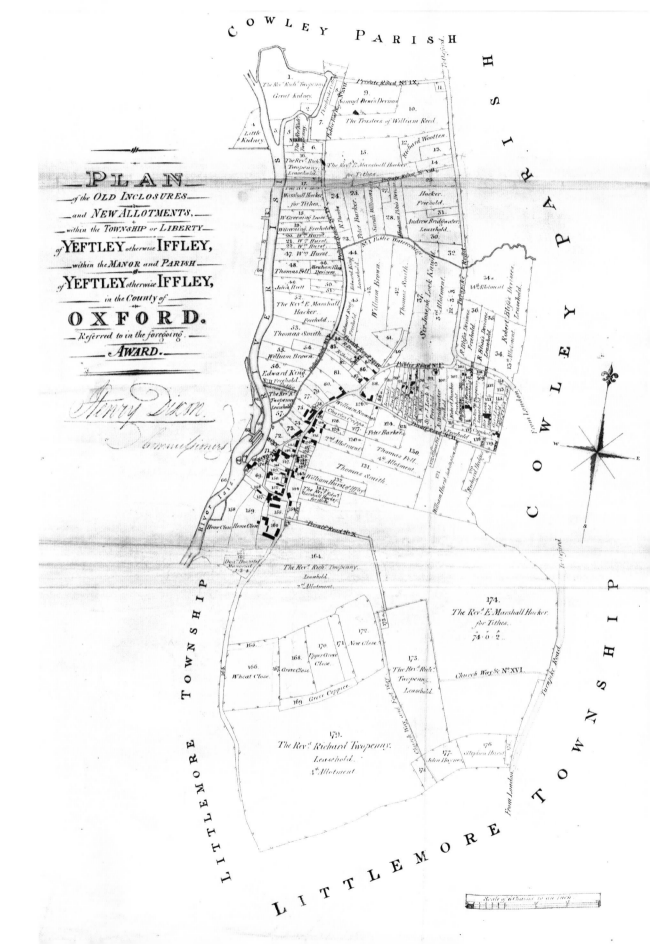

PLAN
of the OLD INCLOSURES
and NEW ALLOTMENTS,
within the TOWNSHIP or LIBERTY
of YEFTLEY otherwise IFFLEY,
within the MANOR and PARISH
of YEFTLEY otherwise IFFLEY,
in the County of
OXFORD.
Referred to in the foregoing
AWARD.

Henry Dixon
Commissioners

COWLEY PARISH

COWLEY PARISH

LITTLEMORE TOWNSHIP

LITTLEMORE TOWNSHIP

Scale of 6 Chains to an Inch

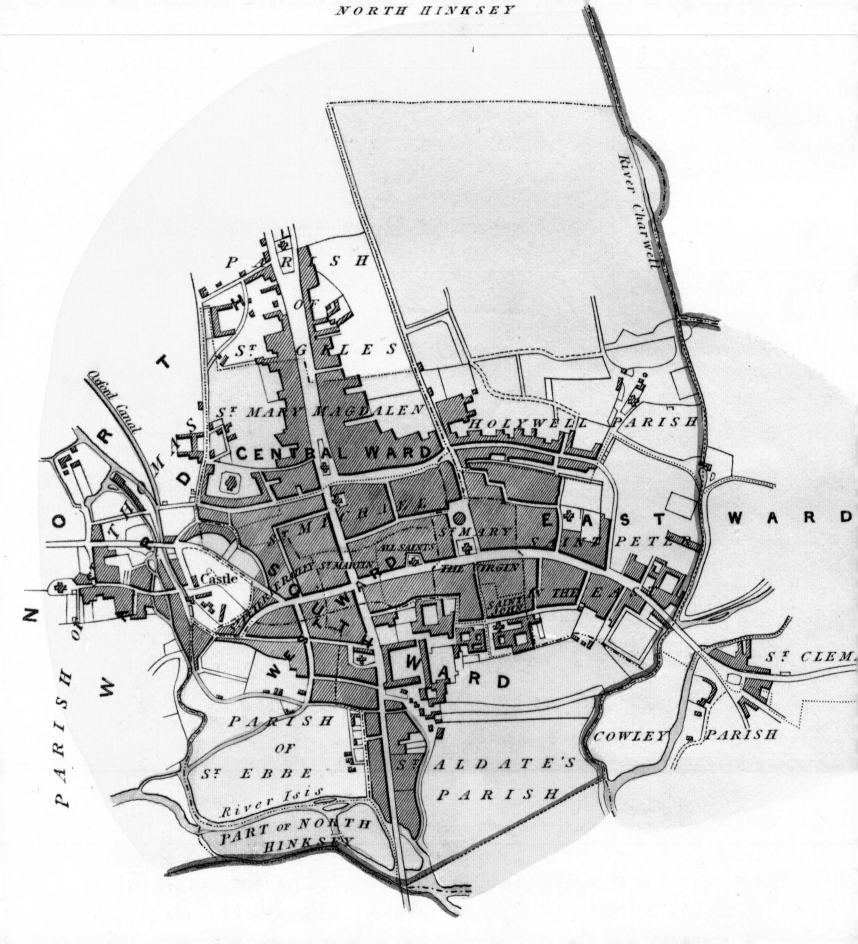

1831a

Charting the demise of the 'rotten boroughs'

As the 1820s drew to a close, Prime Minister the Duke of Wellington – an Irish Anglican and the most astute military brain of his, or perhaps any other, generation [1805] – had come to believe that unless the UK's centuries-old legal framework of discrimination against Roman Catholics were soon removed, Ireland would undergo a violent and possibly successful revolution. Within his own Tory party, which had always been pro-established church to a fault [1724], one of Wellington's few allies in his unlikely and initially quite secret Catholic Emancipation project was the intellectually brilliant Sir Robert Peel, Bt (1788–1850). When at Christ Church, Peel was the first person ever to earn a double first in mathematics and *literae humaniores* – despite having spent the day before the exams playing tennis. This choice of partner made the Emancipation initiative doubly unlikely. Peel, who had been

MP for Oxford University since 1817, was a man of such fixed Protestant opinions that he was nicknamed 'Orange' Peel by the Irish radical leader Daniel O'Connell; and the Protestant 'firebrands' among Peel's Oxford constituents turfed him out with vehement rudeness as soon as his insufficiently anti-Catholic position became known in 1829. In the short run, Peel was able to remain in Parliament only because he was given a 'rotten borough' seat in Wiltshire by Tory MP Sir Manasseh Lopes, Bt, a Jamaican-born Jew who – the times being the times – had been required to convert to Christianity in 1802 as a precondition of pursuing a political career. Following an inconclusive pistol duel between Wellington and the arch-Protestant Lord Winchilsea, Catholic Emancipation was passed – over the protests of Oxford's town council and at least two of its parishes. O'Connell, 'who had raged against

---

Thomas Drummond/Robert Dawson, 'Oxford From the Ordnance Survey', from House of Commons, *Reports from commissioners on proposed division of counties and boundaries of boroughs* (1832)

Wellington's Government, had now to abuse the "vile cozening Whigs," and . . . admit that the Tories were not so bad after all'. But as one of Wellington's relatives remembered it, the passage of Emancipation had been

> the triumph of the educated classes represented by nomination ['rotten'] boroughs. It had been passed by the few with a complete disregard for the wishes of the many, and the thoughtful and unrepresented in the bigger cities began to combine to prevent this ever happening again. . . . Parliamentary Reform was in the air. Men heard the word in talk on every street corner, caught it in snatches of discussion in clubs, read of it and laughed over it in newspapers and cartoons.

Just days after the beginning of the long polling period in the British general election of 1830, which would eventually return the Wellington/Peel government to power, the July Revolution erupted in France. This lent 'colour and reality to fears which had been merely surmises': that something similar was brewing in England. Indeed, the French overthrow of King Charles X (who went into exile, initially in Edinburgh) and his replacement by the 'bourgeois' Duc d'Orléans, amid days of open warfare on the streets of Paris, was part of a wave of serious unrest that would also affect Belgium, Poland, Italy and Brazil before the year was out. This time, however, in Wellington's politico-military estimation, England was in no particular danger; and it was largely from this opinion – frequently and publicly expressed – that the real danger came: for others saw a country in the grip of economic depression, food shortages and preventable epidemics [1848]. After a period of wrangling lasting more than a year, the Great Reform Act was passed in May 1832, in large part because Wellington, no longer in government but still wielding enormous influence over a 'throng' of his fellow Tory peers, chose not to oppose it in the House of Lords.

Long before the bill actually passed, however, the Whigs had sought cartographic answers to questions of what 'Reform' would actually consist of on the ground. In 1831, a 48-member Parliamentary Boundary Commission – of whom 30 members were surveyors or draughtsmen – was placed under the command of Lieutenant Thomas Drummond (1797–1840). Born in Edinburgh and raised in Musselburgh, Drummond had been sent to the Royal Military Academy at Woolwich at the age of 16 and was commissioned into the Royal Engineers one month after Waterloo. From 1820, he became heavily involved in the mapping of Scotland, England, and especially Ireland, under the supervision of the Ordnance Survey's irascible Colonel Thomas Colby (1784–1852), nephew of Major-General John Murray Hadden, surveyor-general of the Ordnance. Their 6-inch-to-the-mile mapping of Ireland, begun for tax-reform purposes in 1824, was so elaborate that they were allowed to teach surveying techniques to three entire companies of the Corps of Royal Sappers and Miners. (The merger of the all-officer Royal Engineers with the enlisted Sappers and Miners did not take place until after the Ordnance became part of the Regular Army in 1855–56.) The resultant maps, published from 1833 to 1847, 'represented a cartographic achievement of world importance' due to their 'detail, accuracy, and pleasing appearance' as well as their staggering cost and the horde of people their production had employed (E. Baigent). While in Ireland, Drummond made significant improvements to Colby's invention known as compensation bars, which are used for measuring base-lines in geodetic surveying, and improved the heliostat

> by adding a theodolite (an instrument for measuring angles), dispensing with the telescopes, and reducing the size of the mirror and connecting it to a stand by a ball-and-socket joint so that overall the heliostat was made smaller, portable, and easier to set up and adjust. (S.H. Palmer)

In addition to mapping 179 towns and cities, many of which had not yet been covered by the Ordnance Survey, Drummond's parliamentary team produced 'mathematical formulae incorporating statistics on the boroughs' population

OXFORD

From the Ordnance Survey

Scale 1 Inch to a Mile

Furlongs 8 7 6 5 4 3 2 1 0   1 Mile

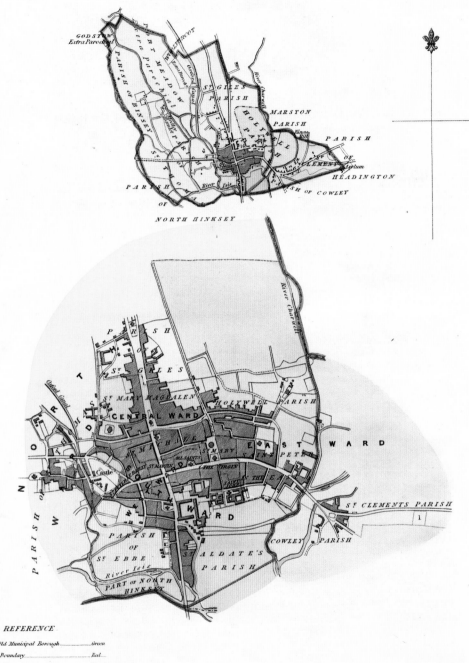

REFERENCE

Boundary of Old Municipal Borough	Green
Parliamentary Boundary	Red
Proposed Municipal Boundary	Purple
Boundaries of Parishes or Townships	
Water	Blue

WARDS
- CENTRAL
- NORTH
- SOUTH
- WEST
- EAST

Portion of Cowley and Iffley Parishes } Marked 1

R. K. Dawson Lt R.E.

Scale 4 Inches to a Mile

0   ¼   ¾   1 Mile

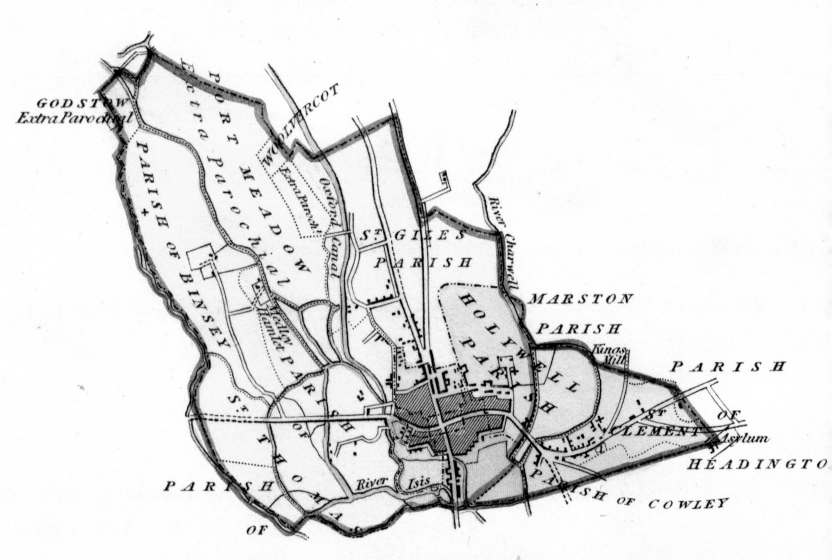

OXFORD

From the Ordnance Survey

Scale, 1 Inch to a Mile

Furlongs 8 7 6 5 4 3 2 1 0   1 Mile

GODSTOW
Extra Parochial

PORT MEADOW

WOOLVERCOT

Extra Parochial

Extra Parish

Oxford Canal

PARISH OF BINSEY

Medley Hamlet PARISH

St GILES PARISH

River Cherwell

MARSTON PARISH

HOLYWELL PARISH

Kings Mill

PARISH OF

St THOMAS

PARISH OF

St CLEMENT

Asylum

HEADINGTO

PARISH

OF

River Isis

PARISH OF COWLEY

NORTH HINKSEY

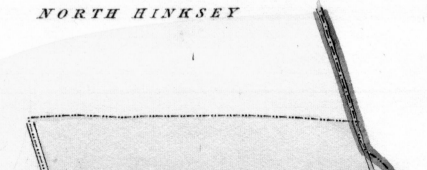

Ri

(houses) and wealth (assessed taxes)', allowing 'scientific' or 'algebraic' decisions to be made regarding the fairness, or not, of pre-Reform representation. Drummond's calculations 'served as a general basis for' the 1832 reform, but would be 'more fully embodied' only in the Electoral Redistribution Act 1885 (Palmer), when the Oxford city constituency lost one of its two MPs. Oxford University, however, would continue to return two MPs of its own until 1950.

Credit for the specific appearance of the reform maps can be assigned to Kent-born Captain Robert Kearsley Dawson (1798–1861); one year younger than Drummond, he graduated from Woolwich one year later but joined Colby's mapping outfit at the same time Drummond did, and was a pioneer of the use of lithography in British maps, including this one. After the passage of the Great Reform Act, he went on to publish *Plans of the Most Capital Cities of Every Empire*. Dawson's maps did not always show streets and hardly ever named them. The great extent of the boundary to the north and northwest of Oxford might seem to suggest that the city's post-1850 expansion into North Oxford was already planned or predicted, but in fact this large still-rural area was the ancient 'ridden boundary' established by the end of the seventeenth century and confirmed annually via the ceremonial 'riding of the franchises' by the mayor's entourage. As the map makes clear, the Commissioners felt that – industrialisation and population growth notwithstanding – major reform of the Oxford constituency was required only in its southeastern part. The red-outlined district on the uppermost map, comprising 261 acres in St Clement's and two in Cowley, was placed within the parliamentary borough, which then covered the whole contiguous built-up area of the city and suburbs.

Quite unfairly, Peel is nowadays remembered almost solely for his role in police modernisation; and Wellington's hard-headed turn in politics, which probably saved the nation from a Continental-style bloodbath, is hardly ever spoken of either. Perhaps we are always least grateful to those whom we owe the most.

Emancipation, of course, did not equate to immediate toleration: 'college servants and others connected with the

Royal Engineers officer Robert Kearsley Dawson was a pioneer of the use of lithography in British maps.

university voted against the Catholic Thomas Stonor in the parliamentary elections of 1832 and 1835 because of his religion' (J. Cooper). Dawson 'was attached to the Tithe Commutation Commission from its first formation' in 1836 [1853] and finished his career as a lieutenant-colonel (S. Moverley). In 1835, Drummond married Maria Kinnaird, ward and principal heir of the wealthy Newfoundland-born critic and *bon vivant* Richard 'Conversation' Sharp, on whom Charles Dickens would base the *Bleak House* character Conversation Kenge. Though a Whig politically, Drummond would spend much of the remainder of his short life remodelling the Irish police forces on Peelite lines. He died of overwork at the age of 42.

1831b

Jericho rising

Inevitably, some British town maps are far more interesting for what they record of the development of the street system than for their own beauty or precision, or their makers' life stories. Others still, particularly in the economically chaotic aftermath of the Napoleonic Wars, presented hoped-for, planned or projected developments as if they had already occurred. This otherwise mundane map, the first of Oxford to be produced since the beginning of the city's 1820s building boom, falls firmly into the latter category.

'Building boom' may, in this case, be too strong a term. Far from being an act of comprehensive re-planning, this was a piecemeal, almost schizophrenic affair. On the one hand, it created Oxford's first bourgeois enclave on the Edinburgh New Town or Clifton Village pattern – albeit in miniature – in the form of neo-classical Beaumont Street, which has been praised by leading architectural critic Sir Niklaus Pevsner as

the finest streetscape in the city. On the other, it 'filled the meadows and garden grounds along the banks of the Isis with hundreds of small two- or three-storey brick cottages . . . [for] mechanics, small shopkeepers, journeymen, tailors, shoemakers and labourers with their wives and children' (R.J. Morris).

Beaumont Street was named for the nearby ruins of Beaumont Palace or 'the manor of Oxford', which had been a favourite residence of Eleanor of Aquitaine; two of her sons, the future kings Richard the Lionheart and John Lackland, were born in it. The luxurious new street is shown here as complete, except for a short stretch in the southeastern part, but this may be our first instance of anticipation or wishful thinking, as the building of it would not be completed until six years after this map was published. Mapmaker John Whessel also shows the newly developed but somewhat less

John Whessel/T. Bartlett, 'A new and improved map of the University and City of Oxford', from *Oxford delineated; or A Sketch of the History and Antiquities and a general topographical description of That celebrated University and City: illustrated by a series of views* (1832)

grand St John Street ('47'), which connects Beaumont Street to Wellington Square ('8'), as substantially complete on both sides and the Regency brick terrace known as Beaumont Buildings ('48') as finished. Numbers 4–28 Walton Street were also explicitly built for middle-class residents at around this time. Curiously, Walton Street (here 'Walton Place'), Beaumont Buildings and St John Street are shown as equidistant from each other and nearly parallel, which can only mean that the map's creator positioned one or more of them wrongly. Hoggar and Jones's far more accurate map from two decades later [1850] confirms that St John Street as actually built was precisely parallel to the Beaumont Buildings, which in turn lined up almost perfectly with the west front of the Wellington Square Workhouse. Alfred Street ('59', now Pusey Street) is also incorrectly shown here as transitioning smoothly into Beaumont Place at its western end. As such, it is safe to say that this area of the present map was the product of either *very* shoddy surveying or – as seems more likely – nearly pure guesswork based on the builders' written statements or even oral hearsay.

Only a couple of buildings are shown as fronting directly onto Little Clarendon Street ('60'), and Walton Place is only about half occupied by completed buildings on either side along the whole of its length from Worcester College ('r') to the new University Press building ('t'), which had opened as a replacement for the Clarendon Building as recently as 1830 but was not yet closed off on its western end. Only a shallow ribbon development stands between the west side of Walton Place and the canal. A narrow gap labelled '50' signals the approximate future location of Worcester Place, but the eventual locations of Walton Crescent, Richmond Road and Nelson Street have not even been guessed at.

From the Press northward, Walton Place's eastern side has no buildings at all, but there seems to be evidence of considerable planning coordination in the layout and appearance of

Great Clarendon, King, Wellington, Union (now Hart) and Cardigan streets, here numbered 53–57 respectively, and Jericho Street, which is not numbered. Again, however, this is fantasy. The western side of King Street's northern half had only two buildings on it, not five, 19 years after this map was published. The houses in the area were of widely varied sizes and shapes, with those between King Street and Walton Street generally the smallest, and those on the north side of Great Clarendon Street the largest – but nearly all were narrower across the front than they were deep, i.e. the opposite of what is indicated here. And Union/Hart Street, though shown correctly as being much wider than King Street, was not actually parallel to it. The unnamed and unnumbered street to the immediate north of and parallel to Little Clarendon Street would be blocked off by new building at its eastern end before 1850.

In the city centre, it is worth noting that the modern names Queen Street for Butcher Row and St Aldates Street for Fish Street have at last taken hold. In St Ebbe's, we see the 1818 gasworks in its correct position, but the same criticisms regarding the orientations of the streets and the shapes of houses in Jericho apply here too – egregiously so, in the case of Friars Street ('93') and Bull Street ('94'), which in actuality were nowhere near parallel and would have crossed each other at the Tan Yards if they had continued a bit farther eastward. Bull Street would be renamed New Street by 1865.

This is also the first map of Oxford made after the 1824–27 reconstruction of the medieval Folly Bridge, as South Bridge was by this time generally known. This involved the removal of the city's waterworks to a new site a little way upstream. The relative positions and sizes of this, its weir and the new bridge are all shown more or less correctly; but given that the new waterworks was described as being in a 'street', the complete absence of any other buildings near it does not tend to re-inspire confidence in Whessel's methods.

Opposite. The map's depiction of Jericho, Beaumont Street, and the area between them was largely conjectural.

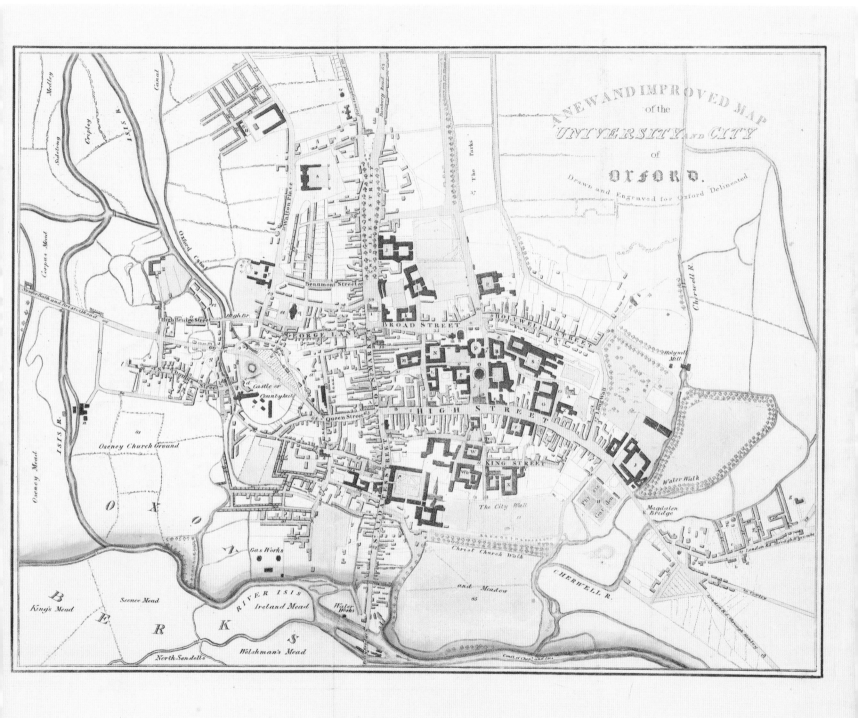

A NEW AND IMPROVED MAP
of the
UNIVERSITY AND CITY
of
OXFORD.
Drawn and Engraved for Oxford Delineated

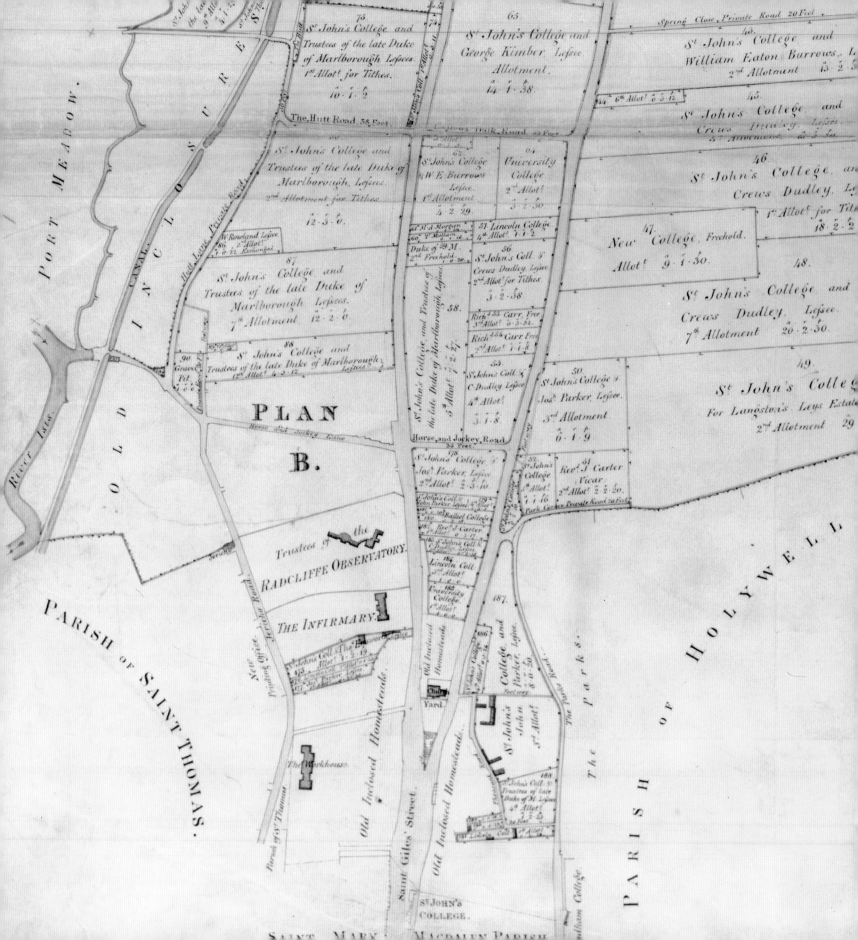

PLAN B.

PORT MEADOW.

PARISH OF SAINT THOMAS.

PARISH OF HOLYWELL.

75.
St. John's College and
Trustees of the late Duke
of Marlborough Lessees.
1st Allott. for Tithes.
10.1.2

65.
St. John's College and
George Kimber, Lessee.
Allotment.
14.1.38

45.
St. John's College and
William Eaton Burrows, L.
2nd Allotment. 13.2.5

Spring Close Private Road 20 Feet

44. 6th Allott. 0.3.12

45.
St. John's College and
Crews Dudley, Lessee
5th Allotment. 10.3.5.

The Hutt Road, 35 Feet.

Congroves Walk Road 35 Feet

80.
St. John's College and
Trustees of the late Duke of
Marlborough, Lessees.
2nd Allotment for Tithes.
12.3.0

62.
St. John's College
& W.E. Burrows
Lessee.
1st Allotment.
4.1.29

64.
University
College
2nd Allott.
3.2.30.

46.
St. John's College and
Crews Dudley, L.

1st Allott. for Tithes
18.2.2

87.
W. Rowland Lessee.
86. 2nd Allott.
1.0.12 Exchanged

60. G M A Morgan
Y. Wallam. 16

51. Lincoln College
4th Allott. 1.1.2

47.
New College, Freehold.
Allott. 9.1.30.

48.

87.
St. John's College and
Trustees of the late Duke of
Marlborough Lessees.
7th Allotment. 12.2.0

Duke of 59.M.
2nd Freehold.

56.
St. John's Coll. &
Crews Dudley, Lessee.
2nd Allot. for Tithes.
3.2.38

St. John's College and
Crews Dudley, Lessee.
7th Allotment. 20.2.30

58.
Rich 55 Carr, Free.
3rd Allot. 5.3.32.
Rich 54 Carr Free
2nd Allot. 1.1.8

86.
St. John's College and
Trustees of the late Duke of Marlborough
Lessees.
12th Allott. 4.3.12

90. Gravel
Pit.

St. John's College and Trustees of
the late Duke of Marlborough Lessees.

53.
St. John's Coll. &
C. Dudley, Lessee
4th Allott.
3.1.8

50.
St. John's College &
Jos. Parker, Lessee.
3rd Allotment.
6.1.9

49.
St. John's College
For Langston's Leys Estate.
2nd Allotment 29

Horse and Jockey Road 35 Feet.

Horse and Jockey Road

178.
St. John's College &
Jos. Parker, Lessee
2nd Allott. 2.3.10

52.
St. John's
College
4th Allott.
1.1.16

51. Rev J. Carter
Vicar
2nd Allot. 2.2.20

Park Corner Private Road 20 Feet

St. John Coll &
Jos Parker, Lessee

Balliol College

Rev J. Carter
Lessee

St. John Coll &
Lessee

Lincoln Coll.
3rd Allott.

University
College

Trustees of the
RADCLIFFE OBSERVATORY.

THE INFIRMARY.

St. John Coll. The
Allott.
Jos Parker, Lessee

Church
Yard

College and
Jos. Parker, Lessee

St. John's College
3rd Allott.
8.0.30

St. John's College
Jos. Parker, Lessee

St. John's
Coll.
3rd Allott.

The Parks.

The Workhouse.

St. John's Coll. &
Trustees of late
Duke of M. Lessees
4th Allott.

Lincoln Coll. 1st Allott.

ST. JOHN'S
COLLEGE.

SAINT MARY MAGDALEN PARISH

1832

Gateway to the north

As we have seen [1830], landholders in the still-rural district of Iffley were disproportionately individuals from the middling ranks of society, with three of the largest being the clergymen Richard Twopenny and E. Marshall Hacker, and Oxford's former mayor Sir Joseph Lock, who according to local legend was knighted by mistake. A starkly different pattern of landholding in the parish of St Giles's is shown in this equally detailed cadastral plan, prepared by the same local surveyor, Henry Dixon – who was also probably the architect of Beaumont Street [1831b]. Nor was the Beaumont Street/St John Street/Beaumont Buildings development taking place in isolation, for it was in St Giles Street that Oxford saw its 'greatest concentration of new stone buildings' in the late Georgian period, 'mostly built as residences and offices for leading professional men' (C.J. Day).

Here, within easy reach of the city but outside its walls and therefore not subject to its market tolls, a marketplace for hay, wood and other basic items had arisen naturally at an early date in the unowned and unused space at the junction of the not-quite-parallel roads to Woodstock and Banbury. Its use as a fairground began in or by the Jacobean period with the St Giles's parish wake or feast, and this evolved over the next century and half into a large fair held annually in early September: 'always primarily a pleasure fair' (J. Cooper) but with the selling of miscellaneous items, especially for children. The importance of this activity is underscored by the fact that the city per se had no fairs in 1675, 1684 or 1756; fair tolls in St Giles's were payable not to the city, but to St John's College in its capacity as lord of the manor of Walton. It may have been due to this bustling if intermittent trade that St Giles

Henry Dixon, *Plan, A, of the parish of Saint Giles in the Suburbs of the City of Oxford in the County of Oxford, referred to in the annexed award* (1832)

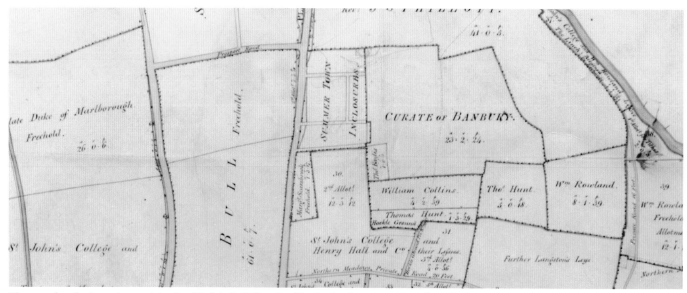

The map foreshadows the crucial role of St John's College land in the development of North Oxford a generation later.

Street was paved somewhat earlier than Broad Street was.

It is still widely recollected that most of the post-1850 development of North Oxford took place on St John's College land [c.1862, 1872]. Thus, it is interesting to note that some of the most valuable plots for potential residential and office construction – in the wedge of land between the two turnpikes, bounded at one end by Horse and Jockey Road (now Bevington Road) and the 'Old Inclosed Homesteads' to the north of the parish church at the other – were owned not only by St John's, but by Lincoln, University and Balliol. Bevington Road would be developed for housing beginning in 1865.

From the point of view of the city's near-term development, the other most interesting feature of this map is that a basic street pattern has already been laid out in the 'Summer Town Inclosures' to the northwest and southeast of the junction of Prospect Road (now South Parade) with the Banbury turnpike. Summertown would separate from St Giles's for administrative purposes as early as 1834, when the former's projected growth mandated the creation of a new parish, St Michael and All Angels. Dixon's apparent obsession with road widths was in fact part and parcel of the enclosure process [1819], which required public roads made through enclosed lands to be a minimum of 30 feet in width at this date.

Present-day St Margaret's Road, which would not be developed until 1879, is here referred to in its eastern portion as 'Gallows Balk Road', as being the site of the town's gallows from medieval times, though in those days it was referred to as the Green Ditch. The western part of the same road is here called 'The Hutt Road' because it led to the canal-side pub originally known as Heyfield's Hutt [1768, 1838]. The Martyrs' Memorial, to three Protestant bishops burnt at the stake in Broad Street during the reign of Mary Tudor, would not be put up until 1843, as a riposte to the Oxford Movement [1837].

St Giles's Fair continued to expand in the Victorian era, 'becoming a major holiday for the working people of the whole county and beyond' (Cooper). The city took over control of it in the 1930s, when Sir John Betjeman thought it 'about the biggest fair in England'. It is still held, completely blocking the street for two days in September each year.

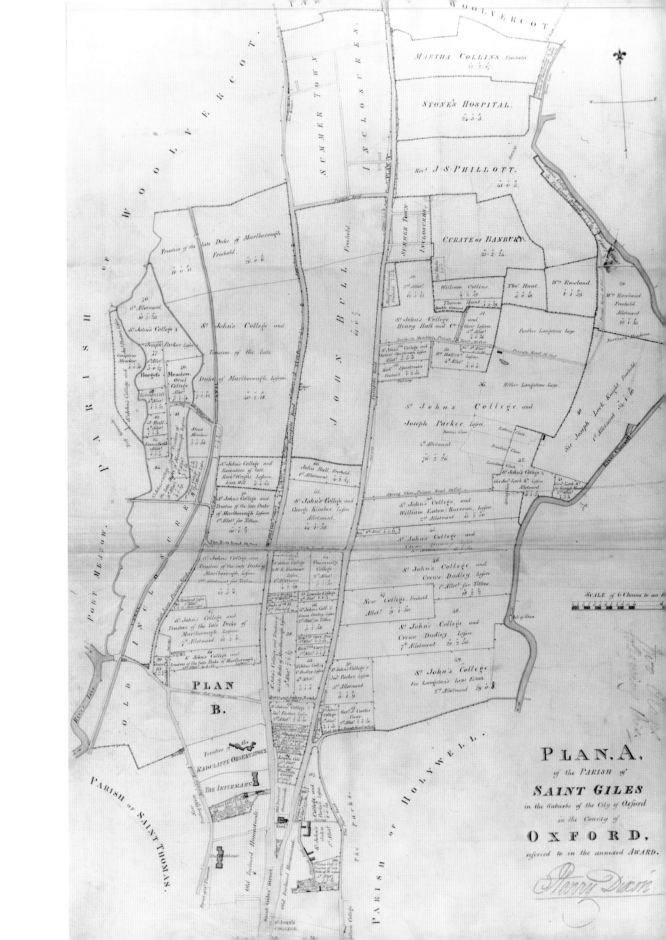

PLAN. A,
of the PARISH of
SAINT GILES
in the Suburbs of the City of Oxford
in the County of
OXFORD.
referred to in the annexed AWARD.

Harry Dixon

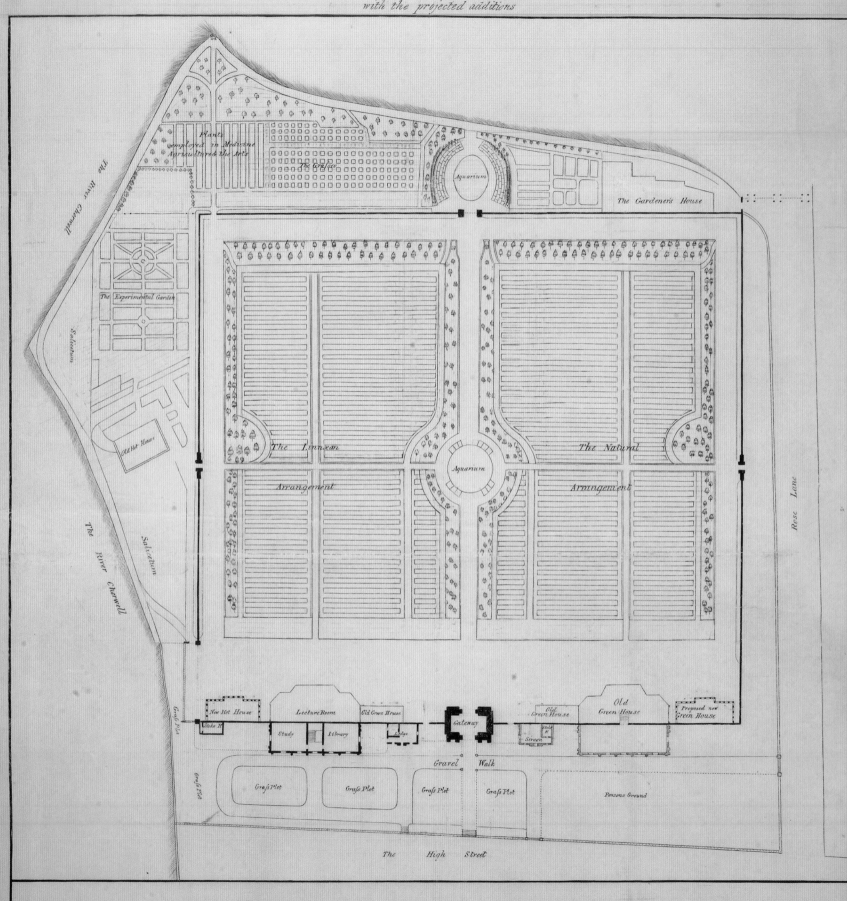

The River Cherwell

Plants employed in Medicine Agriculture & the Arts

The Grasses

Aquarium

The Gardener's House

The Experimental Garden

Salicetum

Old Hot House

The Linnæan Arrangement

Aquarium

The Natural Arrangement

Rose Lane

The River Cherwell

Salicetum

Grass Plot

New Hot House

Stove H.

Lecture Room

Study

Library

Old Green House

Lodge

Gateway

Old Green House

Screen

Stove H.

Old Green House

Proposed new Green House

Grass Plot

Grass Plot

Grass Plot

Gravel Walk

Grass Plot

Grass Plot

Persons Ground

The High Street

c.1834

The Physic Garden comes of age

Throughout medieval Europe, 'physic gardens' dedicated to the cultivation of plants with medicinal properties were maintained by monasteries, universities and other institutions connected with the medical profession. It was in the mid sixteenth century, however, that the physic-garden concept first began to evolve into the 'botanic garden', reflecting a more general interest in the collection of living plants simply for the sake of extending botanical knowledge, rather than for their instrumental use as cures (or poisons). Interest in these scientific, but not specifically medical gardens spread rapidly, in a process intimately bound up with the discovery of new plant species in far-flung parts of the world that were being visited and settled by Europeans for the first time. The Oxford Botanic Garden was laid out on a 5-acre site to the south of Magdalen College between 1621 and 1633, hard upon the English colonisation of Virginia, Bermuda, Amboina,

Surat, the Gold Coast, Massachusetts, Barbados and Connecticut. Though often described as the first *botanical* garden in England, it was in fact founded as a traditional physic garden; in 1659 it was producing a 'physick-drink' made of 'scurvy-grass', and it was not officially termed the Botanic Garden until nearly two centuries later.

The site, which included a medieval Jewish cemetery, required thousands of cart-loads of earth and 'dunge' to raise it above the level of the Cherwell's flood-line. The £5,000 cost of the project – more than £13 million at today's prices – was donated by Henry, 1st Earl of Danby (1573–1644), a Wiltshire-born Protestant soldier of fortune and accused murderer who had been ennobled for his role in the battle of Kinsale, climax to the Tudor reconquest of Ireland. Despite its immensity, this sum was less than half of Danby's annual income, which by this time came from official appointments

H.J. Underwood/C. Mathews, *Plan of the Botanic Garden with the projected additions* (n.d.)

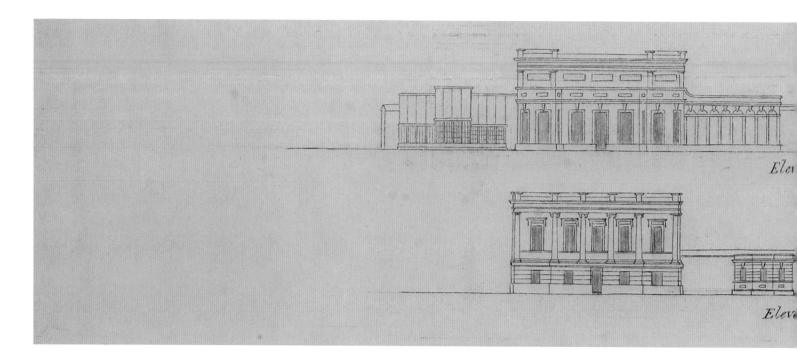

Elev

Eleva

including the governorship-for-life of the Isle of Guernsey; in his defence, Danby was probably one of the few people in the world who had been both a warship captain and a cavalry general.

The garden's magnificent Danby gateway was built by Devon-born Nicholas Stone (d.1647), master mason to the crown. Many have claimed that Stone worked to a design by Welsh architectural master Inigo Jones (1573–1652), though this should be taken with a grain of salt, given that Stone was by this time styled 'architect' in his own right, as well as being 'England's leading sculptor in stone and marble' both artistically and commercially (A. White). Be that as it may, his gateway of 1632–33 is one of the earliest English examples of the ever-controversial baroque mode in architecture. Stone's 1637 baroque porch for Oxford's medieval church of Mary the Virgin struck contemporaries as so papal in style that it formed part of the evidence against Archbishop Laud during his 1644 trial for treason.

Elevating the ground level of the Physic Garden site and erecting its gates and walls proved so expensive that there was

initially nothing left with which to buy plants. It would take nine years after the completion of the monumental gateway for the garden to acquire its first curator, Jacob Bobart (c.1599–1680), 'a veteran of the German wars' born in Brunswick, and another seven would pass before he was paid for his efforts. Fortunately, in the intervening period of pennilessness, sales of fruit were brisk; the proceeds enabled Bobart not only to form a significant collection of more exotic plants, notably from Canada, but to publish a 64-page catalogue of them in 1648. Prominent visitors from the era of Bobart's curatorship included Elias Ashmole as well as the Prince of Orange and the Grand Duke of Tuscany – though a far less illustrious one complained in 1664 that the place was 'small, ill-kept, and more like an orchard than a garden'.

The collection was greatly expanded by Bobart's son of the same name, an academic disciple of Robert Morison [1673] who wrote 'the sole complete exposition of Morison's classificatory system' (D.E. Allen). Sadly, Bobart the Younger was sacked in 1719 for exceeding the garden's budget, which was still less than £100 per year, and he died shortly after-

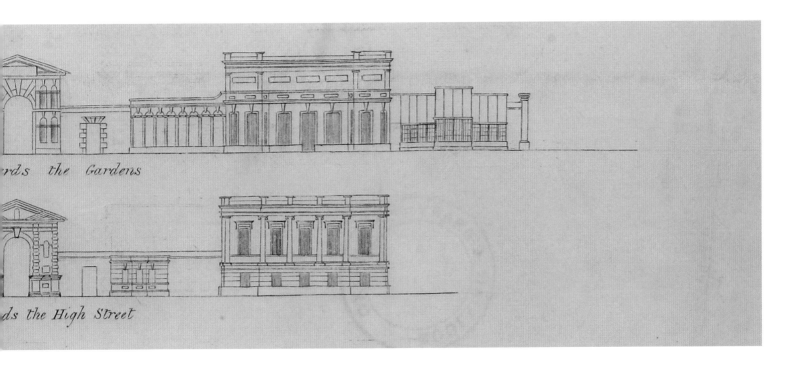

rds the Gardens

ds the High Street

wards, still inhabiting the garden-house. A more generous endowment of £150 per year followed in 1728, and the great Carl Linnaeus (1707–1778) named *Bobartia*, a genus of African irises, after the Bobart family.

The garden-house in which Bobart had lived and died was removed in 1790 during the reconstruction of Magdalen Bridge [1771]. The present plan, engraved at a scale of around 1:550 by C. Mathews after a drawing by Oxford-based church architect Henry Jones Underwood (1804–1852), shows the latter's scheme to quadruple the space of the original 1730s orangeries, which were single-storey structures entirely on the inside of the garden's boundary wall. More or less as shown, this was achieved in 1835 – hence our provisional dating – by extending the existing buildings upward by one storey, and then outward, as new two-storey structures beyond the wall on the High Street side. In the event, however, the upper storeys on the garden side were given windows of a normal Georgian 'portrait' format. Also, through most of the remainder of the century and in contrast to the rooms' internal labelling here, maps identified the northwestern pavilion as

'Lecture Room' or 'Lecture Hall' and the southeastern one as 'Professor's House' [e.g. 1850, 1895]. The engraver, Mathews, was a local Oxford artist who eventually became an excellent botanical illustrator as a result of his long-term collaborations with William Baxter, who was appointed curator of the garden in 1813.

Finances in the nineteenth century, though greatly improved, remained problematic at times. A scheme to charge people a shilling each to see the *Victoria amazonica* water lilies in the 1850s seems to have attracted more angry letters than visitors, though Samuel Pepys appears to have paid as much to visit the garden nearly two centuries earlier. Arguably Oxford's most versatile site of literary inspiration, the Botanic Garden influenced Lewis Carroll and J.R.R. Tolkien, and features prominently in Evelyn Waugh's *Brideshead Revisited* and Philip Pullman's *His Dark Materials* trilogy. For good measure, the 1594 murder of Henry Long, which garden founder Lord Danby probably committed as part of a long-running interfamilial feud, is thought to have been part of the basis for Shakespeare's *Romeo and Juliet*.

1834

The outer limits: Wolvercote and the Duke's Cut

Readers will by now be familiar enough with Henry Dixon's splendid draughtsmanship [1830], and with the general pattern of landholding in rural areas immediately adjacent to the city of Oxford [1832] or administered by city parishes [1819]. Here, Dixon captures the immediate pre-railway state of the villages of Upper and Lower Wolvercote: the former stretching from the eastern side of the Oxford–Coventry Canal [1768, 1838] to the Woodstock turnpike along present-day Godstow Road (here marked 'Lower Woolvercot Road') and First Turn ('The Church Road'); and the latter centred on its important Thames-side paper mill ('34'), already more than a century old, at the end of the unnamed street now called Mill Road.

The publisher of the *Jackson's Oxford Journal* newspaper, established in the 1750s, leased the originally water-powered mill from the 4th Duke of Marlborough in 1782. It was converted to run partially on steam power in 1811, which necessitated the delivery of thousands of tons of coal per year. This was achieved via narrowboats, which would come south along the canal, turn west into the Duke's Cut (dug in 1789) and then south along 'Branch of the River Isis' – more generally referred to as the Wolvercote Mill Stream – where they were unloaded at a coal wharf specially built for the purpose.

The permanent preservation of Port Meadow as common land [1695] ensured that Lower Wolvercote would remain effectively isolated from the city, despite the employment opportunities provided by papermaking and, by 1898, a small gasworks. It is not immediately clear, however, what factors impeded neighbouring Upper Wolvercote's absorption by/as Oxford's northern suburban fringe for so long. The Ordnance

Henry Dixon, *Map of the old inclosures and new allotments in the Parish of Woolvercot in the County of Oxford, referred to in the within award* (1834)

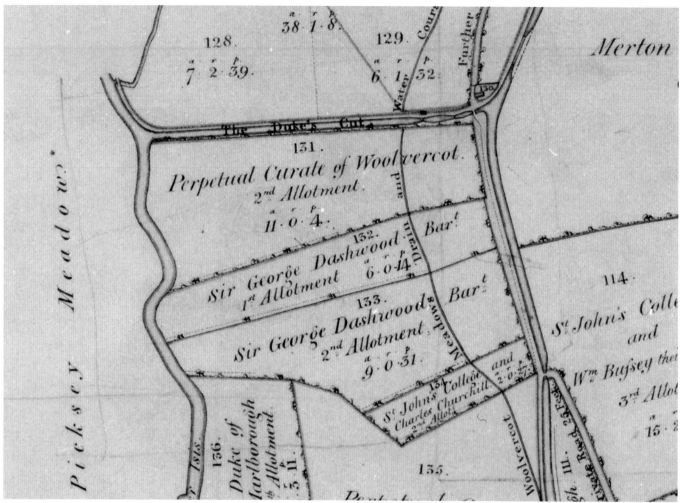

The Duke's Cut connected the Wolvercote Mill Stream (left) to the Oxford–Coventry Canal (right), and allowed the delivery of coal directly to Wolvercote's paper mill.

Survey maps of the area that were surveyed in the 1870s and revised in 1898 show little change, even in terms of field boundaries, despite the Oxford & Rugby Railway having been driven through the western half of Goose Green in 1846, and the Buckinghamshire Railway line of 1850 skirting the edge of Upper Wolvercote on its other side. The long and the short of it seems to be that neither railway saw fit to provide a halt in the immediate vicinity until 1905; and that the Duke of Marlborough, Joseph Parker and Sir George Dashwood did not sell their respective parcels '86', '93' and '94' to developers. This by itself would have connected Upper Wolvercote to Summertown a short distance to the southeast, as of course did happen in the following century.

The Wolvercote Paper Mill operated its own narrowboats from the 1850s down to the First World War, and coal continued to be delivered via canal boat until the modernisation of the mill in the 1950s. It closed in 1998 and was torn down in 2004.

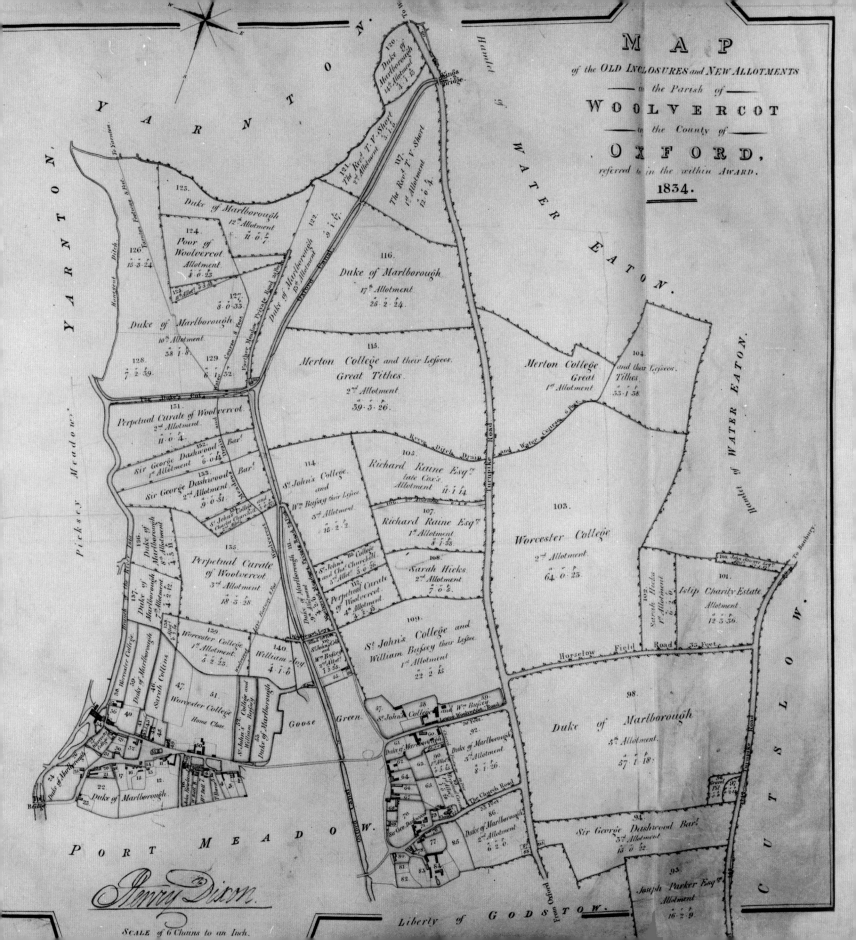

MAP
of the OLD INCLOSURES and NEW ALLOTMENTS
in the Parish of
WOOLVERCOT
in the County of
OXFORD,
referred to in the within AWARD.
1834.

Henry Dixon.

SCALE of 6 Chains to an Inch.

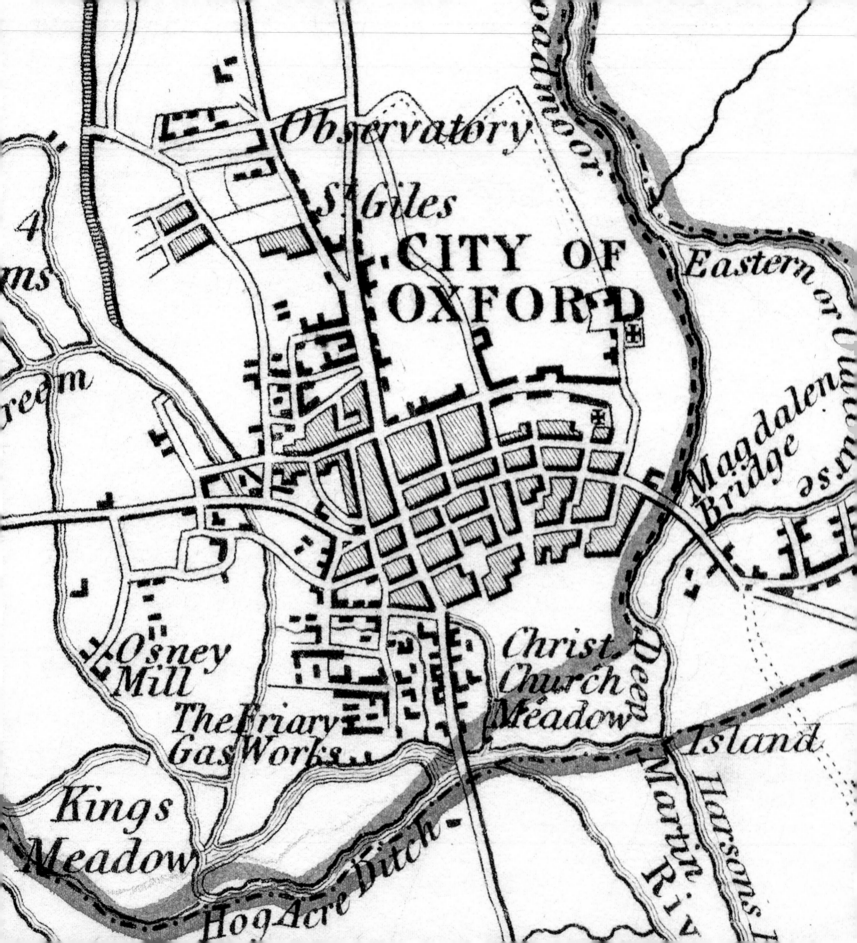

Observatory

St Giles

CITY OF OXFORD

Eastern or Cherwell

Magdalen Bridge

Osney Mill

The Friary Gas Works

Christ Church Meadow

Deep

Island

Kings Meadow

Hog Acre Ditch

Martin Riv

Harsons R

1835

Towards a modern city government

The royal charter granted to the city of Oxford by King James I in 1605 would continue in use as the basis of civic administration for the next 230 years. The present map, in some respects merely a version of Dawson's [1831a] that has reverted from the state-of-the-art technique of lithography to the ancient craft of engraving, was produced in connection with the Municipal Corporations Act 1835, which ensured that the boundaries of the municipal borough matched those that the Great Reform Act had established for the parliamentary borough.

More generally, the 1835 act was a response to a parliamentary select committee's June 1833 finding that, while many towns had far outgrown their ancient borough boundaries, others had shrunk to the point that they now claimed an absurd authority over 'distant' places 'more properly falling within the jurisdiction of the county magistrates'. For the time being, Oxford's administration arguably fell into both these categories: having too little authority in built-up places immediately to the south, and too much in rural places a long way to the north. A follow-up Royal Commission report in 1835 was far more damning, finding that 178 of the 285 town governments it had investigated in England and Wales, including Oxford, were secretive and corrupt self-perpetuating oligarchies that systematically discriminated against religious minorities and had little or no popular support among the townspeople they governed. The existing systems in these towns were promptly swept away, and in Oxford, all ratepayers were now allowed to vote for the new city council that replaced the 'Mayor, Bailiffs, and Commonalty'. As a collateral benefit, municipal reform also overthrew centuries-

R. Creighton/J. & C. Walker, 'Oxford', from R. Creighton and
S. Lewis, *View of the Representative History of England* (1835)

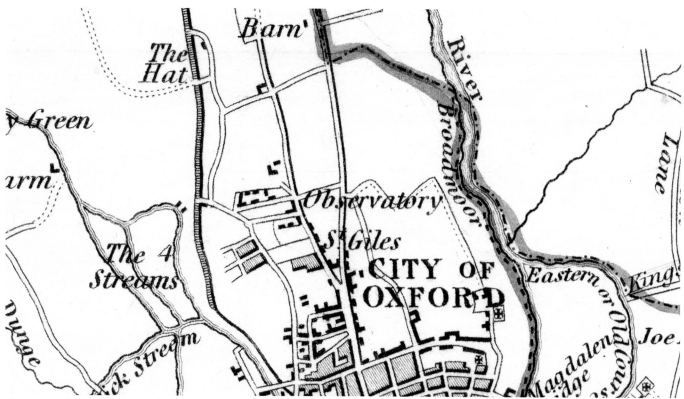

The haste with which all maps of this sort were prepared is reflected in the mislabelling of the canal-side pub known as the Hutt: here, 'The Hat'.

old 'conservative and restrictive attitudes towards the town's economy', by allowing persons who were neither members of the university nor freemen of the city to legally engage in trade there for the first time (C.J. Day). In the event, however, a Liberal Party stranglehold on local politics and a range of public institutions would ensue from the 1850s to the 1880s; this 'inevitably aroused suspicion and envy, exacerbated by the arrogance and tactlessness of some of Oxford's rulers' (C. Colvin), including a failed attempt to shut down six pubs owned by Tories.

There was a time-lag of more than two decades between Benjamin Disraeli's Second Reform Act of 1867, which enfranchised most working-class urban men, and the enlargement of the Oxford municipal borough to match its associated boundary changes. In the event, this delay resulted in the city council area being very slightly larger than the parliamentary borough as of 1889: with the council acquiring formal control over 32 acres at the southern end of Grandpont, in addition to 447 acres in the parish of St Giles, 293 in St Aldates, 216 in Headington, 90 in Iffley, 82 in New Hinksey and 24 in Marston, and those parts of Cowley that were already represented on the Local Board [c.1862, 1872]. The Oxfordshire/Berkshire border was also moved, so that the municipal corporation area would once again be entirely in Oxfordshire. After this, however, the tables were turned. Rampant urban growth led to nearly 3,600 acres coming under the city's jurisdiction in the 1920s, but this was not reflected at Westminster until 1948.

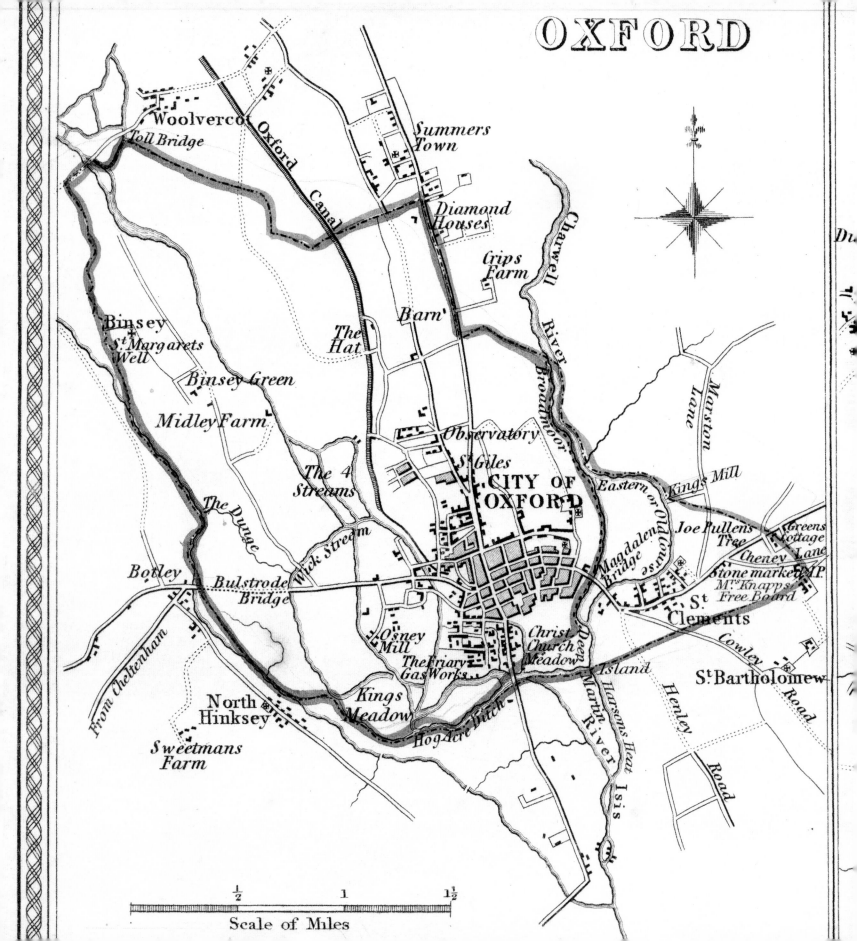

OXFORD

Woolvercot

Toll Bridge

Summers Town

Oxford Canal

Diamond Houses

Crips Farm

Charwell River

Barn'

The Hat

Binsey

St Margarets Well

Binsey Green

Broadmoor

Midley Farm

Observatory

St Giles

The 4 Streams

CITY OF OXFORD

Eastern or Oldcourse

Kings Mill

Marston Lane

The Dunge

Joe Pullens Tree

Greens Cottage

Wick Stream

Magdalen Bridge

Cheney Lane

Botley

Stone market M.P.

Bulstrode Bridge

Mrs Knapps Free Board

St Clements

From Cheltenham

Osney Mill

The Friary Gas Works

Christ Church Meadow

Deep Island

Cowley

St Bartholomew

Road

North Hinksey

Kings Meadow

Hog Acre Ditch

Marsons Heat River Isis

Henley Road

Sweetmans Farm

Road

Du

| ½ | 1 | 1½ |

Scale of Miles

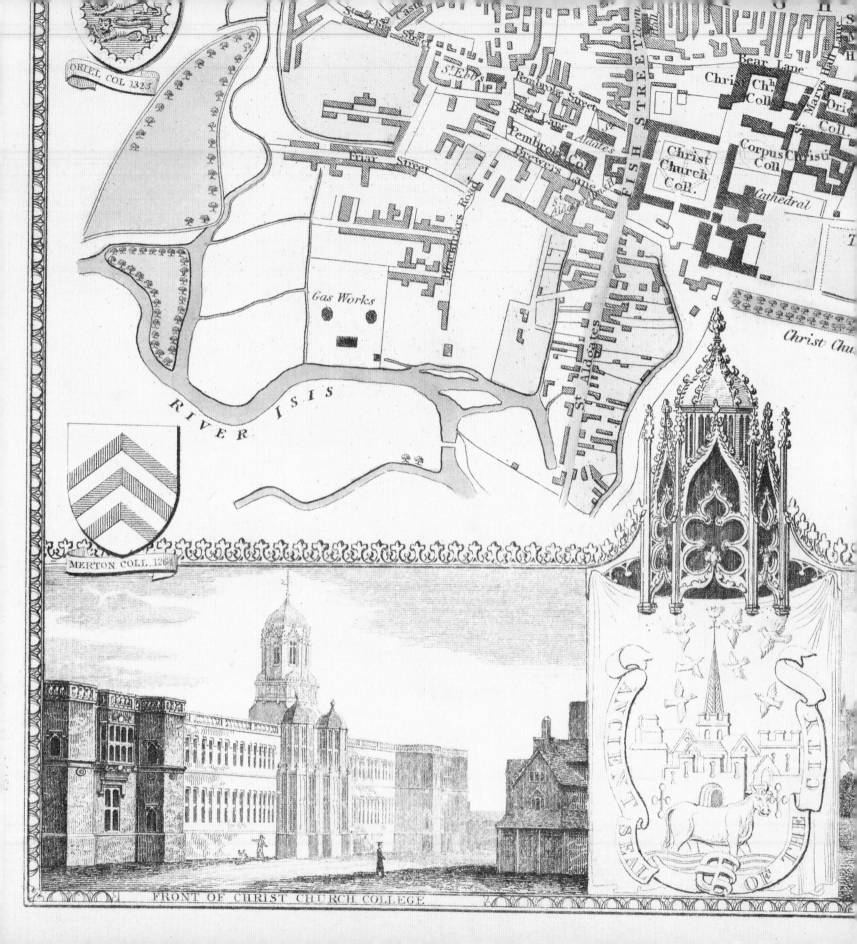

ORIEL COL. 1323

St. Ebbs F

Castle

St. Ebbs

St. Ebb's

Bear Lane

Christ Ch. Coll.

Marys Hall

Oriel Coll.

Pembroke Street

Beef Lane

St Aldates

Corpus Christi Coll.

Pembroke Coll.

FISH STREET

HIGH

Friar Street

Blackfriars Road

Brewers Lane

Christ Church Coll.

St. Aldates

Cathedral

Gas Works

St. Aldates

Christ Chu.

RIVER ISIS

MERTON COLL. 126

ANCIENT SEAL OF THE CITY

FRONT OF CHRIST CHURCH COLLEGE

1837

Announcing the Gothic revival

No book of this kind would be complete without at least one map that is more significant for its peripheral decoration than for its main cartographic content. This magnificent, not to say grandiose plate from Thomas Moule's two-volume *The English Counties Delineated, or, A Topographical Description of England*, published in the year of Queen Victoria's accession, marks the return of a hyperactive heraldicism that had scarcely been seen since Stuart times, in maps or out. It is no coincidence that one of the inset views prominently features Christ Church's 1682 Tom Tower, an early and isolated forerunner of the neo-medieval architectural style – a style further encapsulated in the map's central design motif – that would go on to beat neo-classicism in the 'battle of the styles' and dominate 'good' architecture in Britain right down to the end of the Victorian era. The newfound respectability of Gothic architecture was not unconnected to Catholic Emanci-

pation [1831a], and Oxford, long a bastion of both small-c and big-c conservatism, rapidly added Gothic-c conservatism to its quiver. One of many aspects of this was the Anglo-Catholic, Tractarian or 'Oxford Movement' in religion, which was launched in 1833 and led to the establishment of orders of monks and nuns within Anglicanism by the 1860s. College heraldry dominates the upper third of the map, conveniently blotting out the new working-class suburb of Jericho (though the neighbourhood's 'University Print'g Office' mounts an astonishing fight-back); and this decoration is unusually replete with ecclesiastical headgear, including Christ Church's cardinal's hat, which is nowadays hardly ever seen or discussed.

Given that there were business connections between Moule and John Whessel, it would not be surprising if the strictly cartographic content of this map had been simply lifted

Thomas Moule/J. Cleghorn, 'City and University of Oxford', from Thomas Moule,
The English Counties Delineated; or, a Topographical Description of England . . . vol. 2 (1837)

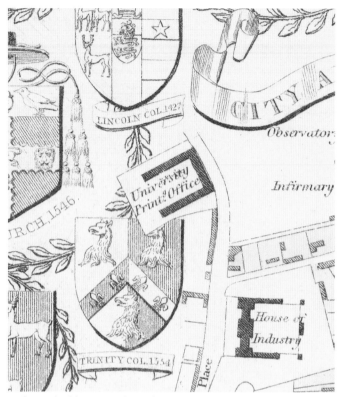

Only one building in working-class Jericho was deemed important enough to burst through Moule's forest of heraldry.

wholesale from Whessel's deeply flawed effort of six years earlier [1831b]. The reality is more complicated and rather more interesting. First, Moule or his engraver John Cleghorn has eliminated Whessel's 'scenic' treatment of the city's churches – presumably because this was an embarrassing reminder of Whessel's over-reliance on Taylor [1750] or more likely Longmate [1773] – and yet has retained Whessel's lone 'scenic' non-ecclesiastical building, the Holywell Music Room, and even increased its level of detail. The churches, moreover, have simply been darkened, without their shapes being changed. St Martin's therefore appears here with a strange lobe on its northwest corner, which had been its tower back when it was a side view as seen from the south.

Fish Street's name has been restored, but only in its northern half. The west side of St John's Street and the

Beaumont Buildings, wrongly shown as complete by Whessel, are empty space again; and the southern and western sides of Paradise Square have likewise been 'de-built' in Moule and Cleghorn's map.

The possibility of inaccuracies around the new Folly Bridge, as in Jericho, have been eliminated through framing the area out. Moule's failure to note the northward expansion of the Physic Garden's two pavilions [c.1834] could be chalked up to the usual survey-to-publication time-lag, but his St Ebbe's – too central to be omitted, but perhaps too nauseating to be surveyed, either – is the site of a series of astonishing errors. First, disorientatingly, Bull Street has been mislabelled as Friars Street and Commercial Row as Blackfriars Road. The real Blackfriars Road and everything to the south of it is in all respects a copy of Whessel's work, far too perfect for this to be any sort of coincidence. But the real Friars Street, which should appear here south of 'Friars Street' (i.e. Bull Street) and north of the real Blackfriars Road, is simply missing: a garden of peculiar immensity, served by three side-streets that lead to nothing.

Moule's frankly bizarre career included deciphering letter-writers' bad handwriting for the General Post Office, writing about medieval coins for the *Numismatic Chronicle* and living for three decades in the stable-yard of St James's Palace as an employee of the Lord Chamberlain. But it probably reached its apogee with the 1842 publication of his *Heraldry of Fish: Notices of the Principal Families Bearing Fish in their Arms*, illustrated with woodcuts. Given that Moule lived his life as an exemplar of the idea that the medieval way of doing things was better than the modern way, it is rather funny that the present item has been the map of Oxford most reproduced in the digital age, to say nothing of the analogue reprints of it that appeared in assorted books by Moule and others across the nineteenth and twentieth centuries. But then again, Moule was not quite as old-fashioned as he seemed. As well as frequently collaborating with his daughter Sophia, he had his maps engraved on steel in preference to copper, in part to ensure 'a reasonable price . . . within reach of every class'. In this, he has now succeeded beyond his wildest imaginings.

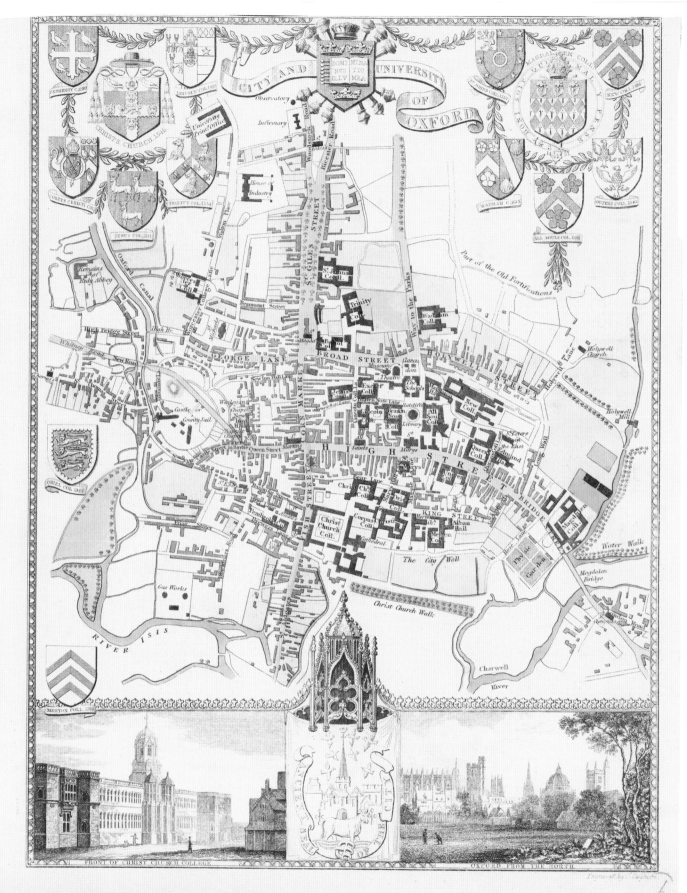

CITY AND UNIVERSITY OF OXFORD

FRONT OF CHRIST CHURCH COLLEGE.

OXFORD FROM THE NORTH.

London. Published by G. Virtue, 26. Ivy Lane.

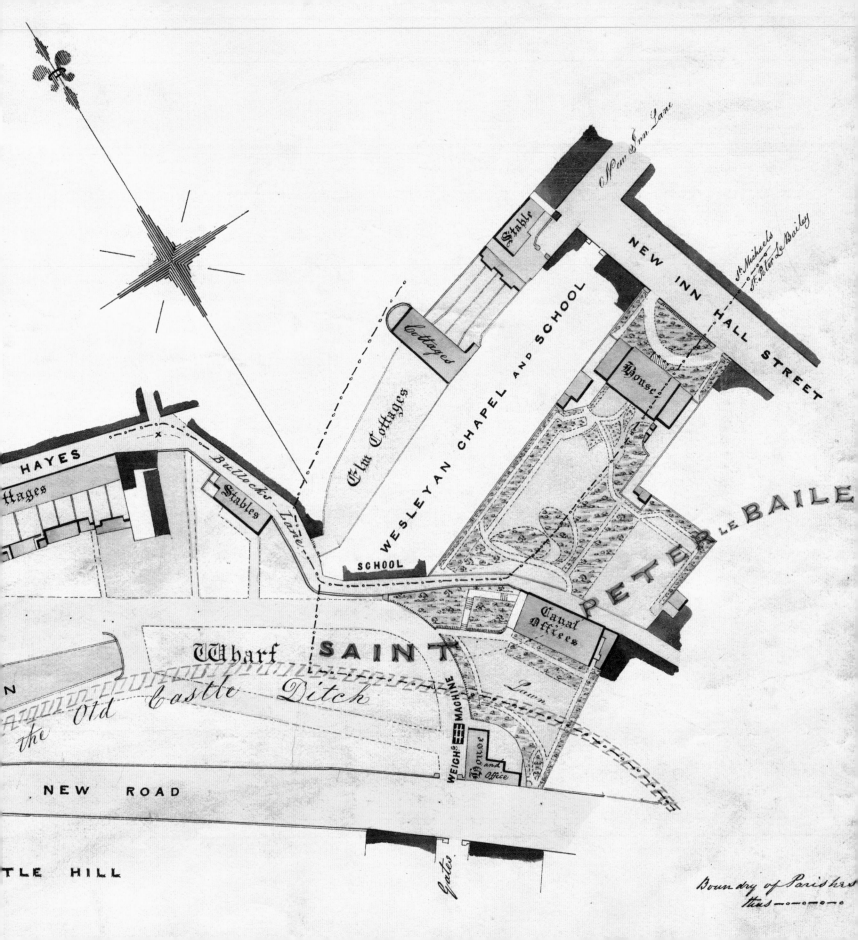

1838

Canal-led industrialisation and convict labour

Carrying thousands of tonnes of coal, timber, building stone and slate, pottery and porcelain, foodstuffs and a range of other heavy goods, the canal from Coventry to Oxford [1768] was an immediate commercial success. Less than three years after its ceremonial opening on New Year's Day 1790, its owners sought to augment James Brindley's original canal basin – now, the 60-year-old 'temporary' car park between Worcester Street and the Castle Mill Stream – via a second group of wharves immediately east by southeast of the same site.

With the canal-abetted industrial revolution in full cry, the new basin would specialise in coal shipments only, despite the existence since 1789 of a dedicated coal wharf by the North Oxford inn known as Heyfield's Hutt (but called the Anchor Inn or Dolley's Hut since the Victorian period, and rebuilt in a mock-Tudor style in the inter-war years; Hayfield

Road seems to have been named after the original inn, which in turn was named for a proprietor who died in the 1770s). The 2-acre St Ebbe's Gasworks, Oxford's first large industrial complex, was built in 1818 and was supplying gas for the city's streetlights by the following year; and in 1825, the Eagle Ironworks moved to a canal-side site in Jericho. Between 1800 and 1830, industrialisation nearly doubled the size of the city's population – from under 12,000 to nearly 21,000 – and dramatically altered its socioeconomic profile. There was grotesque overcrowding in St Ebbe's, St Thomas's and St Clement's, leading to the construction of additional low-quality housing in Jericho, and a predictable range of severe public-health and sanitation problems [1848, 1872, 1893].

Canal-boat workers, too, rapidly multiplied in numbers, and the rootless lifestyle of these inland sailors aroused suspicion and sympathy in equal measure. Thomas Beesley,

C. Gilbert, *Plan of the Wharf and Premises belonging to the Oxford Canal Company at Oxford* (1838)

from a large and prominent boating family, bludgeoned to death a younger man who had accused him (rightly) of poaching a duck from the common stock on Port Meadow, and was sentenced to 14 years' transportation in 1829. One of the measures taken to succour and/or control the boatmen was the creation, ten years later, of a floating chapel and schoolroom for their exclusive use. Paid for by a donation from H. Ward, coal merchant, and moored immediately to the north of Hythe Bridge, it was Anglican in character and technically speaking a chapel of ease for the parish of St Thomas.

It did not long escape the notice of the authorities that a bigger, poorer city population meant more crime. In 1836, a municipal police force of about a dozen men was created, replacing the parish constables, though it operated only in the daytime due to Oxford University's traditional control of the Night Watch – a right in which it had been confirmed as recently as 1825. Oxford Gaol's governor from 1786 to 1809, Daniel Harris (c.1761–1840), 'was a journeyman carpenter when he came to Oxford' but gradually gained acceptance as an engineer and architect. This was in part due to his rebuilding of the gaol itself to a modern design by William Blackburn (1750–1790), leading prison architect of the age, renowned as much for his humane concern for ventilation as for his provision of 'panoptical' surveillance and water traps to prevent tunnelling. Perhaps emboldened by Blackburn's ideas for deadly water obstacles, Harris was hired in the early 1790s to construct three masonry locks on the 32-mile stretch of the Thames between Oxford and Lechlade in Gloucestershire, and also was asked to build 'a weir on the side of Port Meadow, to Mr Simcock's plan and estimate'. In 1797, Harris's Isis or 'Louse' Lock replaced the flash-lock that had connected the new canal wharves of Worcester Street (still then known by the medieval name of Stockwell Street) to the Castle Mill Stream, and it remained in use until 1844. In what now might be called 'synergy', Harris combined his two seemingly disparate roles: ordering the convicts in his custody to provide free labour for his engineering projects, including the Louse Lock as well as the new city coal wharf and warehouses seen in this magnificent 1838 manuscript, now in the care of the Warwickshire Record Office. A cadastral plan of the Oxford Canal Company's property, it was not drawn by Harris himself – though he had, when nearly 70 years old, designed the company's headquarters in New Inn Hall Street, here marked simply 'House' in a neat Gothic script.

Inevitably, however, the railways came [1844], revolutionising the nation's inland trade in terms of speed, as much as the canals had done in terms of bulk. In a fitting and timely epitaph to the canal-building period as a whole, the Oxford boatmen's chapel sank in 1868, though it was replaced by a permanent structure in Hythe Bridge Street two years later. Most of Britain's canals were nationalised in 1948, with many closing for good, and the last animal-drawn coal-boat in the country, *Friendship*, retired from service on the Oxford Canal in 1959. Original basins aside, the Oxford Canal is still open along its entire length, thanks in part to a dramatic intervention in the mid 1950s by Sir John Betjeman, the noted poet, architectural preservationist and Magdalen College dropout; and it is now held to be one of the prettiest such waterways in the world. One of the canal's chief drawbacks is the scarcity of temporary moorings for canal-boating visitors within the city of Oxford – especially in contrast to their ready availability in Banbury.

Though Governor Harris's skill as a designer of canal locks was severely criticised in his lifetime and beyond, he remains highly respected for his 1799 re-design of Braziers Park: Vice-Admiral Isaac Manley's house in the village of Ipsden, which was hailed by Pevsner as the only important 'Gothick' or 'Strawberry Hill'-style building in the whole county of Oxfordshire. It was also, briefly, one of the childhood homes of *James Bond* creator Ian Fleming. Harris's canal-company headquarters building also survives, as the master's house of St Peter's College.

Plan *of the* Wharf *and* Premises

BELONGING TO THE

OXFORD CANAL COMPANY

AT Oxford *1838*.

Quantities

The total Area of the Coal Wharf is
9318. Sq.ᵈ Yds: of which 696 are
in the Parish of Saint Peter Le Bailey
being a ⅓ nearly.

Note

The Company's Buildings coloured Red
The d.º Land ——— d.º Green

The Line of the Old Castle Ditch is put on
this Survey in Red Ink correctly transfer'd from
a Map at the Bodleian Library
dated 1750.

George Lane

College Lane

High Bridge Lane

Green Hereford

Warehouse Merchandize

Warehouse

CANAL

Warehouse

BASIN

Green Isis

FISH ROW

Warehouse

Warehouse

Bickford's Wharf

Green Witney

Green Banbury

Wharf

Sheds

Warehouse

Warehouse

BROKEN HAYES

Cottages

Stables

Bullock's Lane

Coal

Wharf

SAINT

Canal BASIN

Line of the Old Castle Ditch

NEW ROAD

CASTLE HILL

New Inn Lane

Stable

Cottage

Elm Cottages

WESLEYAN CHAPEL AND SCHOOL

SCHOOL

House

Canal Officers

Lane

NEW INN HALL STREET

St. Nichol's
St. Peter Le Bailey

PETER LE BAILEY

WEIGHⁿ MACHINE

House

Gate

Gates

Boundary of Parishes
———

Scale.

50   1   2   3   4   Chains

Surveyed by C. Gilbert

F. B. Mc Cook

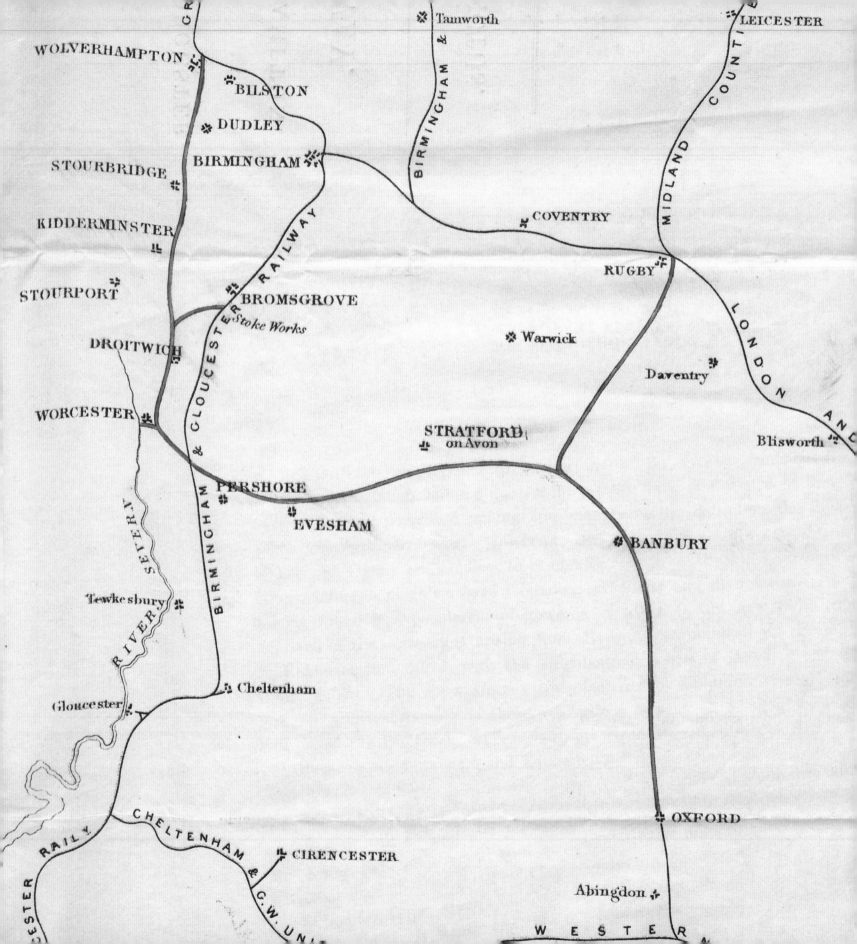

1844

Steaming into the future

In hindsight, from the viewpoint of the prosperous mid twentieth century, the main idea that underpinned the building of the Great Western Railway (GWR) must have seemed absurd: namely, that the relatively tiny, medieval port of Bristol could take on mighty Liverpool for the control of Britain's transatlantic trade – and win. A bright glare of justifiable hero worship surrounds the GWR's chief engineer, Isambard Kingdom Brunel (1806–1859), who by 1843 had designed the world's longest bridge and the world's biggest ship. But Brunel's controversial northerly 'hump' in the GWR's main line of 1838–41 must have seemed inspired by an equally medieval notion: that its most important branch-line destinations were Oxford and Gloucester, almost as if rail transport were a direct successor to the packhorse trade in wine and wool.

Whatever Brunel was really planning, the resultant development of branch lines northward from Didcot and Bristol immediately placed Oxford and Gloucester in the front line of the so-called 'gauge war'. The GWR and the Bristol & Gloucester Railway both used rails 7 feet ¼ inch apart, for which Brunel was a passionate advocate on both passenger-comfort and load-carrying grounds. But most other companies used a much narrower gauge of 4 feet 8½ inches, devised by George Stephenson (1781–1848) based on his early experience with the mining industry. Trains running from Oxford north to Wolverhampton and south to Basingstoke in the 1850s would therefore run on 'mixed-gauge' track with a total of three unevenly spaced rails, of which the outermost pair were on Brunel's gauge and one outer and one inner made up Stephenson's gauge. But this mixed-gauge compromise was still to be arrived at when the present map was published, as part of a prospectus for the lines shown in red, in August 1844.

Isambard Kingdom Brunel, Map of the proposed routes of
the Oxford, Worcester & Wolverhampton Railway (1844)

The text consists largely of a paean of praise for the proposed routes' mineral resources and existing industries, the latter including especially 'The great Carpet Manufactories of Kidderminster [which] are too well known to need comment'. Unsurprisingly, Kidderminster carpet-manufacturers Thomas Lea and George Hooman were on the scheme's Management Committee. The former Inspector-General of Railways, Colonel Sir J.M.F. Smith RE (1790–1874), was quoted regarding the 'favourable nature of the country' and 'skilful' choice of the route; and the picturesque appeal of the cities of Oxford and Worcester, particularly to travellers from Ireland and the North of England, was also prominently mentioned.

The first railway station for Oxford, which had opened as recently as June 1844, was owned by GWR and sited to the south of Folly Bridge; this led directly to the 'greenfield' development of New Hinksey three years later [c.1862]. Construction of the broad-gauge Oxford-to-Rugby line commenced in 1845. It opened as far as Banbury in September 1850 and to Fenny Compton, Warwickshire 25 months later; but the planned continuation to Rugby was abandoned due to insurmountable gauge-compatibility issues. Nevertheless, the failed initiative would involve the construction of a station in 1852 at the east end of the Botley Road, on the site of the current Oxford Railway Station, one year after the Buckinghamshire Railway (closely affiliated with GWR's rival, the Liverpool-focused London & Northwestern Railway (LNWR)) had built a station of their own immediately to the east of the same site. LNWR was the result of an 1846 merger of three of the railways shown on this map – the London & Birmingham, Manchester & Birmingham, and Grand Junction – aimed in part at blocking the advance of GWR and its hated broad gauge north from Oxford into the industrial Midlands. Beyond simple rivalry, the newer of the two GWR stations in Oxford was built to end the prevailing situation whereby its trains heading to Banbury from the old station first had to go nearly a mile south to Millstream Junction and reverse direction there: a problem that the maker of this map failed to anticipate, or perhaps chose not to reveal.

The longer of the two new routes shown, from Oxford to Wolverhampton via Worcester, was open along its entire length by 1853, but the mere fact of this conceals a tangled history indeed. Brunel, who surveyed the route, had underestimated how much it would cost to construct, and by the summer of 1849 the GWR proxy company running the project was broke. It would take a hostile-takeover attempt by LNWR and Midland, and a riot by workers over pay arrears, before GWR finally agreed to pay for the completion of the line (as the original agreements had required) in 1851. Nicknamed 'Old Worse & Worse', the Oxford, Worcester & Wolverhampton Railway was responsible for an avoidable derailment in 1858 that killed 14 passengers and severely injured 50 others. The Board of Trade inspector referred to this as 'Decidedly the worst railway accident that has ever occurred in this country'.

The battle of the gauges was won by Stephenson's gauge, known as 'narrow gauge' at the time, but now termed 'standard' or 'normal' around the world. Stephenson himself later expressed regret that it had not been somewhat wider. The Bristol & Gloucester and Birmingham & Gloucester railways merged in 1845 and were absorbed the next year by Midland, who replaced the line south of Gloucester with Stephenson gauge by 1854. In Oxford, 1872 marked the end of both Brunel's gauge and the original station, which had continued in use as a goods station for 20 years after the opening of the new one. Interestingly, the 1880s building of Oxford's southern suburb of Grandpont was only economically feasible because a large area comprising the old station site, station road and embankment had already been raised above the flood-line by the railway's engineers. GWR would fully convert to standard gauge only in 1892.

Opposite. The share capital of the 'Old Worse & Worse' represented at least £114 million at today's values.

OXFORD, WORCESTER, AND WOLVERHAMPTON
RAILWAY.

CAPITAL £1,000,000.—SHARES £50 EACH.—DEPOSIT £2. 10s.

COMMITTEE OF MANAGEMENT:

FREDERICK PRATT BARLOW, ESQ., London, ⎫
THOMAS RICHARD GUPPY, ESQ., Bristol, ⎪
HENRY SIMONDS, ESQ., Reading, ⎬ Directors of the Great Western Railway Company.
WILLIAM TOTHILL, ESQ., Bristol. ⎭

JOHN ROGERS, ESQ., Chester.
GEORGE B. THORNEYCROFT, ESQ., Iron Master, Wolverhampton.
JOSEPH WALKER, ESQ., Merchant, Wolverhampton.
WILLIAM MATHEWS, ESQ., Iron Master, Corbyns Hall, Dudley.
BENJAMIN GIBBONS, ESQ., Ironmaster, Shut End House, Dudley.
J. JOSEPH BRAMAH, ESQ., Ironmaster, Dudley.
MICHAEL GRAZEBROOK, ESQ., Iron Master, Audnam, Stourbridge.
RICHARD HICKMAN ESQ., Clay Works, Stourbridge.
JOSEPH KING, ESQ., Clay Works, Stourbridge.
THOMAS SIMCOX LEA, ESQ., Carpet Manufacturer, Kidderminster
GEORGE HOOMAN, ESQ., Carpet Manufacturer, Kidderminster.
ARTHUR SKEY, ESQ., Spring Grove, Bewdley.
ENOCH BALDWIN, ESQ., Iron Founder, Stourport
FRANCIS RUFFORD, ESQ., Banker, Bellbroughton.
WILLIAM LEWIS, ESQ., Mayor of Worcester
JOHN LILLY, ESQ., High Alderman of Worcester.
GEORGE B. HUDSON, ESQ., Wick, near Pershore
THOMAS N. FOSTER, ESQ., Merchant, Evesham.
E. F. FLOWER, ESQ., Brewer, Stratford-on-Avon.

ENGINEER:
I. K. BRUNEL, ESQ.,

BANKERS:
MESSRS. SPOONER, ATTWOODS, and Co., London.
MESSRS. RUFFORDS AND WRAGGE, Stourbridge.

SOLICITORS:
MESSRS. W. O. & W. HUNT, Whitehall, London.
MR. ROBERT RISING, ⎫
MR. FRED THOS. ELGIE, ⎬ Worcester.

The Line is proposed to branch out of the Grand Junction Railway at the station near the important manufacturing town of Wolverhampton, containing a population of 93,000 inhabitants. It will pass then

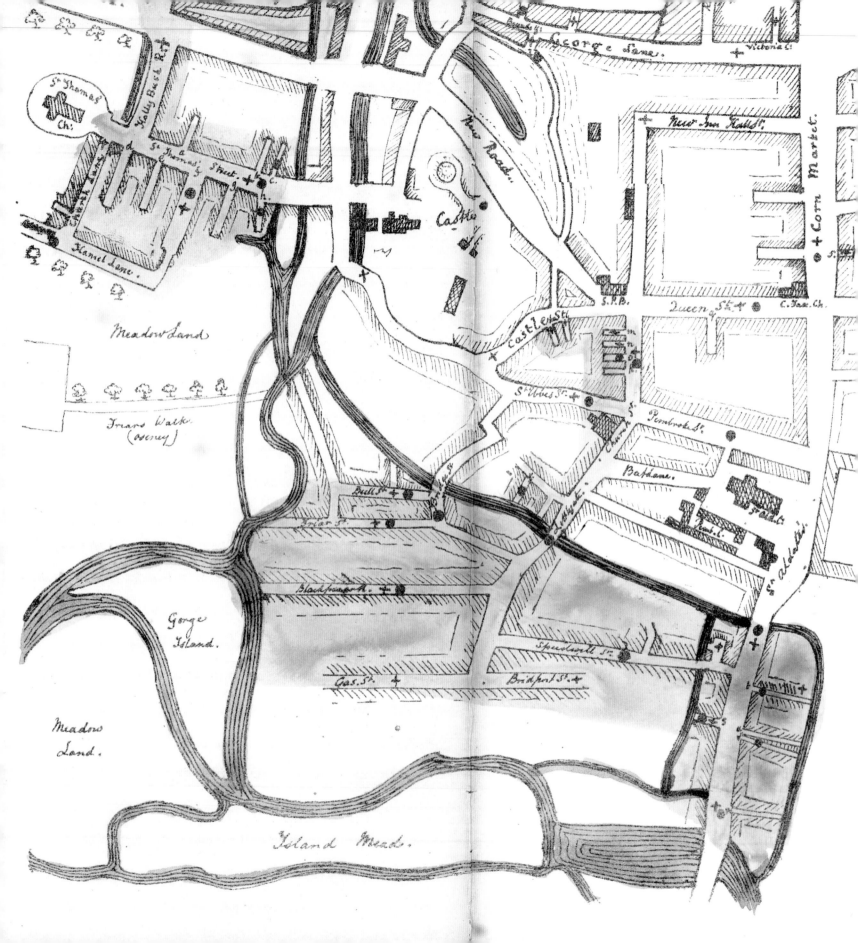

1848

Inspiring Snow?

Epidemic diseases were nothing new in Oxford. The Black Death hit the town hard, and in 1378, the future site of New College was 'a dump for filth and corpses, [and] a resort of criminals and prostitutes' (J. Cooper). Living sufferers of the bubonic plague were banished to 'cabines' on Port Meadow in 1605, and while the royal court and Parliament often fled from London to Oxford to avoid the disease during the remainder of the seventeenth century, they sometimes brought it in their wake. Plague gradually gave way to smallpox, and in the greater Oxford area – where inoculation for it caused 'great terror' and was banned in the mid 1770s – it was responsible for 9.5 per cent of all deaths not ascribable to old age or homicide in 1844. Tuberculosis caused another 25.9 per cent of the city's fatalities in the same year.

A bacterial infection of the small intestine, cholera is usually spread through the contamination of drinking water by human faeces, although the consumption of shellfish grown in sewage-contaminated waters is a major secondary cause. It manifests as profuse diarrhoea and the vomiting of a watery fluid. In conditions of generally poor sanitation and primitive sewage disposal, the sufferers' symptoms lead directly to the contamination of clothing, bedding and the waterways, and thus to the infection of others. Children, the undernourished and those with type O blood are the most susceptible. In a severe case, the infected person rapidly becomes dehydrated and may develop bluish skin, a rapid heart rate, low blood pressure, muscle cramping, seizures and delirium. Without effective rehydration treatment, death occurs in around half of cases, sometimes as little as four hours after infection.

Hardly any of this was yet understood in the 1830s, at the height of the nineteenth century's second cholera pandemic, which claimed the life of France's exiled King

W.P. Ormerod, 'Plan of Oxford shewing the parts visited by Cholera and Fever', from *On the sanatory condition of Oxford* (1848)

Charles X among more than a quarter of a million others in Europe alone. Unknown outside of India prior to 1817, the disease first struck England via trade with the Russian Empire in late 1831, and was popularly blamed on a range of causes including sin, alcohol, unripe fruit, raw vegetables and even the drinking of water that was too cold. Eighty-six people, 49 per cent of those infected, died of it in Oxford in 1832, with further outbreaks in 1849 and 1854 killing 44 and 78 persons, respectively.

One of the best-loved tales in the histories of both cartography and epidemiology is that Dr John Snow (1813–1858) created a dot-map of London cholera fatalities to demonstrate conclusively that the disease was spread by contaminated well-water and not through the air. But this did not occur until 1854; and it has recently been pointed out by H. Brody et al., writing in *The Lancet*, that the first, 1849, edition of Snow's book *On the Mode of Communication of Cholera* did not include a cholera-distribution map, whereas his colleague Thomas Shapter's 1849 *History of the Cholera in Exeter in 1832* did.

It need not detract from the importance of Snow's work, or Shapter's, to point out that both of their cholera maps were preceded into print by a considerable margin by the present 'Plan of Oxford shewing the parts visited by Cholera and Fever'. Drawn in February 1848 and published one month later, it appeared as a fold-out at the end of a precise and thoughtful treatise on mortality trends by the man who drew it: William Piers Ormerod, Surgeon to the Radcliffe Infirmary. Ormerod readily admitted that many others had preceded him in associating cholera with a particular nexus of 'physical conditions . . . [and] classes of persons'. He appears to have personally visited each street or court in Oxford in which a cluster of any infectious disease had been reported, and found the common thread of poor drainage coupled with inadequate rubbish disposal running through nearly all of them. A reasonably typical example was the now-vanished Cock's Row, a 'long . . . chiefly unpaved' residential court that ran westward between present-day nos. 17 and 19 Woodstock Road in St Giles's and contained 'two large cesspools'. There, Ormerod saw

the side of the court . . . flooded with black filthy water, communicating with a boarded hole, full of the same fluid, from which bubbles of gas were escaping. There was a heap of vegetable rubbish in one corner. The south side of this court has open gardens, in which there are pigsties.

Pigs were kept at Nergrove Court in St Thomas's as well as east of Magdalen Bridge, both in the Plain and in 'an open space of ground' between Cherwell Street ('perhaps the most untidy street in St Clement's') and George Street. Most were probably descendants of the 'immense number' of Irish pigs driven overland from Bristol in the previous decade, as part of an improbable but apparently quite successful scheme to establish the city of Oxford as a centre of the English bacon trade.

It was also in Cherwell Street that Ormerod encountered a household who relieved themselves into a hole in their own cellar floor that was stoppered with a large cork when not in use. The 'new streets' of Jericho were low-lying, 'often full of stagnant drain water', and 'almost completely surrounded on three sides' by open sewers 'of the filthiest kind'. The worst places in the city, however, were States' Yard, Godfrey's Row, and Coach and Horse Yard, all in St Ebbe's, which collectively presented 'a degree of neglect and filth rarely witnessed' in Oxford or anywhere else. Special mention was also made of a unique 'large depository of sweepings and nightsoil amounting to several tons' near the western end of Hythe Bridge, where yet more pigs were also being raised. The treatise taken as a whole suggests that, while Ormerod believed implicitly in the miasma theory of disease [1893], he was also grasping towards other explanations in which the mixing of faeces with standing water played some more specific role than merely giving rise to noisome odours.

The most damning aspect of the recent critique of the John Snow 'myth' is that Snow's map was not a tool whereby he arrived at his hypothesis, but mere cartographic propaganda for a hypothesis he had been nursing for years. Considered through this lens, Ormerod as a cartographic communicator falls short of Snow and far short of Shapter, whose eye-

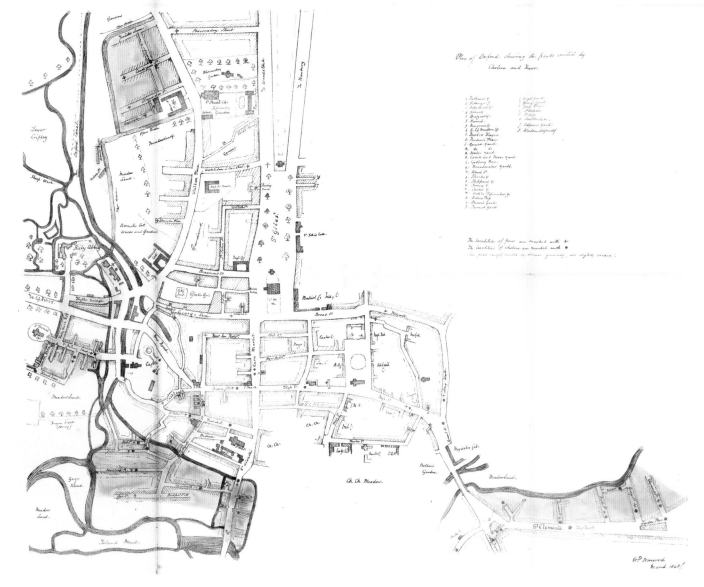

grabbing concentrations of red dots prefigure the marvellous temperance propaganda maps of later decades [1883]. Ormerod's pale-grey shading does not instantly bespeak 'parts highly visited by disease', any more than his bright blue water suggests filth and corruption. Nonetheless, it would not have escaped *every* reader's notice that the four largest of the areas 'highly visited' – Jericho, St Thomas's, St Ebbe's and St Clement's – were all much nearer to the rivers than the areas less badly hit; and the text reinforced the fact that the three latter places together saw 78 per cent of the city's total cholera infections in 1832. Ormerod's accompanying tables also made it clear that in the non-cholera years 1844–46, the number of deaths from diarrhoea and dysentery in St Thomas's and St Ebbe's outnumbered the deaths from the same causes in all 12 of the other city parishes put together. A version of this map, updated with new data from the 1854 cholera outbreak, would be included in an 1856 book by Sir Henry Acland, Bt (1815–1900), who established that the incidence of cholera in Oxford was positively correlated with population density and negatively correlated with altitude.

Tragically, Ormerod suffered from epileptic seizures that forced him to retire from medicine later in 1848, aged just 30, and he died at 42 from injuries sustained in a fall. But regardless of whether it directly inspired Shapter, or Snow himself, Ormerod's last work is a grossly underappreciated artefact of epidemiological cartography on the brink of its pivotal triumph.

1850

Oxford in unparalleled detail

Like Taylor and Anderton's of exactly 100 years earlier, this beautiful map – at 1:528, far and away the most detailed cartographic depiction of Oxford up to its time – was surveyed by a newcomer to the profession who would soon afterward be deemed a failure. Robert Syer Hoggar had previously only surveyed Morpeth in Northumberland, a far smaller place; and his next project, an 1852 survey of Wolverhampton for the purpose of sewerage improvement (as required under the cholera-inspired 1848 Public Health Act), would be over budget and late by more than a year. Worse, in the crucial aspect of elevation, the plan that Hoggar eventually produced was 'just plain wrong, and hindered the cause of town improvement in Wolverhampton for many years' (S. Briercliffe). The evident similarities between the Oxford and Wolverhampton maps – both are dissected and laid to linen, with full-wash colour – tend to raise one's suspicions that the former was also flawed in some fundamental way. It may be, in terms of altitude: as G.M. Howe explains, Hoggar's 'original' method of contour mapping involved working 'downwards from Carfax . . . drawing contours every five feet below its summit' rather than upwards from a base level. Nevertheless, in terms of lateral distances, the present map became the 'gold standard' for studies of Oxford, and remained so for many years after Ordnance Survey maps of the area were finally made available to the public, in 1885. Indeed, even my own detailed critique of Whessel [1831b] and Moule [1837] would have been rendered far more difficult, not to say impossible, had the present map not been made. The tree-by-tree, outbuilding-by-outbuilding level of detail supplied by Hoggar and engraved by Thomas Jones speaks for itself, and readers are encouraged to make their own comparisons of Beaumont and St John streets, Jericho and St Ebbe's across the three maps.

Robert Hoggar/Thomas Jones, *To the Chancellor Masters & Scholars of the University and the Mayor, Aldermen & Citizens, of the City of Oxford This Plan from actual survey Is most respectfully Inscribed . . .* (1850)

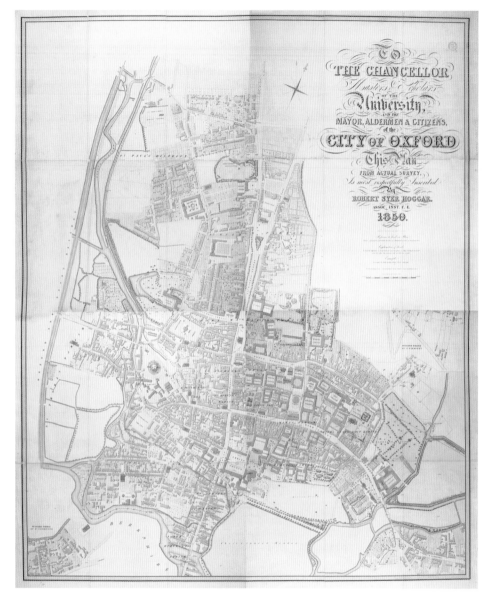

Left. The city's north–south elongation is already becoming apparent.

Opposite. Early Jericho in house-by-house detail.

Overleaf. In cartography, the Gothic revival was often manifested as an astonishingly miscellaneous assortment of text styles.

Hoggar had arrived in Oxford by June 1848, when he was the next person after William Ormerod [1848] to address the Ashmolean Society – on Ormerod's pet subject of drainage in Jericho – and his mapping of the city was intimately bound up with the public-health investigations led by the prominent engineer Sir William Cubitt (1785–1861) [1872]. Denied his full fee of £274 for the Wolverhampton survey, on the grounds that it had been 'thoroughly flawed' and 'completely unfit for purpose' (Briercliffe), Hoggar sued the town's council, and lost. In or by 1856, he created 'the most elaborate in the whole series of cholera maps' at 1:6,336 for Acland's *Memoir on the Cholera at Oxford in the Year 1854*, based on an 'unpublished survey' (Howe); but after this, the unfortunate Hoggar was seldom heard of again.

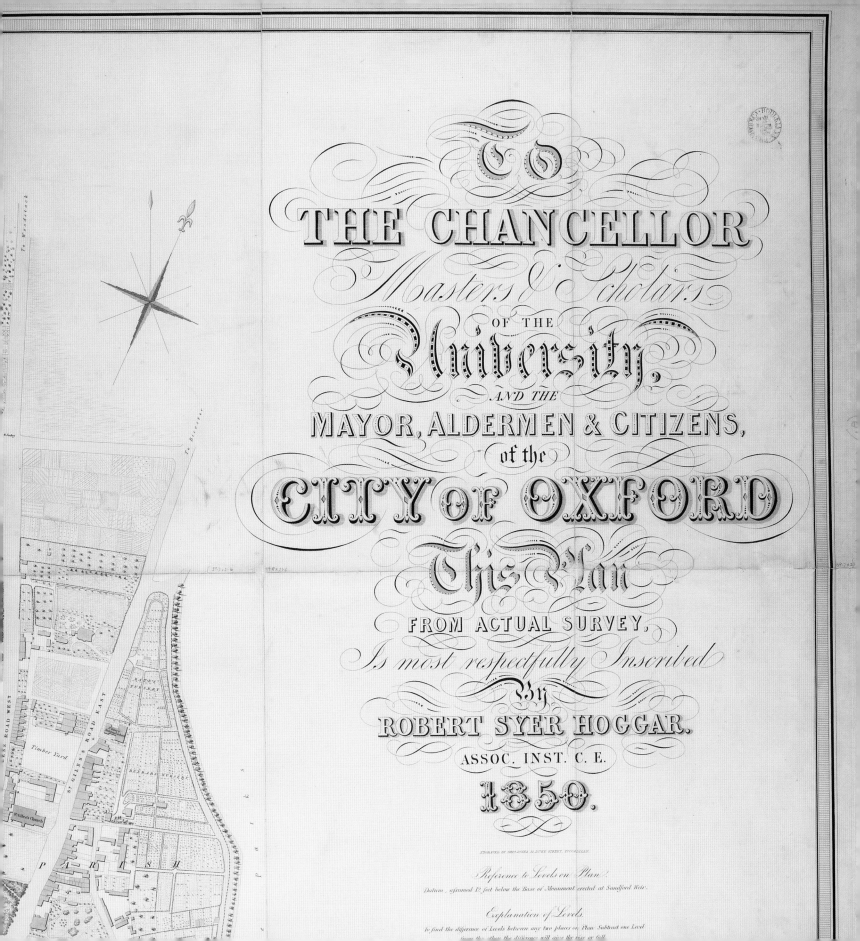

To
THE CHANCELLOR
Masters & Scholars
OF THE
University,
AND THE
MAYOR, ALDERMEN & CITIZENS,
of the
CITY OF OXFORD
This Plan
FROM ACTUAL SURVEY,
Is most respectfully Inscribed
By
ROBERT SYER HOGGAR.
ASSOC. INST. C. E.
1850.

ENGRAVED BY THOS JONES 31 DUKE STREET, PICCADILLY.

Reference to Levels on Plan.

Datum, assumed 12 feet below the Base of Monument erected at Sandford Weir.

Explanation of Levels.

To find the difference of Levels between any two places on Plan. Subtract one Level from the other, the difference will give the rise or fall.

Map labels:

To Woodstock

To Banbury

To Bicester

St GILES ROAD WEST

St GILES ROAD EAST

ROAD WEST

Timber Yard

St Giles's Church

BAXTER'S NURSERY

BULWARKS STREET

P A R I S H

P a r k s

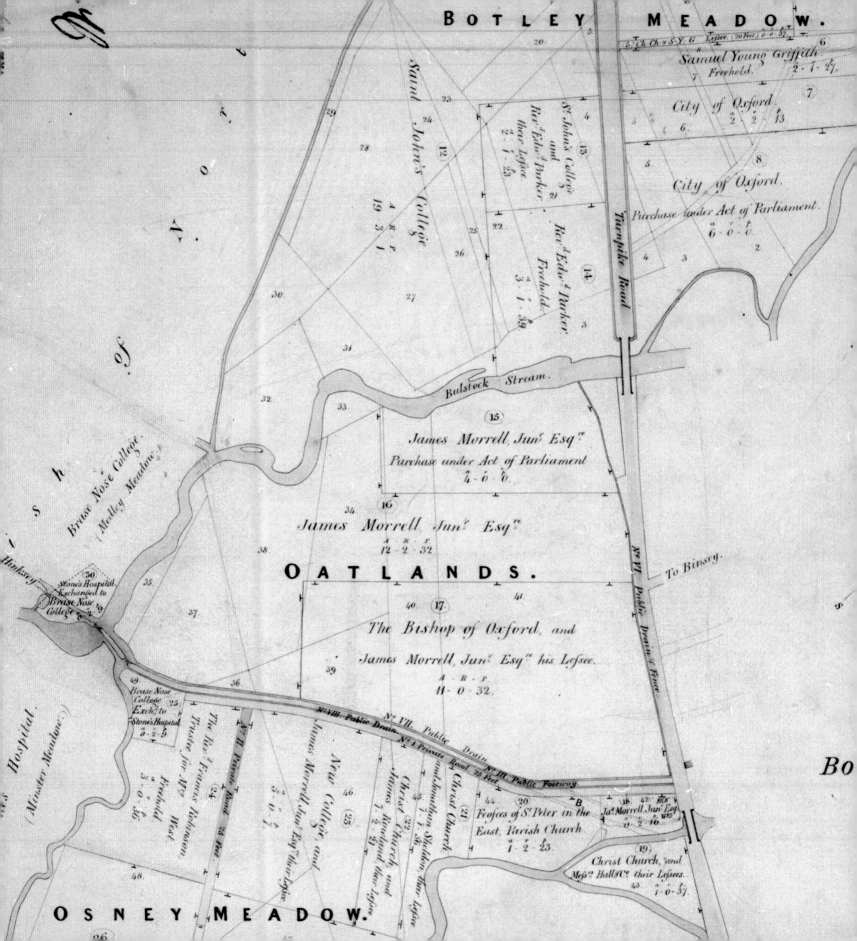

BOTLEY MEADOW.

5 Ch. Ch. + S. y. G. Lessee (20 Feet) 0 · 0 · 37

20

3

6

Samuel Young Griffith.
Freehold. 2 · 1 · 27

7

City of Oxford.
2
2
2 · 13

6

5

7

5

City of Oxford.

8

Purchase under Act of Parliament.

6 · 0 · 0

2

29

23

24

4

28

12

Saint John's College
and
Rev.ᵈ Edw.ᵈ Parker
their Lessee.
2 · 1 · 23

15

5

21

Saint John's College
A · R · P
19 · 3 · 1

25

22

26

14

Rev.ᵈ Edw.ᵈ Parker
Freehold.
3 · 1 · 39

4

3

27

3

Turnpike Road

31

Bulstock Stream.

32

33

15

James Morrell, Junᵣ Esqᵣᵉ
Purchase under Act of Parliament
4 · 0 · 0

No VI Public Drain of River

To Binsey.

5

Brase Nose College.
(Medley Meadow.)

34

16

James Morrell Junᵣ Esqᵣᵉ
A · R · P
12 · 2 · 32

OATLANDS.

Hinksey

30

Stone's Hospital
Exchanged to
Brase Nose
College. 0 · 2

9

35

38

40

17

41

The Bishop of Oxford, and

James Morrell, Junᵣ Esqᵣᵉ his Lessee.
A · R · P
11 · 0 · 32

39

49

Brase Nose
College 25
Exchᵈ to
Stone's Hospital
0 · 2 · 5

36

No II Private Road 25 Feet

No VIII Public Drain.

No VII Public Drain.

No I Private Road 25 Feet

No III Public Footway

Hospital.
(Minster Meadow.)

48

The Rev.ᵈ Francis Robinson,
Trustee for Mrs West.
24
Freehold.
3 · 0 · 36

New College, and
James Morrell Junᵣ Esqᵣᵉ their Lessee.
23

46

Christ Church, and
James Rowland, their Lessee.
22
1 · 2 · 24

45

and Jonathan Sheldon their Lessee.

44

20

B

Feofees of St Peter in the
East, Parish Church.
21
1 · 2 · 23

18

42
BRICK
YARD

Jaᵉ Morrell Junᵣ Esqᵣ
0 · 2 · 16

19

Christ Church, and
Messᵣˢ Hall & Cᵒ their Lessees.
43
1 · 0 · 37

Bo

OSNEY MEADOW.

26

1853

Funding the Church with colts, acorns and hay

By the end of the eighteenth century, the Age of Improvement in agriculture had crashed headlong into the overcomplicated and wasteful system of tithes: the small de facto income tax payable by landholders to the local representatives of the Church of England (and to some others, about whom we shall hear a little later). To say 'system' is really far too generous, as local custom dating back to a largely pre-monetary economy dictated that a high proportion of tithes would be paid in a welter of rural products, many of them bulky or perishable or both, including wheat, hay, live animals, eggs, honey and milk. So the Church did not necessarily get things that it needed. But simply getting what it was owed was problematic, too, for farmers could 'avoid the payment altogether by fallowing arable land, by allowing it to revert to uncultivated waste, by converting it into park or warren, or by planting it with trees' (H.C. Prince). In many areas, however, various by-products of trees such as acorns, fruit and even charcoal were subject to in-kind tithe requirements. And no one ever seemed quite sure whether the farmer was meant to carry the stuff to the vicar, or the vicar meant to come and get it. Fish were not tithable, but a person's profits from engaging in fishing as a business were. Wild birds were exempt, and partridges certainly fit that description, but what about wild birds brought in specially from foreign countries to serve as a food source or quarry, such as turkeys from North America and pheasants from China and Japan? Lawsuits over such matters were commonplace, and expensive. Nor did all tithes actually go to the Church, for perpetual rights to collect the ones pertaining to monasteries and nunneries had been sold off at the Reformation to various laypeople known as 'impropriators'. Many impropriators also bought and occupied monastic land, and were thus only entitled to receive tithes from themselves. This was very far from universal,

Matthew Hastings, *Plan of Botley Meadow, Oatlands, and Osney Meadow, in the Parish of Saint Thomas, in the County of Oxford* (1853)

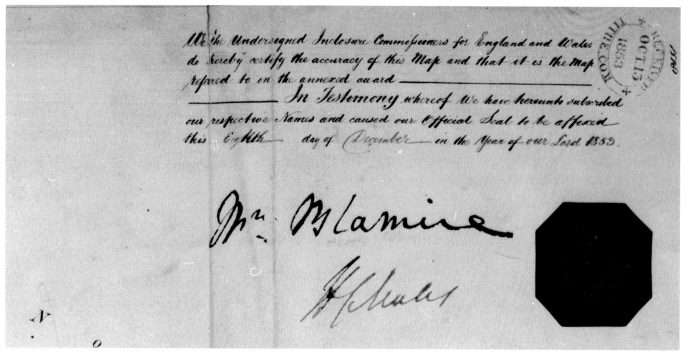

Some tithe maps were specially commissioned, and some adopted from other projects. Standards of accuracy were stringent in both cases, however, and only a minority were approved.

however, and the original impropriators' descendants and other successors – including a number of schools and colleges – were still collecting 23.7 per cent of the more than £4 million worth of tithes that were paid annually in the 1830s.

Far more important than any of this, to keen observers of the national economy considered as a whole, was the negative impact on agricultural productivity and the food supply: places 'subject to a reasonable annual money payment in lieu of tithes were generally farmed on improved methods, whereas lands liable to pay tithes in kind were often abandoned to almost total neglect' (Prince). A solution to the problem was initially applied piecemeal: more than 2,200 of the Enclosure Acts that were passed down to 1835 [1819] aimed at the abolition of in-kind tithes in particular areas, with just over three-quarters giving the former tithe recipients plots of land they could cultivate themselves or rent out, in lieu of the nearly random trickle of commodities they had previously received.

The Tithe Commission was created in 1836 to see to the complete conversion of in-kind payments to money payments across England and Wales, and in the process created arguably the best-ever record of agriculture in the country. Prepared by Matthew Hastings and approved by the same Colonel Dawson RE who mapped the city of Oxford in preparation for the Great Reform Act [1831a], this map was considered one of the best, as only around one in six of completed tithe maps received the Commissioners' seal of approval. It is, however, exceptionally late, with almost all such maps having been prepared before 1851, and its indication of north is also incorrect by perhaps 40 degrees: for the road marked 'No. VI Public Drain' is the modern east–west running Botley Road; the route 'to Binsey' is present-day Binsey Lane; and 'No. 1 Private Road' is the broadly north–south running Ferry Hinksey Road. Of the five new streets that have since been created in the area here marked Oatlands, only the easternmost, Hill View Road, was laid out

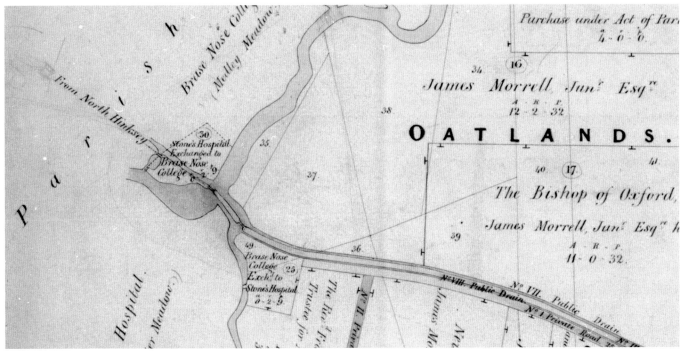

This area of the map records an exchange of land between Stone's Hospital and Brasenose College, for the sake of tidying up the local tithing system.

or built upon by the end of the nineteenth century.

In all, the Tithe Commission's *c.*11,800 surveys covered around three-quarters of England and Wales by area, and 44 per cent of Oxfordshire. Despite the extra effort involved in valuation, this was achieved 'in about one-tenth of the time taken by the Ordnance Survey to complete its 25-inch plans . . . without sacrificing accuracy' (Prince); and the Ordnance Survey simply took their parish-boundary information from the Tithe Commission surveys in some cases.

One of the Tithe Commission's subsidiary concerns was to try to keep tithe-payers and tithe recipients on the same side of parish boundaries, where possible. Thus we see here that Brasenose College has 'Exchang'd' its small plot on the North Hinksey side of the Bulstake Stream for one of equal size on the city's side. Another thorny problem expressed in the map was that of 'Lammas lands', which operated as common pastures between Lammas (1 August) and Candlemas

(2 February), but were formally owned by certain people at other times of the year. Until the tithe award now before us, Botley Meadow had operated on such a system continuously from 1168, when it was known as the King's Mead after Henry I who had given it to Abingdon Abbey. Also noteworthy are the presence of two famous surnames from Oxford's most venerable industry, brewing. The James Morrell Jr referred to here was not, however, from the branch of his family that owned the Lion Brewery in St Thomas Street, but an even wealthier branch of solicitors, bankers and political managers who have been fairly described as the nearest thing Oxford ever had to a 'first family' or local strongmen. The noted literary hostess Lady Ottoline Morrell, a half-sister of the Duke of Portland and great-grand-niece of Wellington, married into this family in 1902. 'Messrs. Hall & Co.' were the proprietors of the Swan in Paradise Street, but would acquire a number of other breweries in the city before 1900.

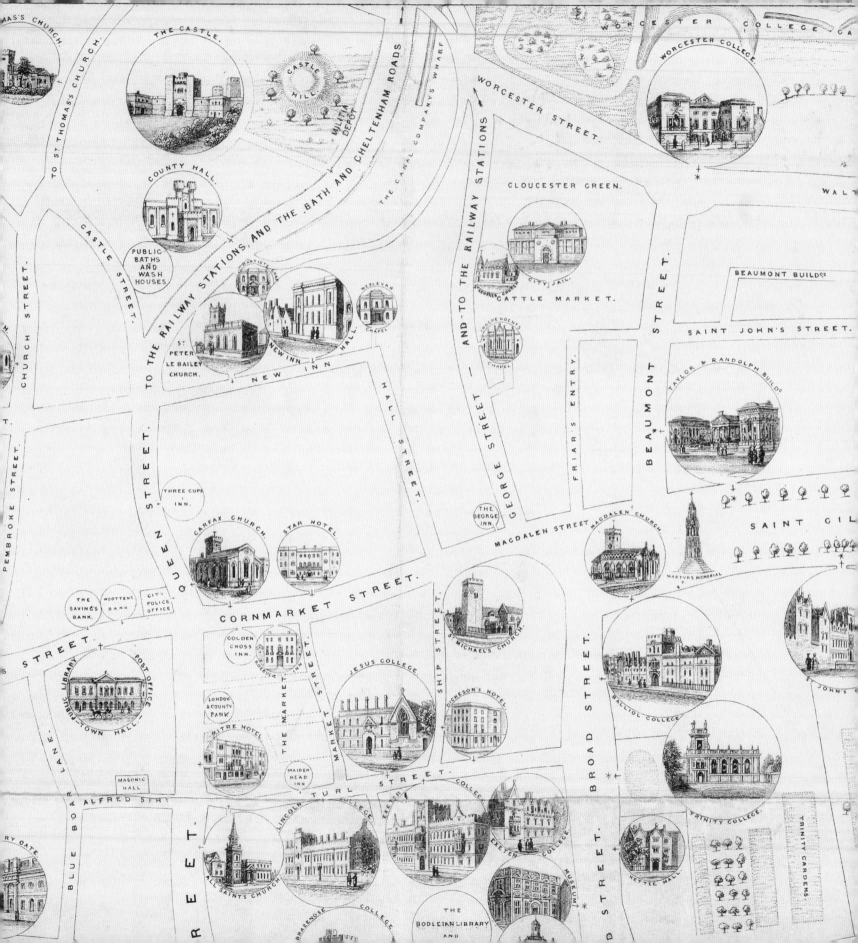

MAS'S CHURCH.

TO St THOMAS'S CHURCH.

THE CASTLE.

CASTLE HILL.

MILITIA DEPOT.

THE CANAL COMPANY'S WHARF.

WORCESTER STREET.

WORCESTER COLLEGE.

WORCESTER COLLEGE.

CHURCH STREET.

CASTLE STREET.

COUNTY HALL.

PUBLIC BATHS AND WASH HOUSES.

TO THE RAILWAY STATIONS, AND THE BATH AND CHELTENHAM ROADS

CLOUCESTER CREEN.

CITY JAIL.

St GEORGE'S CHURCH.

CATTLE MARKET.

WALT

BEAUMONT BUILDS

SAINT JOHN'S STREET.

PEMBROKE STREET.

BAPTIST'S CHAPEL

St PETER LE BAILEY CHURCH.

NEW INN HALL.

WESLEYAN CHAPEL

NEW INN HALL.

HALL STREET.

GEORGE STREET.

AND TO THE RAILWAY STATIONS

FRIAR'S ENTRY.

INDEPENDENTS CHAPEL

BEAUMONT STREET.

TAYLOR & RANDOLPH BUILDe

SAINT GIL

QUEEN STREET.

THREE CUPS INN.

THE GEORGE INN.

MAGDALEN STREET.

MAGDALEN CHURCH.

MARTYRS MEMORIAL.

SAINT GIL

CARFAX CHURCH.

STAR HOTEL.

STREET

THE SAVINGS BANK.

WOOTTENS BANK.

CITY POLICE OFFICE

CORNMARKET STREET.

St MICHAEL'S CHURCH.

SHIP STREET.

BROAD STREET.

JOHN'S

PUBLIC LIBRARY

POST OFFICE

TOWN HALL.

GOLDEN CROSS INN.

ROEBUCK

LONDON & COUNTY BANK

MITRE HOTEL

THE MARKET INN.

MARKET STREET.

JESUS COLLEGE.

DICKESON'S HOTEL.

BALLIOL COLLEGE.

BLUE BOAR

ALFRED ST

MASONIC HALL

MAIDEN HEAD INN

TURL STREET.

COLLEG

TRINITY COLLEGE.

TRINITY CARDENS

RY GATE

REET

LINCOLN COLLEGE

EXETER COLLEGE

EXETER COLLEGE

MUSEUM

KETTLE HALL

ALL SAINTS CHURCH.

BRAZENOSE COLLEGE

THE BODLEIAN LIBRARY AND

1855

The railway tourist cometh

As we have seen [1762], Oxford was attracting enough tourists by the middle decades of the eighteenth century to merit its own guidebooks, a distinction that in the pre-railway age was generally accorded only to cities of the first rank in size, along with a handful of spas. After the coming of the railway [1844], however, one very rapidly stops hunting for tourist maps in a sea of others and instead struggles to find maps of Oxford that are *not* for tourists, or at any rate not compatible with a touristic vision of Oxford and Cambridge as a matched pair. Among the jetsam from the first flood-tide of low-quality Oxford tourist products, we find an 1850 map by the aptly if improbably named F. Trash of 111 High Street, constructed to a very approximate scale of 1:3,000 using nothing other than typographic elements such as dashes and slashes. The present map, at roughly 1:3,500, was streets ahead of Trash in both quality and usefulness; but tellingly, it labels both

George Street and New Road as 'To the Railway Stations', quite as if this is a part of their names.

Like previous maps by de Gomme [1646], Taylor [1750] and others, *Dewe's Pictorial Plan of the University & City of Oxford* gives the city a part-ichnographic, part-scenic treatment of a sort that can be traced all the way back to local estate maps of the late Elizabethan and Jacobean periods [*c*.1600]. In the Victorian age, which notoriously made a religion out of progress, this persistence or resurgence of an ancient cartographic choice is on the face of it rather surprising, though Whittock's bird's-eye view of five years earlier [pp. x and xiv] was perhaps pointing the way. In architecture, too, as we have seen, the 1830s 'battle of the styles' had been won by neo-Gothic rather than by a very mature neo-Classicism which was, by then, arguably just the modernism of its own time. It would be unrealistic to expect

J. Fisher, *Dewe's pictorial plan of the University & City of Oxford* (1855)

Oxford: where heraldry grows on trees.

J. Fisher makes mention of the workhouse, the gasworks, the cattle market and the city police office, and actually presents a picture of the city gaol, built on Gloucester Green in the late eighteenth century as a replacement for the Bocardo [1773]. The gaol was demolished in 1878, having apparently been unfit for purpose from the beginning, but the nearby cattle market soldiered on until the early 1930s.

To allow each buyer of the map to match up the vignettes more precisely to the structures standing before him in real life, the buildings' main frontages are marked with tiny crosses, and 'those places most worthy of notice' merit an additional star. One of the only non-university properties to receive the star treatment is the Martyrs' Memorial, though uniquely among the buildings illustrated, it is not provided with a circle or rectangle. One wonders if the members of the colleges with no star – including Brasenose, Corpus Christi, Exeter, Jesus, Lincoln, Oriel and Wadham – agreed that they were less 'worthy of notice' than the others. The fact that, out of the city's hundreds of pubs and inns, Dewe's only showed 11 – the Three Cups, Golden Cross, Star, George, Roebuck, Wheatsheaf, Angel, Mitre, Maiden Head, King's Arms and the Lamb & Flag – naturally raises the question of whether these particular businesses paid to be included. However, direct sponsorship of maps by commercial advertisers is not believed to have arisen until 1877, or in Oxford before the 1890s [1898].

In fairness, central Oxford can be quite confusing without an illustrated guide of some sort, and particularly so when approached from the railway-station end; so at the very least, Dewe's booksellers should be applauded for identifying this gap in the market and leaping into it with both feet. They also regularly produced 'New and Correct' small-scale (c. 1:195,000) maps of the environs of Oxford, again prominently featuring the railways, from at least 1852. The 1865 instalment, according to an advertisement in a monthly newspaper published by Henry Alden [1872], was 'Constructed from the latest Ordnance and Local Surveys', though the remainder of the description strongly suggests it was yet another chapter in the long afterlife of the seventeenth-century circle-maps of Benjamin Cole [1805].

cartography to stand aloof from 'retro', which was – belief in progress notwithstanding – the dominating and inescapable cultural feature of this map's era.

Dewe's Pictorial Plan, a strange world in which heraldry literally grows on trees, places west at the top: a perhaps unintentional direct inversion of medieval mapmaking practice, with the city's railway stations standing in for Jerusalem. A near-masterpiece of 'cartographic silences', it reduces Oxford to a set of streets, roads and walks connecting some 70 circular vignettes, representing the sights that sightseers need to see, and glances in passing at the services they might require: chiefly, banks and hotels. The things that do not need to be seen – including every factory and workshop, every shop, every private house – just magically disappear. And in a city filled with churches and chapels of all sorts, St Ignatius's, Oxford's only Roman Catholic church down to 1875, is conveniently 'off screen' to the lower left. In a few surprising violations of his own rules, however, mapmaker

OXFORD GUIDE BOOK WITH THIS PLAN,
PRICE ONE SHILLING.

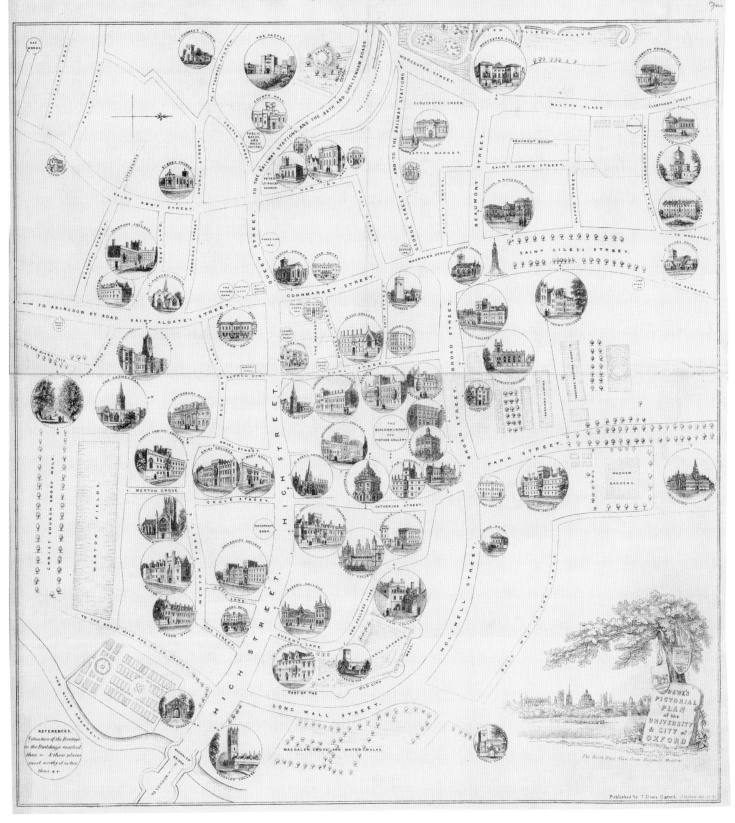

DEWE'S PICTORIAL PLAN of the UNIVERSITY & CITY of OXFORD

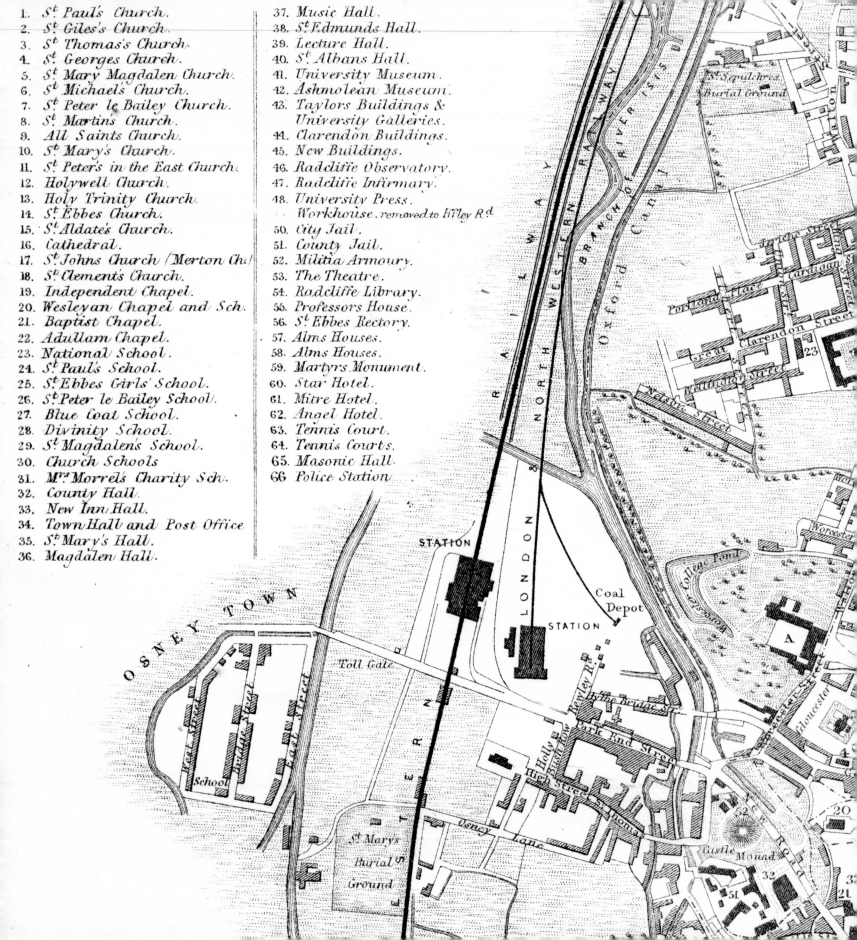

1. St Paul's Church.
2. St Giles's Church.
3. St Thomas's Church.
4. St Georges Church.
5. St Mary Magdalen Church.
6. St Michael's Church.
7. St Peter le Bailey Church.
8. St Martins Church.
9. All Saints Church.
10. St Mary's Church.
11. St Peter's in the East Church.
12. Holywell Church.
13. Holy Trinity Church.
14. St Ebbes Church.
15. St Aldate's Church.
16. Cathedral.
17. St Johns Church (Merton Cha.)
18. St Clement's Church.
19. Independent Chapel.
20. Wesleyan Chapel and Sch.
21. Baptist Chapel.
22. Adullam Chapel.
23. National School.
24. St Paul's School.
25. St Ebbes Girls' School.
26. St Peter le Bailey School.
27. Blue Coat School.
28. Divinity School.
29. St Magdalen's School.
30. Church Schools
31. Mrs Morrel's Charity Sch.
32. County Hall.
33. New Inn Hall.
34. Town Hall and Post Office
35. St Mary's Hall.
36. Magdalen Hall.

37. Music Hall.
38. St Edmunds Hall.
39. Lecture Hall.
40. St Albans Hall.
41. University Museum.
42. Ashmolean Museum.
43. Taylors Buildings & University Galleries.
44. Clarendon Buildings.
45. New Buildings.
46. Radcliffe Observatory.
47. Radcliffe Infirmary.
48. University Press.
Workhouse, removed to Ifley Rd.
50. City Jail.
51. County Jail.
52. Militia Armoury.
53. The Theatre.
54. Radcliffe Library.
55. Professors House.
56. St Ebbes Rectory.
57. Alms Houses.
58. Alms Houses.
59. Martyrs Monument.
60. Star Hotel.
61. Mitre Hotel.
62. Angel Hotel.
63. Tennis Court.
64. Tennis Courts.
65. Masonic Hall.
66. Police Station

c.1862

'Removed to Iffley Rd.': struggling to keep pace with changes on the ground

The completion of Oxford's LNWR station in 1851 was followed in short order by the development of Osney Town to the west of the line, specifically as a place for railway workers to live. Many hotels were also built in St Thomas's, including several that survive. Construction activity intensified in 1852, when GWR relocated their Oxford passenger services to the site of the current railway station from the original [1844] location south of Folly Bridge, which became a goods station.

In the 15 years since Robert Syer Hoggar had mapped the city in stunning detail [1850], Oxford had seen a number of other very significant changes, including the initial development of 'exclusive' planned housing estates at Park Town beginning in 1853 and Norham Manor from 1860. However, because the present map is based fundamentally on Hoggar's (even unto the choice of a curious north-northwest-at-top orientation), Park Town is 'off screen' to the north, and

Norham Manor is obscured by the title at upper right. A similar pattern is repeated in the south, with the map framing-out most of Cowley and the whole suburb of New Hinksey, which had been laid out beginning in 1847, chiefly for railway workers at the original GWR station. In other words, the development of Oxford across an extraordinarily long north–south area had already begun to cause headaches for 'general purpose' mapmakers accustomed to fitting country towns neatly onto book pages of standard shapes and sizes, while retaining an adequate level of detail at the centre.

There is a persistent urban myth that North Oxford was developed for college fellows newly allowed to marry. But such marriages were not actually permitted until the late 1870s, a quarter of a century after Park Town was begun, and the first-generation occupants of the area were mainly the owners of successful businesses. Of the parts we can see here, Plantation Road and Observatory Street were both laid out

J.W. Lowry, 'Oxford', from John Cassell, George W. Petter and Thomas Dixon Galpin, *Cassell's Complete Atlas* (1865)

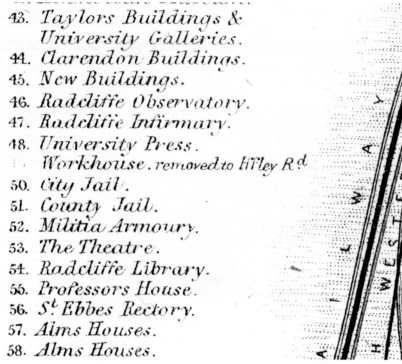

43. *Taylors Buildings & University Galleries.*
44. *Clarendon Buildings.*
45. *New Buildings.*
46. *Radcliffe Observatory.*
47. *Radcliffe Infirmary.*
48. *University Press.*
  Workhouse. removed to Iffley Rd
50. *City Jail.*
51. *County Jail.*
52. *Militia Armoury.*
53. *The Theatre.*
54. *Radcliffe Library.*
55. *Professors House.*
56. *St Ebbes Rectory.*
57. *Alms Houses.*
58. *Alms Houses.*

The hasty and inaccurate alteration of the key's item 49 reflects the high costs of both surveying and engraving.

in the early 1830s, and the whole area between them developed by 1850; but the little shopping street called North Parade, auctioned off for development in 1833, saw no significant building until 1855. Architect Charles Buckeridge (c.1832–1873), active in the development of Norham Manor, also designed Oxford's new Court House in New Road, which opened in 1863 – but is not mentioned here.

The original version of this map was produced for the *Weekly Dispatch Atlas*, published serially in the newspaper over several years from 1858 and complete by 1863. The following year, its plates were sold to Cassell's who rushed them into the production of their own atlases of 1864–67. The original mapmakers clearly did not foresee the removal of the city workhouse from Wellington Square and the erection of a new one in Cowley: for, in the present map's key, the words 'removed to Iffley Rd.' have been hastily inserted after

'Workhouse', and its number, 49, deleted. Worse, though several locations in Iffley Road had been considered (along with others in Holywell, Summertown and on the Abingdon Road), the 12-acre site eventually chosen for the new workhouse – as far back as 1861 – was actually not in Iffley Road but on the north side of Cowley Road. Building commenced in 1864 and was completed by 1866. It is almost with a sense of relief, therefore, that we see the mapmakers have included the new University Museum of 1860 at its correct size and position.

This map was also made at a pivotal moment in the history of the city's administration. The 1771 Paving Commission was finally being wound up, and replaced by the Local Board: a 47-person body that included 15 members from the university and colleges, 16 provided by the council and 16 sent by individual parishes, including some that were well beyond the main built-up area of the city but were implicated in its water-supply issues. The acquisition of the South Hinksey Reservoir in the 1850s had led by 1856 to the building of a pumping station on Lake Street in New Hinksey and the closure of the 'new' Thames-side waterworks of the 1820s [1831b] – though the latter's status as defunct is not noted on the present map.

Founded in 1801, the *Weekly Dispatch* newspaper became the *Sunday Dispatch* in 1928 and merged with the *Sunday Express* in 1961. In addition to British town plans, the *Weekly Dispatch Atlas* included railway strip-maps in emulation of Ogilby's road maps [1675], British counties and American Civil War campaigns, as well as to the countries and continents of the world. Many of these maps were by Edward Weller, who also created the 1887 map reconstruction of medieval Oxford that appears on p. xiii.

By the time of 'his' company's buyout of the *Weekly Dispatch Atlas*'s plates, the radical and teetotal activist John Cassell (1817–1865) was already a sleeping partner at best, having been rescued from near bankruptcy in 1855 by Thomas Galpin and George Petter. Cassell's last published ex-*Dispatch* maps in 1867, and sold the plates on to George Washington Bacon [1909] in or by 1869.

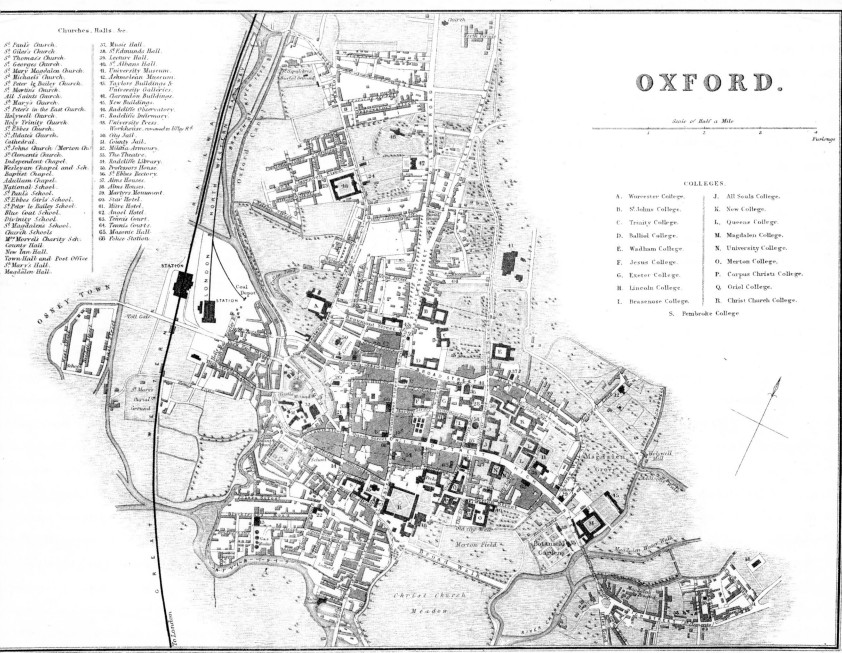

OXFORD.

Churches, Halls, &c.

St Pauls Church.
St Giles's Church.
St Thomas's Church.
St Georges Church.
St Mary Magdalen Church.
St Michael's Church.
St Peter le Bailey Church.
St Martins Church.
All Saints Church.
St Mary's Church.
St Peter's in the East Church.
Holywell Church.
Holy Trinity Church.
St Ebbes Church.
St Aldate's Church.
Cathedral.
St Johns Church (Merton Ch.)
St Clements Church.
Independent Chapel.
Wesleyan Chapel and Sch.
Baptist Chapel.
Adullam Chapel.
National School.
St Pauls School.
St Ebbes Girls School.
St Peter le Bailey School.
Blue Coat School.
Divinity School.
St Magdalens School.
Church Schools
Mrs Morrels Charity Sch.
County Hall.
New Inn Hall.
Town Hall and Post Office
St Mary's Hall.
Magdalen Hall.

37. Music Hall.
38. St Edmunds Hall.
39. Lecture Hall.
40. St Albans Hall.
41. University Museum.
42. Ashmolean Museum.
43. Taylors Buildings & University Galleries.
44. Clarendon Buildings.
45. New Buildings.
46. Radcliffe Observatory.
47. Radcliffe Infirmary.
48. University Press.
49. Workhouse, removed to Iffley Rd.
50. City Jail.
51. County Jail.
52. Militia Armoury.
53. The Theatre.
54. Radcliffe Library.
55. Professors House.
56. St Ebbes Rectory.
57. Alms Houses.
58. Alms Houses.
59. Martyrs Monument.
60. Star Hotel.
61. Mitre Hotel.
62. Angel Hotel.
63. Tennis Court.
64. Tennis Courts.
65. Masonic Hall.
66. Police Station.

COLLEGES.

A. Worcester College.
B. St Johns College.
C. Trinity College.
D. Balliol College.
E. Wadham College.
F. Jesus College.
G. Exeter College.
H. Lincoln College.
I. Brasenose College.

J. All Souls College.
K. New College.
L. Queens College.
M. Magdalen College.
N. University College.
O. Merton College.
P. Corpus Christi College.
Q. Oriel College.
R. Christ Church College.

S. Pembroke College

Scale of Half a Mile

LONDON PUBLISHED BY CASSELL, PETTER & GALPIN, LA BELLE SAUVAGE YARD, LUDGATE HILL E.C.

1872

Modern sewers for an ancient city – and vice versa

As one might expect, Oxford's position as an 'island among the swamps' was not conducive to perfect drainage. In the late 1630s, the tenants of Butcher Row emptied their blood and unusable scraps of meat 'into the street channels, which had neither pump nor water-course to cleanse them', and the town ditch to the west of the North Gate was 'a common sewer [and] receptacle of offal' (A. Crossley). During heavy rain, the gate itself – in theory, the most reliable means of access to the town, due to the absence of a river on that side – would be flooded with the most disgusting imaginable mixture of human excrement and rotten animal parts. There were underground drains of late-medieval date near Merton College and the Castle that carried water and muck out through the town walls, but in the early modern period they were not well maintained and no new ones seem to have been built. The burial of animals was at last required in 1661 by a joint order of the town council and university; presenting such a united front was probably prudent, in an age where university officials with the theoretical power to compel street-cleaning were occasionally burnt in effigy by angry townspeople. In 1764, it was noted that the outside of the Clarendon Building was an especially popular site for the tipping of rubbish, an act that the populace may have felt had symbolic as well as practical value.

One of the many responsibilities assigned to the Paving Commission [1773] was that of keeping the streets clean. They allowed a rubbish dump to be sited by the back gate of the Botanical Garden and arranged for the aforementioned sweeping of the streets by workhouse inmates [1771], but integrated approaches to filth and drainage were still inadequate. Covered drains were provided only in the High Street and St Giles during the Commission's first 23 years of existence; everywhere else, the main streets' traditional central gutters known as kennels – 'open sewers' in the true sense – were repaired, not replaced. William Ormerod [1848] also

W.H. White/Henry Alden, *Oxford Local Board. Plan of main and street drainage* (1872)

noted 'great irregularity' in the cleaning-out of the city's hundreds of private cesspools, 'the whole thing being sometimes left almost to chance'.

Mapping of the city's sewerage problems and potential solutions seems to have begun only in 1851, when a 1:18,000 *Plan and Sections of Proposed Water-works & Sewers* was prepared by Sir William Cubitt. Son of a Norfolk miller, Cubitt was 'one of the last of the "self-made engineers"'; after an early career designing improved windmill-sails, treadmills and horse-operated stationary engines, he had been 'responsible for straightening the northern section of the Oxford Canal in the 1830s' (H. Hobhouse). Cubitt was engaged as a direct result of the public debate on cholera inspired by Ormerod [1848] and a failed attempt to refute Ormerod that was made by another member of the Ashmolean Society, G.A. Rowell. Investigations by Cubitt and others revealed that, although the provision of underground sewer pipes had accelerated dramatically since 1795, all sewage emanating from west of the Cherwell was still discharged directly into the Thames, except that of the new leafy suburb of Park Town, which went straight into the Cherwell instead. But shockingly, given that the public-health implications of the status quo were already well known, nothing would be done to correct it for more than two decades. Indeed, the Paving Commission may have simply added to the problem in 1854 by recommending that the Trill Mill Stream south of Paradise Street in St Ebbe's be covered over and formally adopted as a sewer, a course that was actually taken nine years later.

Further inquiries were held, and in 1866, the same year in which Oxford households were first required to equip themselves with rubbish bins (and the city was miraculously spared a fourth visitation of cholera), Cubitt's map was followed by a full-colour Local Board plan for sewerage. A scheme to macadamise the city's 35 miles of streets commenced in 1868 and was 87 per cent completed by 1873, when work on a new, 33-mile modern sewerage system commenced. On its completion in 1880, the system served around 75 per cent of the city's houses, though the proportion was lower in outlying areas, and Summertown would not be served at all

until 1890. A pumping station built at Littlemore ensured that sewage would reach the new 370-acre sewage farm there.

The Oxford-based printer, stationer and bookseller Henry Alden produced this attractive 1:6,336 litho map to a design by Oxford's internationally respected City Engineer, W.H. White. Positioned with east at top, it uses solid red lines to indicate both proposed and useable existing sewer systems in areas controlled by the Local Board, and dashed red lines for proposed sewers in areas 'not yet in the possession of the Board'. This latter category notably included the barely developed area south of James Street in Cowley; Bradmore Road in North Oxford, where the initial phase of house-building would not be completed for a further two years; and nearly the whole of the Walton Manor estate, bounded by Rackham's Lane (since renamed St Margaret's Road) in the north and Plantation Road, here unlabelled, in the south. Given that building in Rackham's Lane would not commence for another seven years, its firm inclusion in the sewerage plan suggests White's long-sightedness. St Hugh's College, which now occupies a very considerable amount of land at the junction of Walton Manor, Norham Manor and Park Town, would not be founded until 1886, and its main building was not begun until 1914. One of the map's more surprising revelations is the quality and quantity of existing and planned sewer provision in St Ebbe's: one of the city's poorest areas in the 1870s, and indeed, in all other eras since records began. Oxford's sewer system would more than triple in linear size between 1880 and the outbreak of the Second World War. Nevertheless, it was described as 'probably the most backward in the country' in 1952. Five years later, the original pumping station in Littlemore was modernised, and a second one constructed near it.

For about seven decades beginning in the 1850s, Alden's shop and printing apparatus occupied the extant late Georgian building at 35 Cornmarket, on the former site of the Bocardo Prison [1773]. In 1861, Alden – then in his early fifties – was living over the shop with his wife, one servant and eight children aged 4 to 22. The eldest child, Edward C. Alden, inherited the business and became a prolific publisher of Oxford guidebooks and tourist maps.

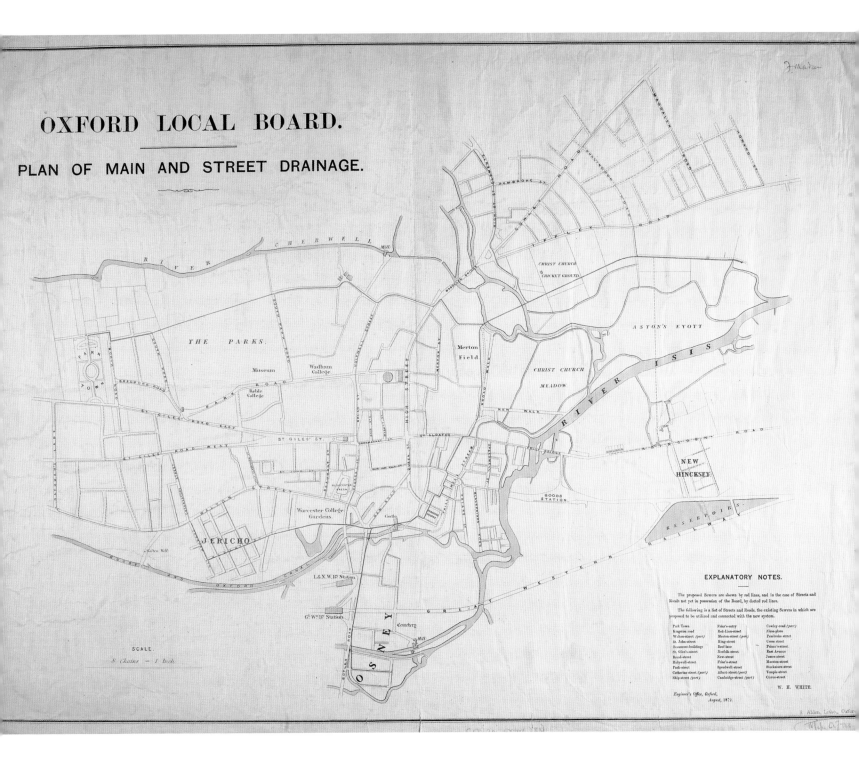

OXFORD LOCAL BOARD.

PLAN OF MAIN AND STREET DRAINAGE.

SCALE.

8 Chains = 1 Inch.

EXPLANATORY NOTES.

The proposed Sewers are shown by red lines, and in the case of Streets and Roads not yet in possession of the Board, by dotted red lines.

The following is a list of Streets and Roads, the existing Sewers in which are proposed to be utilized and connected with the new system.

Park Town	Friar's-entry	Cowley-road (part)
Kingston-road	Red-Lion-street	Alma-place
Walton-street (part)	Merton-street (part)	Pembroke-street
St. John-street	King-street	Cross-street
Beaumont-buildings	Bull-lane	Prince's-street
St. Giles's-street	Norfolk-street	East Avenue
Broad-street	New-street	James-street
Holywell-street	Friar's-street	Marston-street
Park-street	Speedwell-street	Stockmore-street
Catherine-street (part)	Albert-street (part)	Temple-street
Ship-street (part)	Cambridge-street (part)	Circus-street

W. H. WHITE.

Engineer's Office, Oxford,
August, 1872.

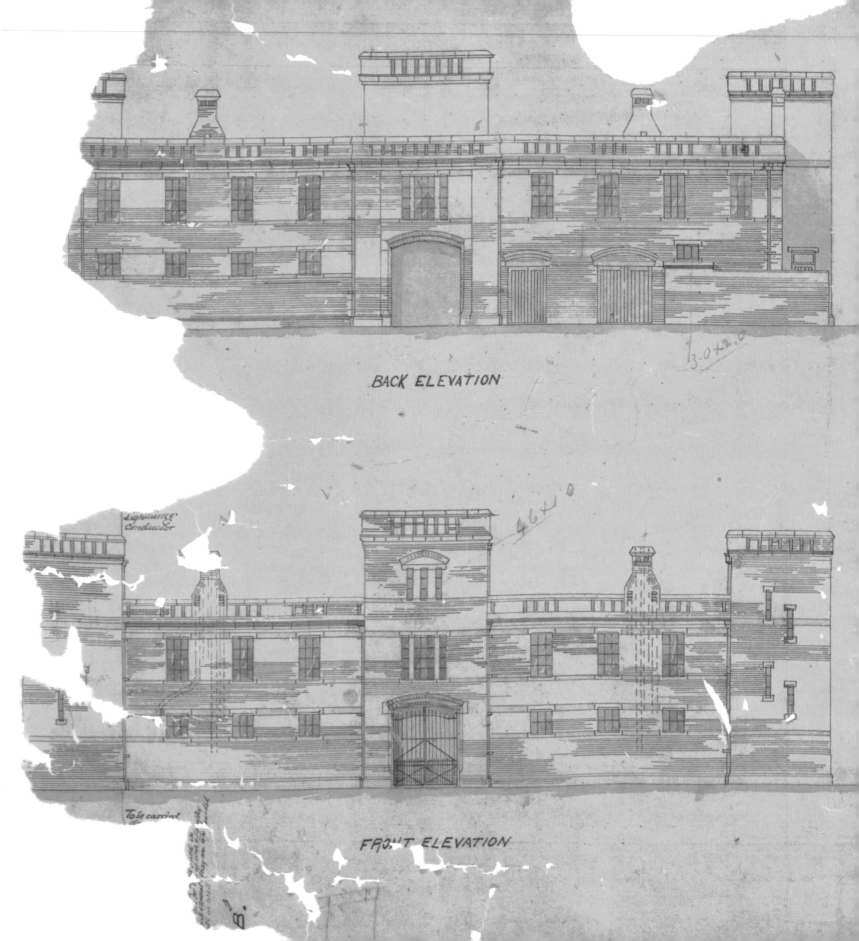

BACK ELEVATION

Lightning
Conductor

FRONT ELEVATION

To be carried

1876

Housing the military

British Army regiments were first systematically linked to counties only in the latter part of the American War of Independence, though such geographic linkages often reflected earlier realities. The 52nd Foot, later the Oxfordshire Regiment, gained a substantial number of recruits at Oxford's Mitre inn during the Seven Years' War invasion scare [1759], and miraculously all survived the wreck of the transport *Pitt* in the Gulf of St Lawrence a few years later. In 1798, 20,000 men were reviewed on Port Meadow by the same grand old Duke of York who reputedly had only half that many; and a grand new militia barracks, later the county police station, was built on the south side of the New Road in 1854 [1855]. Five years later, implausible as it now sounds, the French – who had been our allies as recently as the Crimean War of 1853–56 – threatened to invade again. Though not a shot was fired, the episode loomed large in the public imagination and led to the immediate formation of hundreds of paramilitary rifle clubs and other such uniformed volunteer organisations, which would not be brought fully into the governmental fold as the Territorial Army for another half a century.

The mid-Victorian Regular Army's traditional roles in home defence and internal security were therefore supplemented, some might say challenged, by the rise of the volunteers on the one hand, and of modern professional police forces [1831a, 1838] on the other. The popularity of volunteering among the English-speaking peoples worldwide fed into the decision to make Britain's self-governing colonies responsible for raising their own land-based defence forces, and the concomitant return of tens of thousands of British soldiers to the British Isles between 1869 and 1871. It was at this point that the regular regiments' local affiliations were literally cemented, through an ambitious building programme

M. Moffatt/Royal Engineers, Elevations and sections
of proposed Oxford brigade depot at Cowley (1876)

reflecting the new division of the country into 66 regimental districts. Public and governmental focus on the defence of the home islands was further consolidated by the humiliatingly rapid defeat of France by Prussia in 1870–71, as well as by the runaway success of *The Battle of Dorking: Reminiscences of a Volunteer*. Written by Captain Sir G.T. Chesney RE, this 1871 science-fiction novel depicted the invasion and permanent conquest of the United Kingdom at the hands of an unnamed German-speaking country, leading to civil war in Ireland, an American takeover of Canada, and Australian and Indian independence.

Cowley Barracks on Bullingdon Green, about 2½ miles east-southeast of Magdalen Bridge, was completed in early 1876 as a considerably taller variant of this restrained mock-castle design. Built as the depot for the 52nd (Oxfordshire) and the 85th (Buckinghamshire) regiments, it cost £45,000, and a further £2,400 for the 20 acres of land. As completed, each of its two brick-lined stone accommodation blocks housed 56 unmarried enlisted men on each of its two floors. Officers, and enlisted men who were married, were housed separately, bringing the total garrison population to around 400, exclusive of children. The complex also incorporated a library, workshops, recreation rooms, a hospital, a chapel and a school. The 'keep' controlled access to the site and included the armoury, along with cells for soldiers who had been placed under arrest. In addition to the Oxfordshire Militia, who received their annual training there, the new barracks served as a depot for the Royal Buckinghamshire Militia, Buckinghamshire Volunteers, Oxford City Rifle Volunteers and Oxford University Rifle Volunteers.

Though established in the same year, the barracks complex was not directly affiliated with the nearby Cowley Military College, which was a private institution for educating officers' sons aged 13 and above in any subject, and other boys, 'whether sons of officers or not, for commissions'. The curriculum included 'military riding, infantry drill, lance, sword, carbine drill, swimming and gymnastics' as well as university preparatory subjects. This somewhat schizophrenic arrangement was not a success; the school 'languished and

BACK ELEVATION

FRONT ELEVATION

expired' after less than 20 years, and was purchased by Morris Motors in 1912, becoming the nucleus of its immense Cowley factory two years later [1930].

Use of Cowley Barracks as a regimental depot ceased in 1959, but quasi-military use continued with the arrival of the

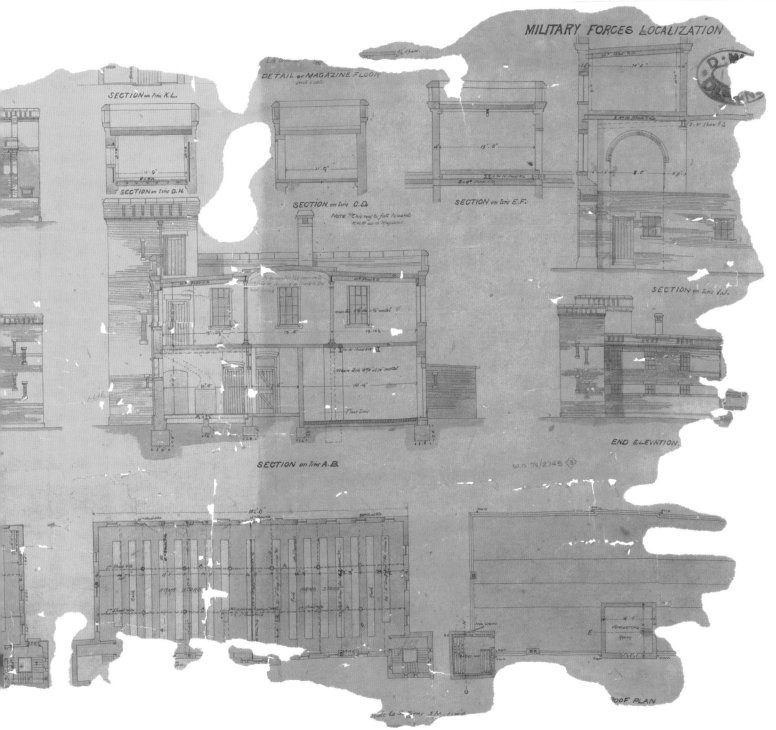

UK Warning and Monitoring Organisation (UKWMO): a Home Office-funded body of volunteers – many of them school science teachers – responsible for detecting nuclear explosions, estimating their sizes and locations, tracking fallout and providing post-Armageddon weather reports. With the end of the Cold War, the UKWMO stood down in the summer of 1991 and was disbanded the following year. All parts of the facility have now been demolished or converted to civilian purposes.

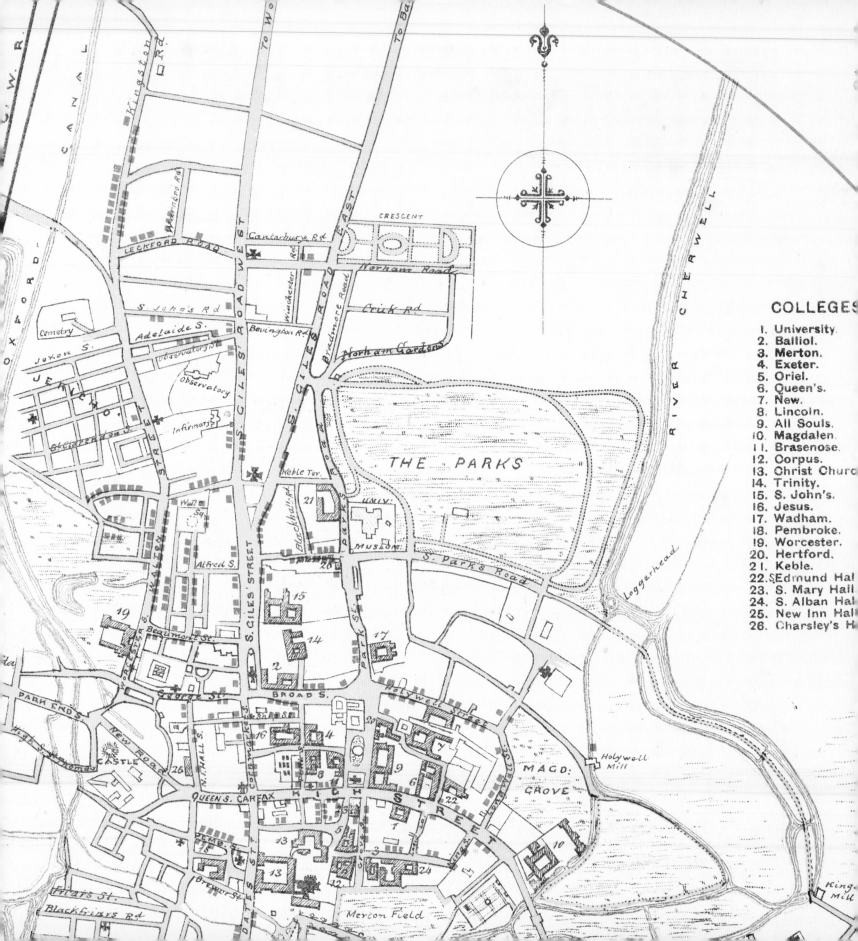

COLLEGES

1. University.
2. Balliol.
3. Merton.
4. Exeter.
5. Oriel.
6. Queen's.
7. New.
8. Lincoln.
9. All Souls.
10. Magdalen.
11. Brasenose.
12. Corpus.
13. Christ Church
14. Trinity.
15. S. John's.
16. Jesus.
17. Wadham.
18. Pembroke.
19. Worcester.
20. Hertford.
21. Keble.
22. S Edmund Hall
23. S. Mary Hall
24. S. Alban Hall
25. New Inn Hall
26. Charsley's H

1878

Controlling the student body

Any town with a population heavily skewed to young, unmarried men, mostly from privileged backgrounds, will inevitably develop a distinctive set of chronic public-order problems. These affected Oxford in a range of subtle and not-so-subtle ways. In the seventeenth century, for instance, the university demanded that the city's taverns be built without back doors, so that the university police would have an easier time apprehending undergraduates illicitly drinking in them. The university remained in charge of all crime-fighting in the city during the hours of darkness until as recently as 1869, despite the existence of an otherwise-normal municipal police force from 1836 onward.

Doubts about the city's ability to cope with its student population came to the fore again with the advent of 'unattached, or non-collegiate' students in 1868. As a result, C.W. Boase wrote two decades later,

the lodging system has been much extended; and in this . . . we have returned to the earlier mediaeval custom, but with much more adequate control and security, for the lodgings, nearly 600 in number, are specially inspected for sanitary purposes, and licensed.

This map's key also reveals some interesting changes in the university's more formal accommodation arrangements. Charsley's Hall was founded under a rule-change of 1854, which allowed anyone aged 28 or above with an MA to apply for a licence to establish a 'permanent private hall', which would be recognised as part of the university, but set its own charges and make its own tutorial arrangements. Charsley's – renowned for high fees, 'vexatious' regulations and the relatively low intellectual abilities of its undergraduates – closed its doors in 1918, having been renamed Marcon's Hall

Anon., 'Limit of Residence within the University of Oxford', from the *Oxford University Gazette* (1878)

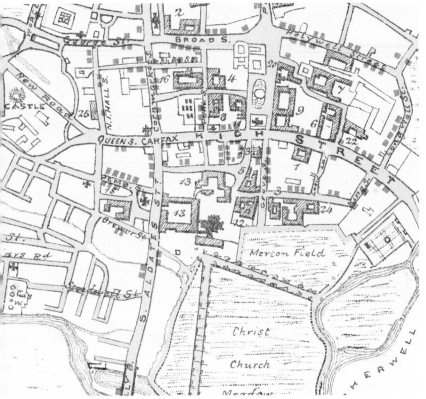

Student lodgings were absent from many western and southern parts of the city, and more than half were located to the north of Mary Madgalen Church.

same pace over its first and second decades of existence, i.e. with a net gain of about 30 houses per year.

One of the most interesting revelations provided by the map's pattern of red squares is how little of the official maximum radius was actually in use. In addition to the huge blank area corresponding to St Ebbe's – presumably still a 'no-go area' for the middle classes generally [1837, 1848] – there was no recognised student accommodation west of the railway lines, east of St Clement's Church, south of Bullingdon Road in Cowley or south of Folly Bridge (though there was at least one licensed house on the island in the Thames that the bridge passed over). Indeed, the outermost boundary was scarcely approached, other than on Kingston Road in North Oxford: where, among the brick terraces completed as recently as 1875, we can see 20 red squares, or more than 6 per cent of the city's total. In an interesting side-light on the rapid growth of North Oxford since Hoggar's time [1850], over half of the approved-lodgings icons in the wider metropolitan area were north of Mary Magdalen Church, as compared to 15 per cent in the old city west of Carfax, 24 per cent from Carfax to Magdalen Bridge and just 10 per cent east of the bridge.

The base map superficially resembles an Alden map [1872]. The 'F. Madan' stamp does not relate to authorship, however, but to the Bodleian Library employee who saw to its preservation. The son of a Gloucestershire vicar, Falconer Madan (1851–1935) was elected a fellow of Brasenose College in 1876. He joined the library four years later and 'was at first engaged in the cataloguing of accessions and arrears of manuscripts' (R.J. Roberts), which would explain the two-year gap between this map's publication and Madan's own first library appointment. His fascination with anything printed in Oxford, however ephemeral, led Madan to collect widely, both for the library and on his own behalf. After years of ugly conflict with head librarian E.W.B. Nicholson, Madan succeeded him in 1912 and went on to win the Bibliographic Society's gold medal in 1932. We may be thankful to Madan for the preservation of this and other seemingly unimportant documents of his own time, as well as for the creation of one of the more peculiar items in the present book [1917].

in 1891 [1910]. As of 1897, a total of three post-1854 permanent private halls were in operation. But whether intentionally or otherwise, the key elides the existence of Oxford's first women's college, Lady Margaret Hall, founded in 1878 in the wake of a decision to allow women to sit certain examinations. Three more women's colleges would be established by 1893.

The present map appears to indicate just over half the number of licensed lodging-houses specified by Boase. However, the key is ambiguous as to how many of these houses each red square represents, stating only that they show 'the parts in which' licences have been issued. If, in fact, the unnamed mapmaker applied *exactly one* icon per licence, the licensing process must have continued at almost exactly the

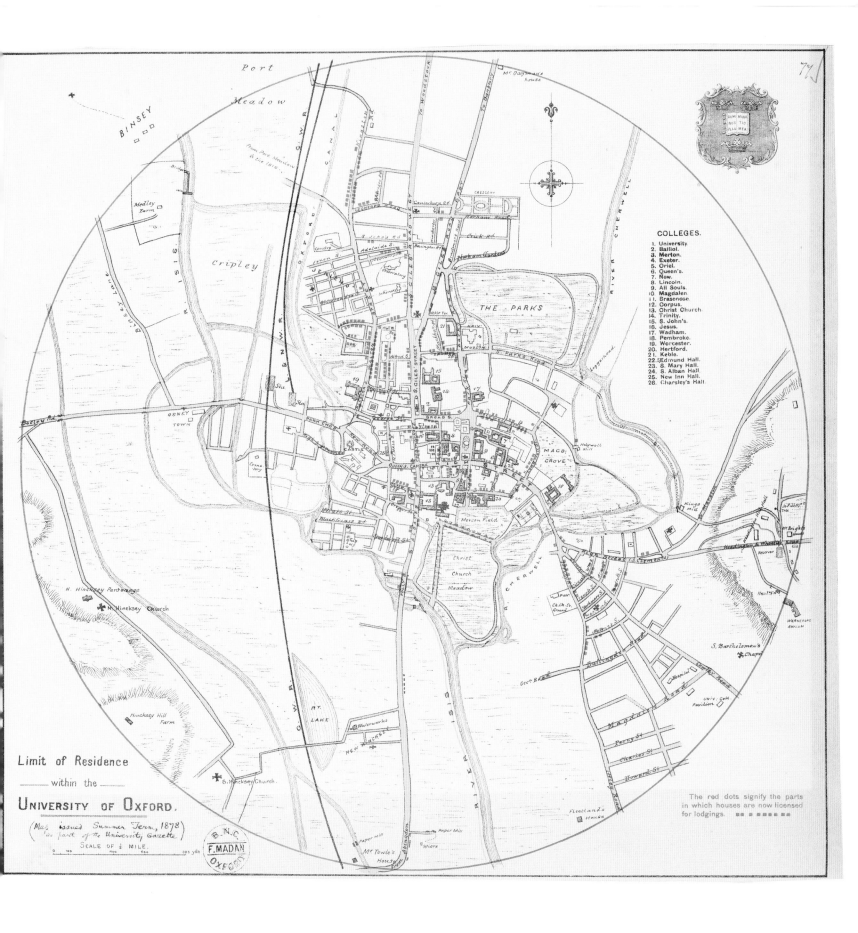

COLLEGES.

1. University.
2. Balliol.
3. Merton.
4. Exeter.
5. Oriel.
6. Queen's.
7. New.
8. Lincoln.
9. All Souls.
10. Magdalen.
11. Brasenose.
12. Corpus.
13. Christ Church.
14. Trinity.
15. S. John's.
16. Jesus.
17. Wadham.
18. Pembroke.
19. Worcester.
20. Hertford.
21. Keble.
22. S. Edmund Hall.
23. S. Mary Hall.
24. S. Alban Hall.
25. New Inn Hall.
26. Charsley's Hall.

The red dots signify the parts
in which houses are now licensed
for lodgings. ▪ ▪ ▪ ▪ ▪ ▪ ▪ ▪

Limit of Residence

—— within the ——

UNIVERSITY OF OXFORD.

(Map issued Summer Term, 1878)
as part of the University Gazette)

SCALE OF ½ MILE.

F. MADAN

1883

Dens of iniquity in the cradle of Methodism

In medieval times, the distinction between inns, taverns and student halls of residence could be blurry: Oxford's oldest recorded inn, Mauger's (later the Golden Cross), served all three functions over the course of the thirteenth century. By 1381, arguably the town's lowest ebb economically, there were still 32 resident brewers, 10 innkeepers, 7 'tapsters', 3 tavern-keepers and a vintner, in addition to 'numerous part-time beer-sellers who had some other principal occupation' (N. Selwyn). Nevertheless, according to Anthony à Wood, public drunk-enness – along with tobacco-smoking – did not become a major social problem in Oxford until the plague years 1603–05. In the 1630s, by which time the city required ale-houses to distinguish themselves with red-painted posts, there were just under 400, of which a quarter were unlicensed. This sheer number and the licence-evasion both greatly troubled the university's chancellor, Archbishop William Laud, who complained bitterly about the licensing power having passed from the university to the city's mayor and aldermen in the time of King Edward VI (r.1547–53). Despite Laud's efforts, and the destruction caused by the Great Fire of 1644, to say nothing of the later military occupation of the city by the Puritan-inclined Parliamentarian army, the number of taverns and ale-houses still stood at 370 in the 1670s, when an ill-judged speech by the proprietor of the Bear Inn provoked a 'town and gown' riot that lasted 'above a week'. The high-living naval administrator Samuel Pepys pronounced Oxford a 'mighty fine place . . . and cheap entertainment', and soon the university's reputation for drunkenness was such that Puritan preachers were advising like-minded gentry not to send their sons to it at all. By 1740, all 13 of the city's coffee-

Committee of the Oxfordshire Band of Hope and
Temperance Union, *Drink map of Oxford* (1883)

houses were also selling wine, and four or five of them 'laying it in by the pipe'[1] (Selwyn).

Methodism grew out of Oxford University's Holy Club, active from 1729 to 1738. Its founders John and Charles Wesley, sons of the Anglican rector of Epworth in Lincolnshire, were both undergraduates at Christ Church in the 1720s, and the former became a fellow of Lincoln College in 1726. 'Methodist' was first used in 1732, as a term of abuse of members of the club, and for decades thereafter most Methodist clergy considered themselves to be Anglicans with a special interest in helping the poor – especially prisoners and the illiterate – and discouraging excess among the well-to-do. It was usual for the early Methodists 'to give away each year all they had after providing for their own necessities' (C.W. Boase); John Wesley himself, after finding he was able to live in a decent middle-class way on £28 a year, gave the poor everything he received above this amount, even as his income rose steadily over the course of the rest of his life. In the end, he was giving away more than three times as much as he kept; and his brother Charles declined a sizeable inheritance from a distant relative in County Meath, Ireland, which as a result eventually passed to the Duke of Wellington instead (the Wesleys and the Wellesleys being almost, but not quite, entirely unrelated). The early Methodists' almost incidental efforts to 'rescue' other students from 'evil company' evolved into a fixed anti-drinking policy only after Charles Wesley passed away in 1788 and Methodism came to be considered a stand-alone Protestant denomination.

Having almost died out within the city of Oxford in the ten years following John Wesley's death in 1791, Methodism revived there over the following half-century, particularly after the completion in 1818 of a fine new chapel by William Jenkins, on a site in New Inn Hall Street purchased from Daniel Harris [1838]. Though ruinously expensive, the building served

1. A barrel holding between 208 and 256 Queen Anne gallons (168–213 Imperial), with 252 being the norm. The Queen Anne gallon remains in use as the US gallon.

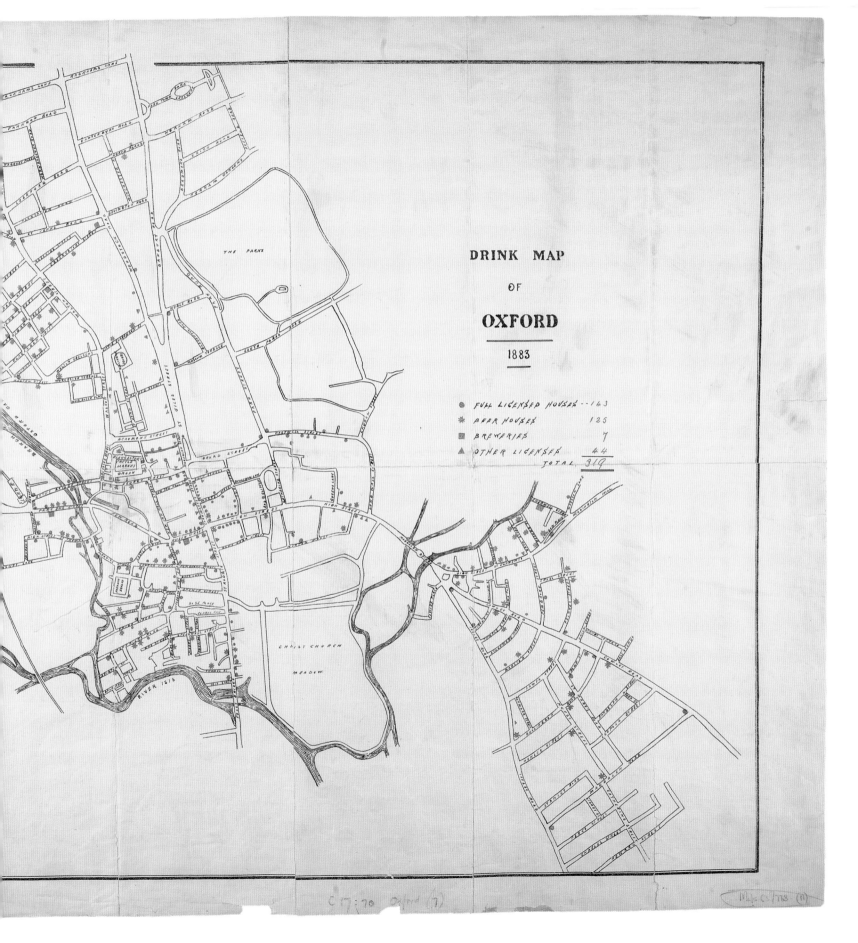

DRINK MAP

OF

OXFORD

1883

●	FULL LICENSED HOUSES	143
✳	BEER HOUSES	125
■	BREWERIES	7
▲	OTHER LICENSES	44
	TOTAL	319

THE PARKS

CHRIST CHURCH MEADOW

RIVER ISIS

its purpose as a magnet for new converts. By 1851, the Wesleyan Methodists could report 600 attendees at evening services and 500 at other times of day. Breakaway Methodist sects operating at the same date in Caroline Street, New Street and Paradise Square boasted a further combined average attendance of 225 in the evening and 183 in the morning.

Remarkably, given that one of the major *raisons d'être* of the university was still the training of Anglican clergymen, half the city of Oxford's population in 1850 reported no religious affiliation and a further quarter were Nonconformists. According to historian Janet Cooper, many poorer residents' 'contact with Christianity in any form was confined to the street preaching of some nonconformist groups' and the receipt of food-bundles in times of general economic hardship; the proportion of people who married in registry offices rather than churches was also 'unusually high' compared to other parts of England in 1849. City premises licensed to sell alcohol in the same era numbered around 400, or (as the *Oxford Chronicle* newspaper pointed out) one for every 60 men, women and children.

Naturally, this degree of godlessness did not go unnoticed among the godly, and the number of chapels would increase from 19 to 26 over the remainder of the nineteenth century. At least eight Methodist churches, chapels and missions had been built in the city of Oxford and its suburbs in the 12 years prior to this map being produced. At roughly 1:6,700, it dates to the ministry of Hugh Price Hughes, who – having been warned (somewhat unfairly) that Oxford Methodism was moribund – embarked on what could reasonably be described as a three-year Methodist blitzkrieg of the city and surrounding countryside, including 'house-to-house' missionising and youth-group appearances in 'gospel chariots'. It was Hughes who first 'made temperance an essential feature of [Methodist] church work' in Oxford (C. Colvin), though it should be noted that at least two different temperance clubs,

a Church Army training house, and of course the Band of Hope who were responsible for this map, had been formed in the city in the two decades prior to his arrival. There was also a Temperance Hall on Middle Way in Summertown from 1876 to 1895, and 'temperance hotels' in Park End Street, Queen Street and Botley Road, among other places. The 'temperance vote' made up largely of Methodists and Baptists narrowly missed unseating popular Tory MP and brewer A.W. Hall in 1880, and then managed to get rid of him the following year on the grounds of electoral malpractice (despite both sides being equally guilty of this).

The map's lengthy accompanying text carefully avoided mentioning that the number of licensed premises it depicted represented a fall of more than 80 per cent since the mid century. Rather, it focused on the fact that the number remaining was still 50 per cent in excess of the British average, and the disproportionate concentration of these loci of 'drunkenness, vice, and crime' in the city's poorest neighbourhoods. Rightly or wrongly, this latter aspect of the problem was ascribed to NIMBYism on the part of the magistrates responsible for issuing licences, whose children were able to play in 'beautiful gardens' rather than 'of necessity' out in the streets among the drunks. Visually, this contrast is mostly between the forest of red markers in Jericho and their relative absence from the wealthier parts of North Oxford; but it is equally interesting to note that more than a dozen beer houses and 'full licensed' houses are shown in southerly parts of Cowley that had not even been inhabited just 15 years earlier. This may have been related to the arrival of Cowley Barracks [1876].

Jenkins's Methodist Chapel in New Inn Hall Street was set back considerably farther from the street than the current Wesley Memorial Church, which replaced it in 1878. After serving as a girls' school, the old chapel was torn down in 1969.

Opposite. As well as the sheer number of licensed premises, the map called attention to the authorities' failure to issue licences in the wealthiest parts of North Oxford, lest vice disturb them in their own 'beautiful gardens'.

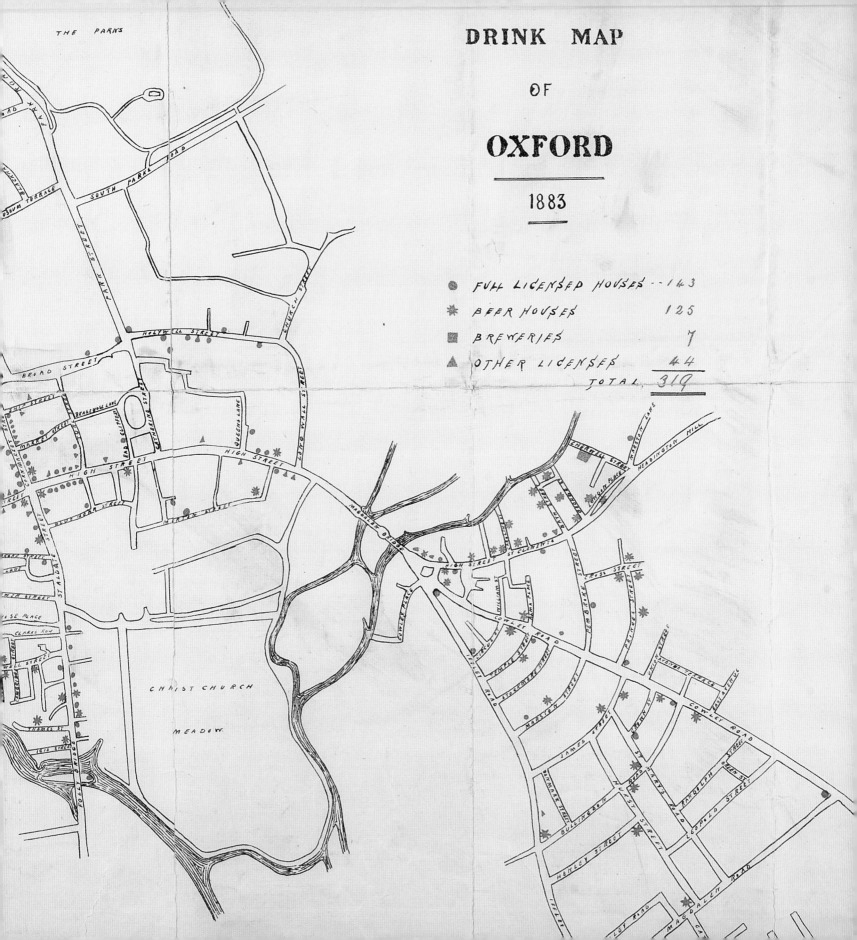

DRINK MAP

OF

OXFORD

1883

FULL LICENSED HOUSES — 143
BEER HOUSES — 125
BREWERIES — 7
OTHER LICENSES — 44
TOTAL 319

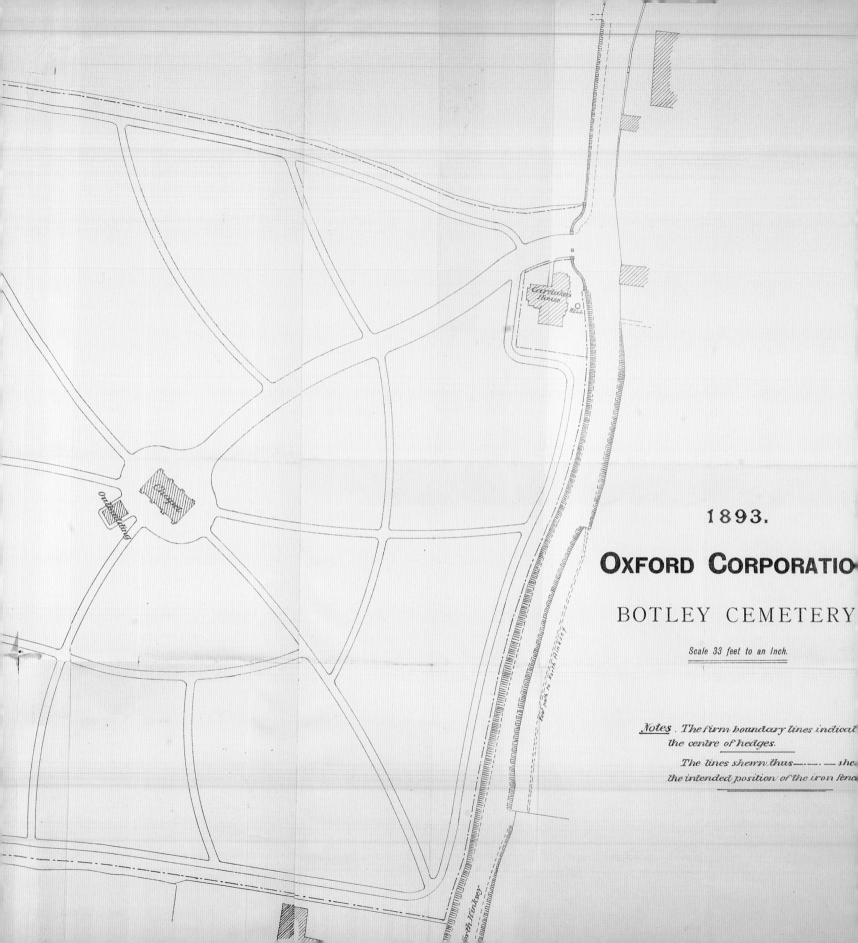

Overlakes House

WELL

Chapel

Outbuilding

Footpath to North Hinksey

North Hinksey

1893.

Oxford Corporatio

BOTLEY CEMETERY

Scale 33 feet to an Inch.

Notes. *The firm boundary lines indicat*
the centre of hedges.

The lines shewn thus ————— she
the intended position of the iron fenc

1893

Accommodating the dead

The plainest and most ordinary-seeming of maps may conceal long, complex and indeed gruesome histories. As one might expect, nineteenth-century Oxford's constrained site, booming population and waterlogged under-layers created a host of problems for those tasked with burying the dead, as much as for the officials responsible for infectious-disease prevention [1848] and drainage [1872]. The miasma theory of disease had led many to blame the national cholera epidemic of 1832 on gases from human corpses putrefying in the small churchyards that were dotted about every town; and 1843 saw the publication of Lanarkshire-born landscape architect J.C. Loudon's enormously influential book *On the Laying Out, Planting and Managing of Cemeteries*. In it, Loudon endorsed the prevailing idea that ill-health among the living could and did result from the 'suffocating effect of the effluvia of decomposition'. He therefore advocated for the now-traditional burial depth of 6 feet; for cemetery trees, hedges and walls to freely admit 'the action of the wind'; and for space and access within cemeteries to be maximised through a system of precise division into 'imaginary squares or parallelograms . . . indicated by numbers and letters on the boundary fence, and by marks inserted in the ground at their points of intersection'.

In 1726, Oxford's twelfth-century church of Peter-le-Bailey had collapsed, due to 'undermining [of] the walls with graves' (H. Hurst). In the same year as Loudon's book appeared, it was found that all of the city's burying-places – whether medieval churchyards, or relatively new facilities like those of the workhouse and the Radcliffe Infirmary – were full to bursting. The workhouse dead were buried seven deep. Even the churchyard of St John the Baptist, Summertown, built as recently as 1832, was far too cramped to be of much use for long; and fine, plain neo-classical St Paul's (completed 1836; now the café-bar called Freud's) had never had any burial facilities to begin with.

Oxford Corporation, *Botley Cemetery* (1893)

183

A single large cemetery for those of all faiths and none was considered but rejected due to qualms on the part of the clergy. The chosen solution was the creation of three new Anglican cemeteries, each serving four parishes. The first of these to be consecrated, in 1847, was Holywell. Built next to St Cross Church on land provided by Merton College, it replaced the parish cemeteries of St John the Baptist, St Martin, St Mary the Virgin and St Peter in the East. Next, in 1848, St Aldate's, St Ebbe's, St Peter-le-Bailey's and St Thomas's were given a new united cemetery in present-day Mill Street, slightly to the west of medieval Osney Abbey. Lastly, St Sepulchre Cemetery was planned on the site of Walton Manor Farm in Jericho for the parishes of St Giles, St Michael and St Mary Magdalen, and St Paul's Chapel. It was objected to by Jonathan Browning (1799–1880), alderman for the North Ward and former mayor (1841–42), on the grounds that Jericho 'was in the midst of a large and increasing population', such that the creation of St Sepulchre Cemetery merely shifted 'the evil . . . from one part of the city to another'. But the scheme went ahead without any apparent modification in 1849.

In May 1855, however, the Privy Council ordered 'for the protection of the public health' that there be no further burials in the city of Oxford, except in airtight vaults, from January of the following year. This covered not only the medieval churchyards and Summertown, but all three of the new four-parish cemeteries, plus the two city parishes that were not served by them, All Saints and St Clement's. Also affected were

> the Roman Catholic Chapel and Burial-ground in the parish of St Clement . . . the George-street Independent Chapel in the parish of St Mary Magdalene . . . the Workhouse and Infirmary Burial-ground in the parish of St Giles . . . the Burial-ground of Oxford Castle or the County Jail . . . (except of persons sentenced to be buried in the Jail by a Court of Justice) . . . the Wesleyan Chapel and Burial-ground in the Parish of St Michael, and at the New-road (Baptist) Chapel[.]

The order provided no clue about what would become of the corpses of those who had not equipped themselves with expensive, free-standing airtight crypts. And burials in churches' indoor crypts had already been made illegal nationally, in 1852.

In practice, then, the Privy Council's 1855 order could not be complied with. The old churchyards of St Clement's and St Thomas's were still receiving new bodies in 1876, and by the following decade the international press was reporting the scandalous state of St Sepulchre: where the bones of the people first buried there, just one generation earlier, could be seen lying about on the surface of graves dug more recently. Only now was the city finally moved to act, buying a total of 32 acres of land for new cemeteries at Botley (then still in Berkshire), Wolvercote and Rose Hill in 1889 and 1890. At 8 acres, Botley Cemetery – illustrated in this planning map of 1893, the year before it opened – was by far the smallest. Nevertheless, as Loudon's book had promised, the site proved able to accommodate many thousands of graves, including those of 672 British and Commonwealth service personnel from the two world wars, as well as 70 foreign war dead, including enemy prisoners, presumably from the nearby Harcourt Hill POW camp.

Chiefly remembered for his theory of the Gardenesque and sometimes called 'the father of the English garden', Loudon produced just three designs for specific (as distinct from ideal) cemeteries before his death. One of the two that was actually built was non-denominational Histon Road Cemetery in Cambridge, whose similarity to Botley Cemetery – both in terms of overall layout and the specific features provided – is abundantly clear. Tragically, Loudon did not live to see the influence of his book, dying of lung cancer in the year of its publication in the arms of his wife, the visionary science-fiction writer Jane Webb Loudon. One can only hope that he did not blame his death on the miasmas he had inhaled during his exhaustive tour of European cemeteries 'from Stockholm to Naples'.

The former churchyard of St Peter-le-Bailey became a garden in 1874 and, from 1900, home to Oxford's first war

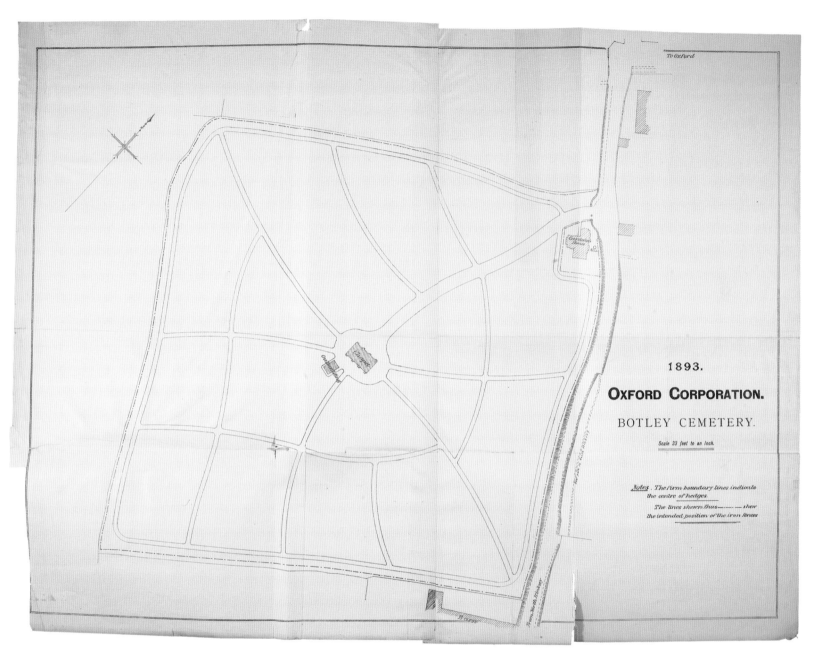

1893.

OXFORD CORPORATION.

BOTLEY CEMETERY.

Scale 33 feet to an Inch.

Notes. The firm boundary lines indicate
the centre of hedges.

The lines shewn thus———— shew
the intended position of the iron fences.

memorial, for 62 officers and men of the Oxfordshire Light Infantry who had recently died in India and Uganda. Bones found during the construction of this monument were reburied at Osney Cemetery, possibly in contravention of the 1855 order. Still standing above the level of the neighbouring streets due to the hundreds of coffins lying beneath it, the St Peter-le-Bailey graveyard area was renamed Bonn Square in 1974 after Oxford's twin town on the Continent, then the capital of West Germany. Human remains are still unearthed in the square from time to time.

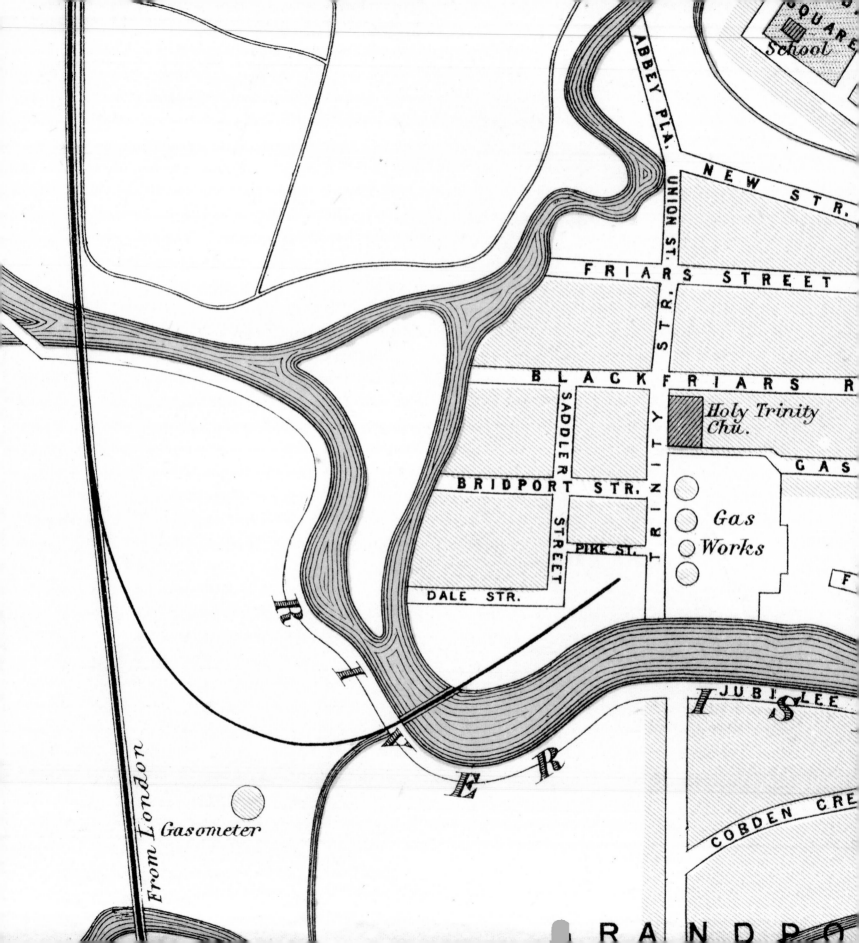

1895

Setting the aesthetic pace for the new century

This deceptively simple map, overprinted in just four colours, manages to indicate a very broad range of Oxford's past and present features in a manner that is legible, uncrowded and generally pleasing to the eye, despite the addition of many new ones since our last 'general purpose' atlas map of a generation earlier [*c*.1862]. The gasworks has expanded across the river, and the two halves are now linked by a special railway branch line and bridge dating from 1886. The terminus for the tramways that were built beginning in the early 1880s is indicated, and those who might be interested could use the map to find their way to the Scotch Church, Synagogue, Salvation Army and Liberal Club, and even to the former site of the Bocardo prison and the so-called Bishop King's Palace: briefly the home of Robert King, the Abbot of Osney who became the first Bishop of Oxford in 1542. Cartography has now caught up with reality in the case of Charles Buckeridge's

Court House – though by this point, it has become a Probate Registry.

The Fire Brigade building in New Inn Hall Street represents the culmination of nearly half a century of faintly bizarre infighting. In 1842, the High Street Post Office and two other buildings burnt down, leading to calls for fire-service and waterworks modernisation and consolidation. Three years later, however, there were still two fire engines owned by parishes, one that belonged to the city, one maintained in the city by the county, nine owned by the university and various colleges, one operated by Sun Insurance and one at the University Press. From 1854 to 1870, there were no public engines at all, and the university and private individuals took on the entire responsibility until another fatal fire revived the issue. Then, from 1871 to 1887, a lone engine operated by a new volunteer fire brigade operated as a rival to a new, two-engine

J.G. Bartholomew, 'Oxford', from *The royal atlas of England and Wales, reduced from the Ordnance Survey . . .* (1899)

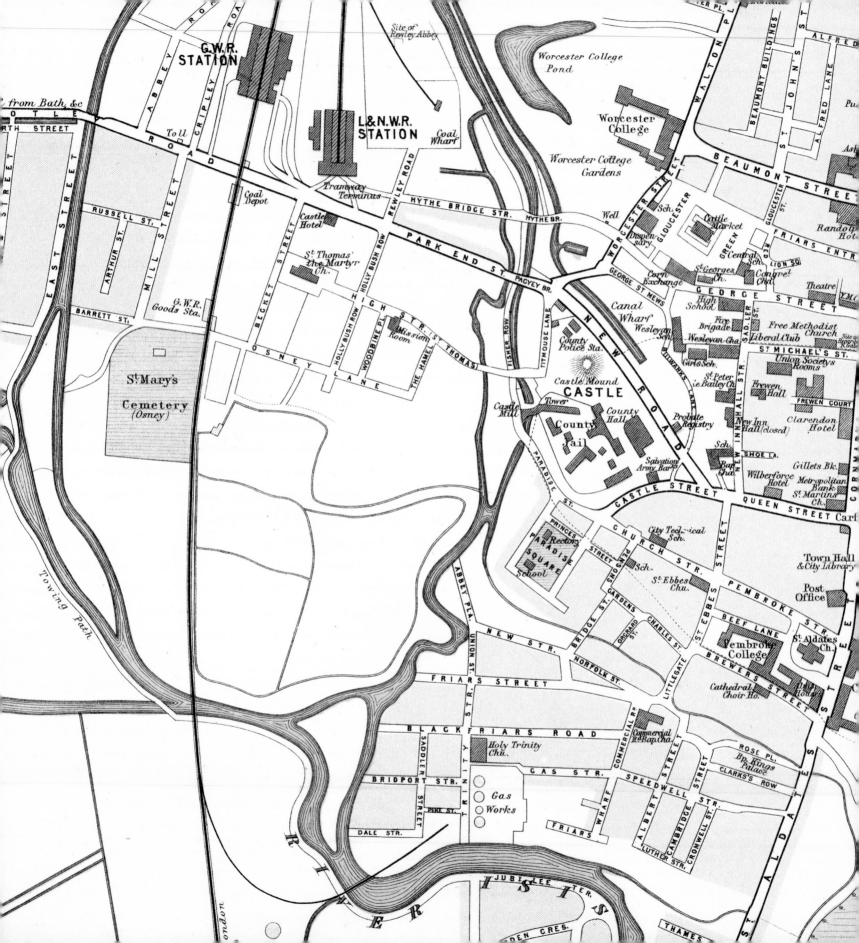

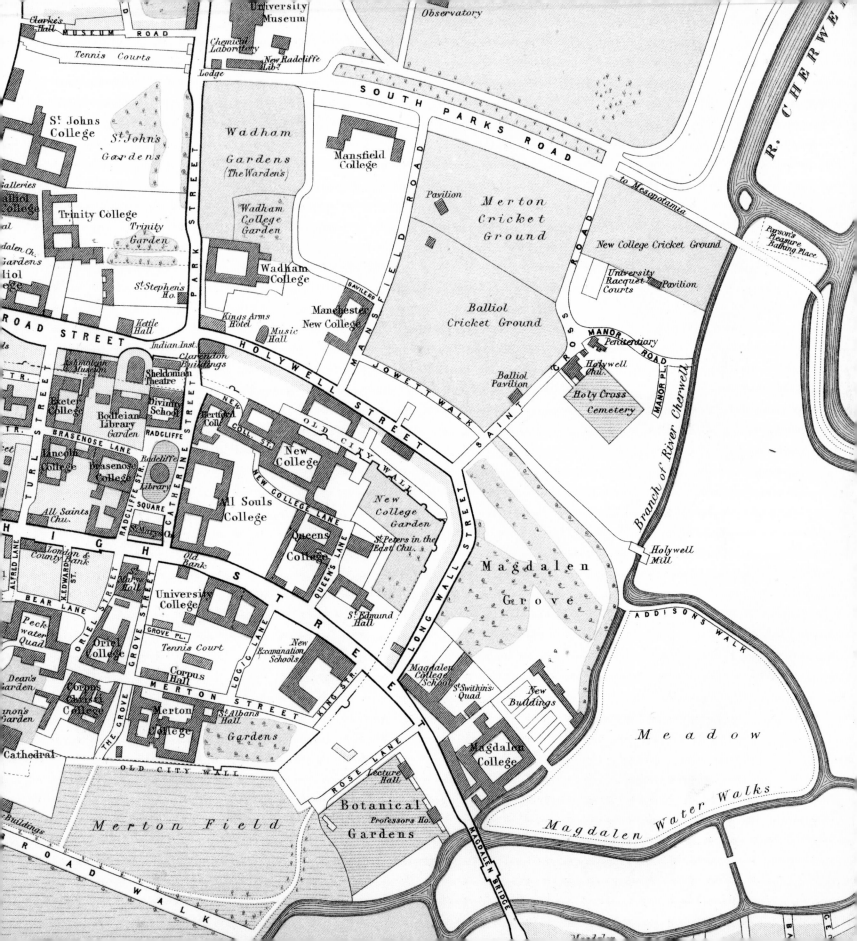

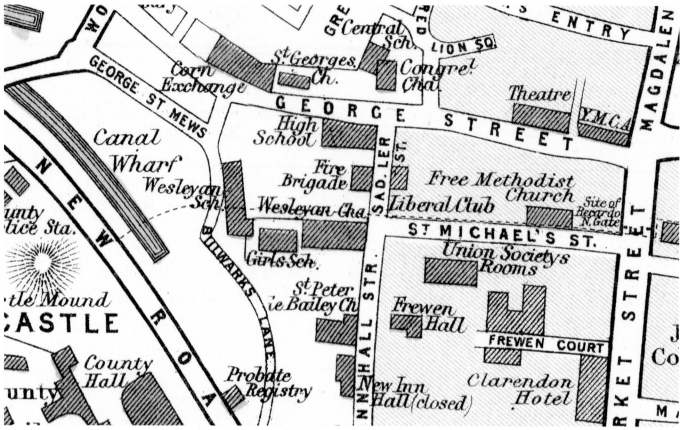

From the range of institutions chosen for depiction here, Bartholomew's map seems to be aimed as much at local residents as at day-trippers.

city fire brigade controlled by the police. This fight was won by the volunteers, who built the headquarters and engine house seen here in 1873–74.

The existence of an additional fire station that was built in George Street in 1896 is not reflected in the map. Neither is the demolition of the body of St Martin's Church for road-widening at Carfax, which also occurred in 1896. The last updating of the map's principal content is most likely to have been 1895, insofar as the new Public Library (now the Museum of Oxford) opened to borrowers in that year, and is not specifically noted as under construction. The new Town Hall in which the new library was located was built over the 1751–53 Town Hall/Corn Exchange and also obliterated

Nixon's School, medieval Knapp Hall (except for its vaulted cellars) and some other buildings in Blue Boar Street, Wheat-sheaf Passage and St Aldates Street.

It is not immediately apparent what the burnt-orange buildings are meant to have in common. Mansfield College had opened in 1886 as the first Nonconformist college in the university, following the abolition of religious tests for non-theological degrees by the first Gladstone government in 1871; but Manchester College – which had hoped to follow suit – would not even be recognised as a permanent private hall for nearly another century. Nor is it only educational institutions that receive the orange treatment, for we find the New Road County Police Station, the George Street YMCA of 1891 and

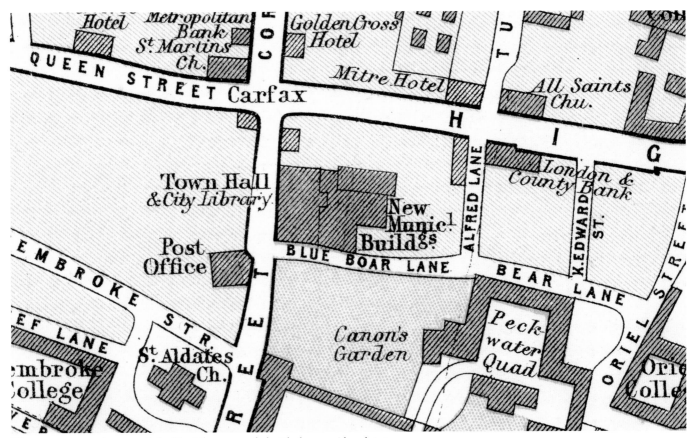

The apparent completeness of the City Library, coupled with the un-widened state
of the northwest corner of Carfax, suggests that the map was compiled in 1895.

even the cattle market are coloured in the same way. It is not about grandeur, either, or the Randolph Hotel in Beaumont Street would surely be among the orangest of all. This leads one to wonder if an absolute distinction has been drawn between institutions that engage in for-profit commerce and those that do not, with the former all being shaded in grey. Mostly, this seems to fit, but the railway stations are orange. Moreover, if pink is intended to indicate the vast undifferentiated blocks of private residential buildings, why has it, and not orange or grey, been chosen for the gasworks? That being said, the use of colour – any colour – coupled with the use of sans-serif typefaces renders the map as a whole considerably more legible than the majority of its recent predecessors.

This map was published as part of *The Royal Atlas of England and Wales, reduced from the Ordnance Survey and edited by J.G. Bartholomew, FRGS.* Bartholomew (1860–1920) was a fourth-generation representative of the dynasty of Edinburgh map engravers, lithographers and publishers that would become John Bartholomew & Son Ltd in 1919. A crusader for better representation of the discipline of geography within higher education, he received the Royal Geographical Society's Victoria Medal in 1905, and five years later was appointed Geographer and Cartographer to the King for Scotland. It is the measure of his advanced ideas on colour and typography, and of his firm's subsequent success, that this map would not have looked out of place in the period 1920–50.

BUSINESS STREET MAP OF OXFORD.

Stephens and Mackintosh
LEICESTER.

Agents for Sale of these Maps, HALL & SON, Printers and Bookbinders, 3A Queen Street, No. ⑧

NOTE.
The numbers shewn ⑤ indicate the positions of places of business advertised in spaces with corresponding numbers.

Tramway Line Shewn thus

1898

Mapping for the consumer society

An early example of what would shortly become a hugely popular genre of 'advertising maps' of middle-sized towns was produced in 1891 by J. Valters of 20 James Street, Oxford, at a scale of 1:14,080. Where *Dewe's Pictorial Plan*'s mighty masthead [1855] had only sold itself, Valters proudly proclaimed, 'ERNEST PIGOTT'S Fresh Butter Delivered to all Parts of the City Daily' from Avenue 4 of the Market (High Street end). A second advert, in the southwestern area of the map itself, was for A. Ballard, 'Practical Watch and Clock Maker and Working Jeweller', and was illustrated with cheap woodcuts of a signet ring, belt buckle and Georgian silver sugar bowl. Eight more similar advertisements adorned the back – though there was space enough for as many more, suggesting that the Valters family's skill as advertising salespeople was limited. A much improved version, with an oval photograph of a stern-faced Fred Valters hovering ominously over Marston Lane, was offered in 1898, presumably due to out-of-town competition from the rather wonderful map shown here.

Over the course of the 1890s, the national market for advertising street maps, aimed at prospective residents of the towns depicted and to a lesser extent at current residents and short-term visitors, came to be dominated by just two firms: Stephens & Mackintosh, who produced the *c.*1:5,000 map now before us, and the Borough & County Advertising Company. Both companies were based in Leicester, where the first-ever item of this kind, a 1:5,280 litho map by E.F. and R.J. Stephens, 'Civil Engineers, Surveyors &c, Market Street', had been produced in 1877. A Leicester Printing & Publishing Company was also active in this niche in the following decade, and what might fairly be described as the 'Leicester deadlock' on the advertising-map market would not be broken until after the First World War, when rivals found success in Cheltenham and elsewhere. For some towns, notably Croydon, the Borough & County map was the first-ever stand-alone street

Stephens & Mackintosh/G. Gibbons & Co., *Business street map of Oxford* (1898)

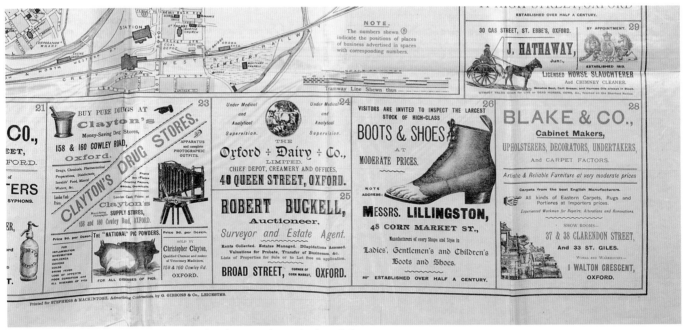

Business specialisation, while a strong trend in this period, was far from being a universal rule – as any horse-slaughterer/chimney cleaner would tell you.

plan ever published. Such maps 'were printed on relatively friable paper and were seen as ephemeral'; their purpose 'was to make money, not to provide national geographical infrastructure' (R. Kain and R. Oliver). Unsurprisingly, many advertising maps that we know were printed in large quantities have since disappeared without trace; and given its extreme flimsiness, the 1891 Valters map discussed above must rate as an incredible survival. The present map certainly fits Kain and Oliver's description of the genre's cartography as 'functional rather than decorative', and as guiding map-users to the advertisers' premises in particular. In a sense, its silence regarding non-advertisers parallels Dewe's silence regarding places of no presumptive touristic interest.

This map has east at the top, probably as the best means of covering the clusters of advertisers whose businesses were located in Jericho and Cowley, as well as those who would presumably soon manifest themselves to the west of the Abingdon Road – an area generally omitted from tourist-focused maps of the same era [1910]. The map-buyer could

have his books printed and bound, his pigs cured of disease, his lands surveyed, and his ecclesiastical vestments and surgical instruments made to order. The city's cradle-to-grave retail sector included prams and baby food at the one end and 'Monumental Masonry' at the other, on the way taking in ginger beer, ale, stout, sherry, port, whisky and 'Havannah' cigars. George Wiggins in the Cowley Road offered one-stop shopping for horse-shoeing and bicycle, tricycle and sewing-machine repair, while those who did not wish to sully themselves by *owning* dishes and cutlery could hire them from Lisemore's Stores – who, despite being 'Cheapest for Everything', offered the finest tea in the world.

By 1903, Edward C. Alden, who had been selling his tourist maps of the city for decades, got in on the act: printing his usual map with adverts on the back for (among others) removal men and coal merchants. By that time, J. Hathaway Jr, since 1813 licensed horse-slaughterers and chimney sweeps of 30 Gas Street in St Ebbe's, had evolved into J. Hathaway & Son, purveyors of pet food.

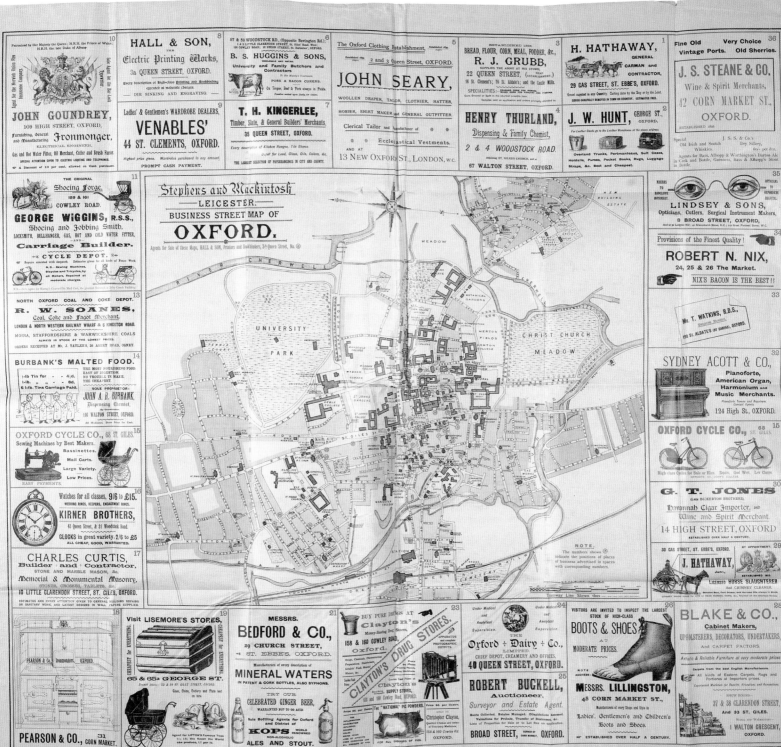

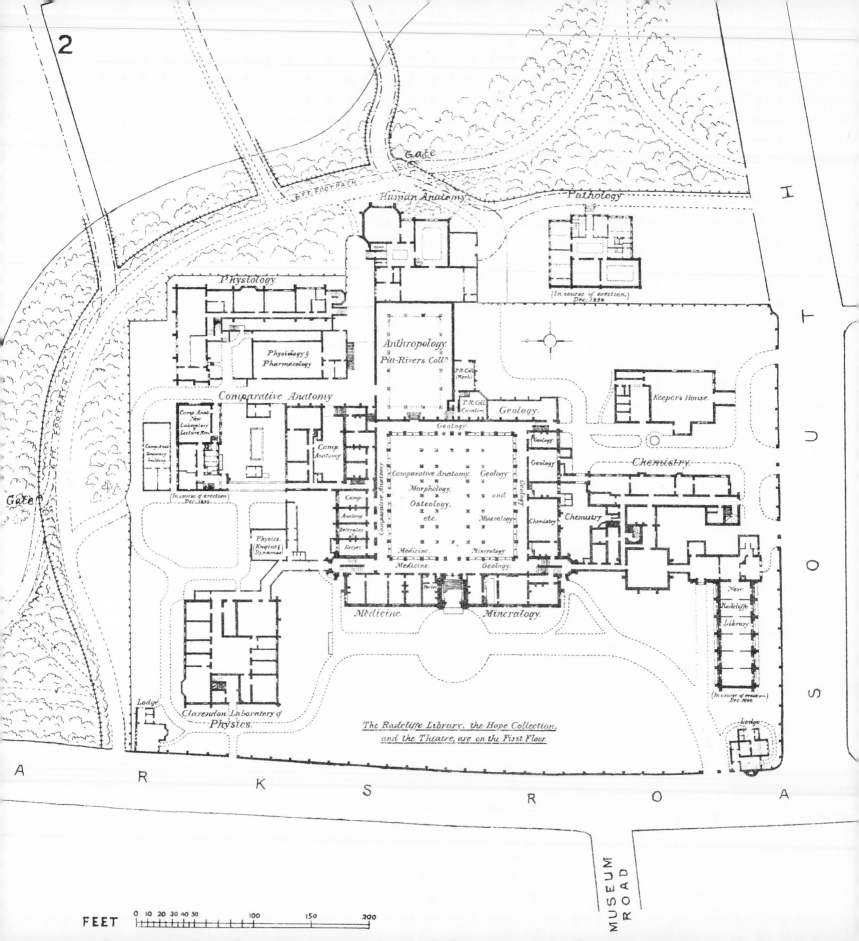

2

Gate

6 FT. FOOTPATH

Human Anatomy.

Pathology.

(In course of erection.)
Dec. 1890.

Physiology.

Physiology &
Pharmacology.

Anthropology.
Pitt-Rivers Coll^n.

P.R.Coll.
(Work)

Comparative Anatomy.

Comp.Anat.
New
Laboratory.
Lecture Rm.

Comp.Anat.
Temporary
Building.

Geology.

P.R.Coll.
Curator.

Geology.

Keeper's House.

Comp.
Anatomy.

Geology.

(In course of erection.)
Dec. 1888.

Comp.
Anatomy.
Delegates
Keeper.

Comp.
Anatomy.

Comparative Anatomy.

Comparative Anatomy.

Morphology,

Osteology,

etc.

Geology.

and

Mineralogy.

Geology.

Chemistry.

Geology.

Chemistry.

Chemistry.

Physics.
(Engine &
Dynamo)

Medicine.

Medicine.

Mineralogy.

Mineralogy.
Geology.

New
Radcliffe
Library.

Gate

6 FT. FOOTPATH

Medicine.

Mineralogy.

Lodge

Clarendon Laboratory of
Physics.

The Radcliffe Library, the Hope Collection.
and the Theatre, are on the First Floor.

(In course of erection.)
Dec. 1890.

Lodge

A   R   K   S   R   O   A

MUSEUM
ROAD

FEET   0 10 20 30 40 50   100   150   200

1900

New peaks to climb

When I was in my teens, a family friend who taught at Cambridge got wind of the fact that I was a Graham Greene fan and gave me a collection of *Night and Day*, the British riposte to *The New Yorker* that Greene edited for six months in 1937. I loved the cartoons, but in light of my family's background in mountaineering I was especially taken by a regular column called 'Night Climbing the Rooftops of Cambridge'. At both of the ancient English universities, this activity almost certainly originated on an impromptu basis among undergraduates on nocturnal sprees trying to get back to their rooms after the college gates were locked. But in 1899 it acquired a bizarre veneer of sporting legitimacy, and new popularity, with the publication of *The Roof-Climber's Guide to Trinity* by Geoffrey Winthrop Young (1876–1958), soon to become one of Europe's great mountaineers. The book could have been quite dull and technical but was written in part as a parody of guides to actual mountains and spawned a number of imitations as well as homages in fiction. Everywhere but Oxbridge, where it is still just 'night climbing', the activity Young described has been known since the 1970s as 'buildering': a portmanteau word made up of 'building' and 'bouldering'. It is at least possible that fears inspired by Young's book were connected to the 'Proposed Unclimbable fence' in this splendidly detailed 1900 plan of building-in-progress around the Oxford University Natural History Museum (1855–60), Clarendon Physics Laboratory (1872), and Pitt-Rivers Museum (1885–86).

If one compares Alfred Robinson's rendering of the buildings' outlines against those shown five years earlier by Bartholomew [1895], the latter does not come off particularly well, possibly having adopted a policy of 'simplicity for simplicity's sake' when it came to structures with particularly

Alfred Robinson, Plan showing work in progress and proposed additions, Natural History Museum, Clarendon Physics Laboratory, Pitt-Rivers Museum and vicinity (1900)

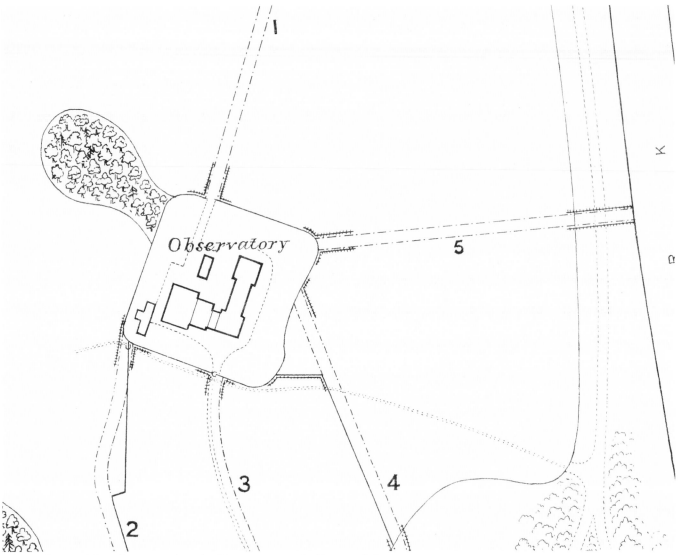

Of these five possibilities for new roads to the Observatory, none had been made by 1919.

baroque floor-plans. The usually hasty and out-of-date George Washington Bacon [1909], on the other hand, gets it more nearly right, though his map is still wholly missing this plan's Physiology/Pharmacology and Pathology blocks, as well as the northward (here leftward) extension of the Observatory. The Ordnance Survey's Oxfordshire Sheet XXXIII.SE, revised in 1898 and published in 1900, shows all the buildings here with the exception of Pathology.

Night climbing aside, Robinson's plan is a fascinating snapshot of the period when the university's non-traditional academic work could still be corralled in a single fairly small area. By the end of the 1970s, all the departments it shows as housed within the museum had been relocated to their own facilities elsewhere.

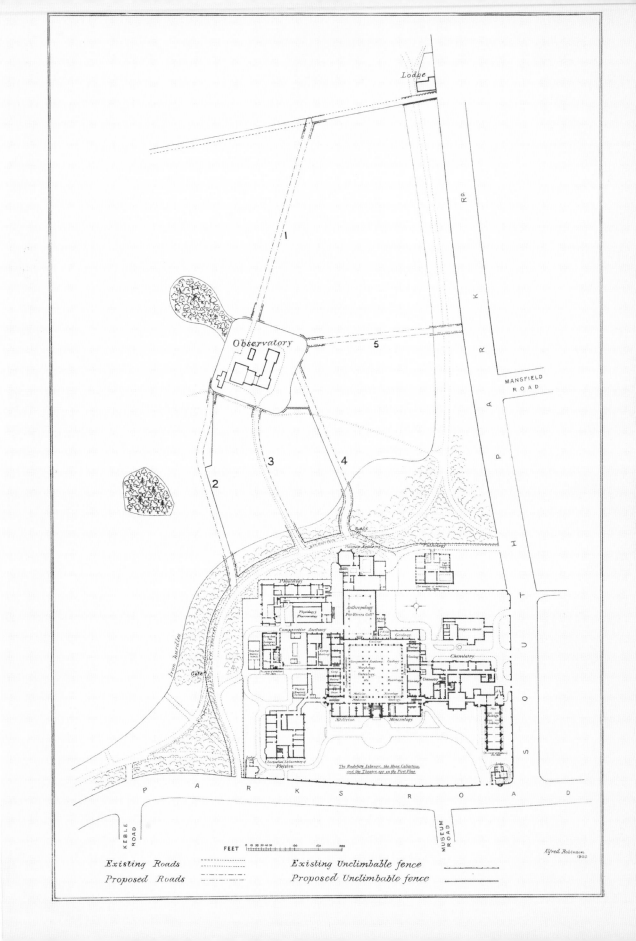

Lodge

Observatory

1

5

3

4

2

PARK RD.

MANSFIELD ROAD

SOUTH PARK

Iron hurdles

Gate

Gate

Physiology

Physiology & Pharmacology

Comparative Anatomy

Human Anatomy

Pathology

Anthropology Pitt-Rivers Coll.

Geology

Keeper's House

Chemistry

Chemistry

Geology

Osteology etc.

Medicine

Mineralogy

Medicine

Mineralogy

Clarendon Laboratory of Physics

Lodge

The Radcliffe Library, the Hope Collection, and the Theater, are on the First Floor.

KEBLE ROAD

PARKS ROAD

MUSEUM ROAD

SOUTH ROAD

FEET 0 10 20 30 40 50   100   150   300

Alfred Robinson 1900

Existing Roads   ....   Existing Unclimbable fence   ————

Proposed Roads   —·—·—·—   Proposed Unclimbable fence   —×—×—×—

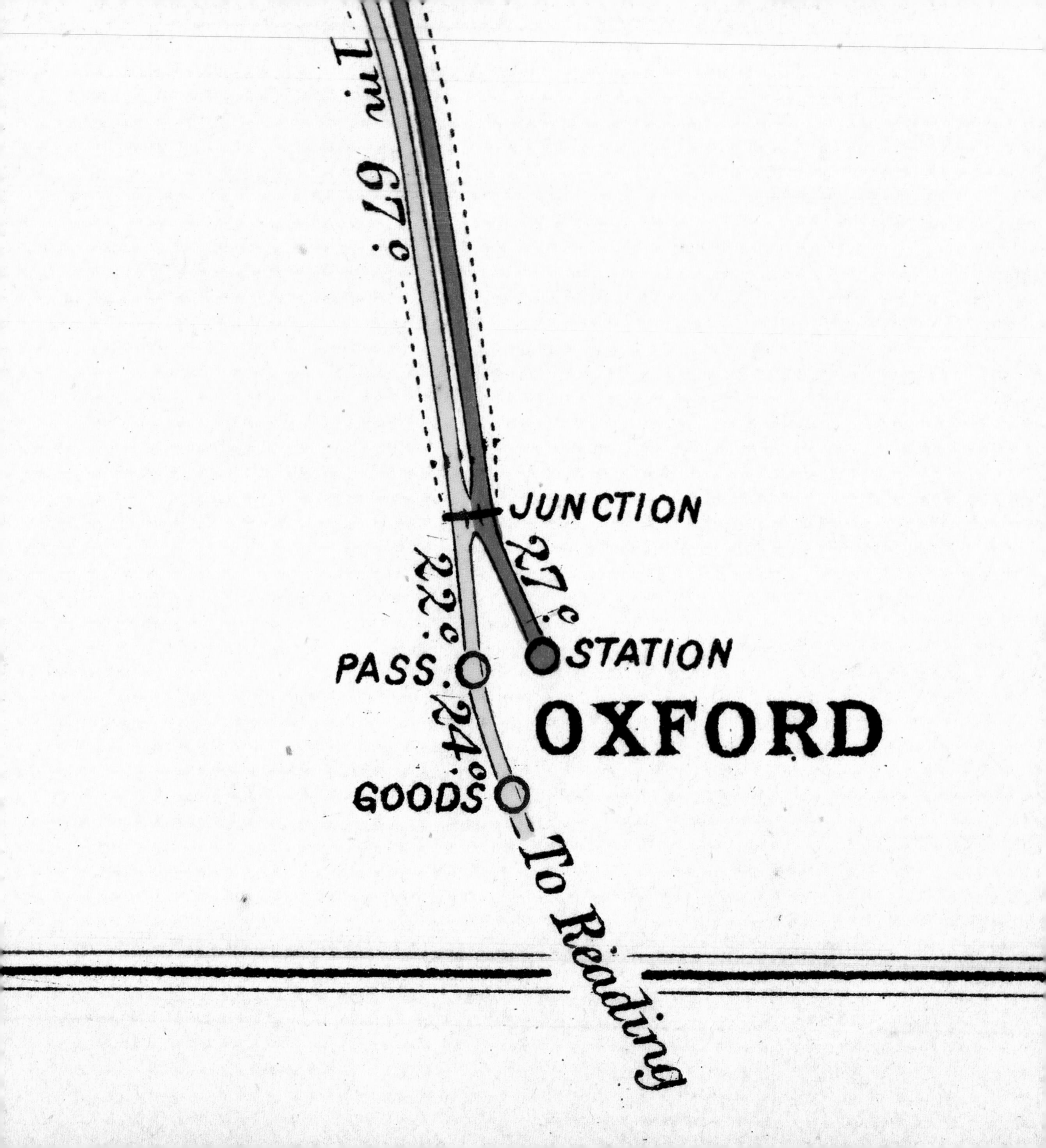

1 in 67.°

JUNCTION

27.°

22.°

24.°

PASS.

STATION

GOODS

OXFORD

To Reading

1902a

Time, money and the railways

The pattern of early railway development seen around Oxford [1844] was repeated across the country: as a series of disconnected local or regional initiatives that were guided by short-term enthusiasm rather than any kind of inter-regional strategic vision. A few brilliant individuals including Thomas Drummond [1831a] foresaw the need for, and even mapped, railway plans at a national scale as early as the 1830s. But in the event, the 'railway mania' of the following decade involved the creation of scores of distinct commercial companies to serve specific routes averaging less than 35 miles in length, and the question of when and precisely how these lines would be connected together was kicked into the long grass.

The 'gauge war' has already been described. But with people and goods suddenly moving at unprecedented speeds, another crucial connectivity problem no one had given much thought to was that of timekeeping. Given a 360-degree globe of the world and a 24-hour day, solar noon varies by exactly four minutes per degree of longitude, and clocks had always been set according to local sundial readings. The bells of Christ Church still ring at five minutes past nine nightly, a reminder of the fact that down to the early Victorian period, when it was nine o'clock in London, it was only 20.55 in Oxford (and 20.50 in Bristol, 20.46 in Exeter, 20.35 in Dublin and so forth, right across the Atlantic and beyond). The grouping of time into zones was very much a product of the railway age.

GWR, in part because it planned to serve routes that were longer in their east–west dimension than those of any other railway company in the British Isles, was the first to adopt Greenwich Mean Time (GMT) – hitherto only of interest to scientists and mariners – on board its trains. But this unilateral action, taken in November 1840, at first only added to the confusion: with some localities adopting 'London Time' a.k.a.

Railway Clearing House, *Oxford & Yarnton* and *Dudley, Great Bridge & Wednesbury* (1902)

'Railway Time', and others stoutly resisting the loss of 'their' time. Nonetheless, many other railway companies quickly saw the merits of using a single coordinated time, not least for the avoidance of accidents.

Then, there were questions of money. A riot of companies of widely differing sizes, profitability levels and ethical practices owned trains, stations and lines that had not been designed from the outset as a network. Though a given journey might take place entirely within a particular railway company's fiefdom, it was commonplace for passengers or goods to begin their journeys at one company's station and end them at another's, and/or to be carried on yet another company's rolling stock. This led to the establishment in January 1842 of the Railway Clearing House (RCH), a Euston-based private consortium dedicated to apportioning railway revenue between the different companies involved in the nearly infinite array of resulting track- and train-usage scenarios. Initially headed by a London & Birmingham Railway employee, and run from premises provided by that company, RCH expanded by the end of 1845 to include 16 member railways, all of which contributed money for its running costs on a per-station basis. Notable by its absence was the GWR. Nevertheless, RCH lobbying in favour of the nationwide use of GMT, beginning in September 1847, was instrumental in its adoption at the grass-roots level, with an estimated 49 out of every 50 British towns accepting GMT as their own by 1855.

New Zealand became the first country to adopt a single time zone throughout its own territory, in 1868. Then, beginning in the late 1870s, the idea of a global system of 24 time zones, with the number of minutes past the hour being the same in each, was popularised by Kirkcaldy-born Canadian surveyor and leading railways engineer Captain Sir Sandford Fleming (1827–1915). In August 1880, the British government at last accepted the railway-led fait accompli and formally adopted GMT for the whole island of Britain, though Ireland would retain Dublin Mean Time for a further 36 years. Time zones were adopted worldwide by 1929, but Fleming's project has still never been completed, to the extent that Newfoundland, Iran, Afghanistan, India, Sri Lanka, Nepal

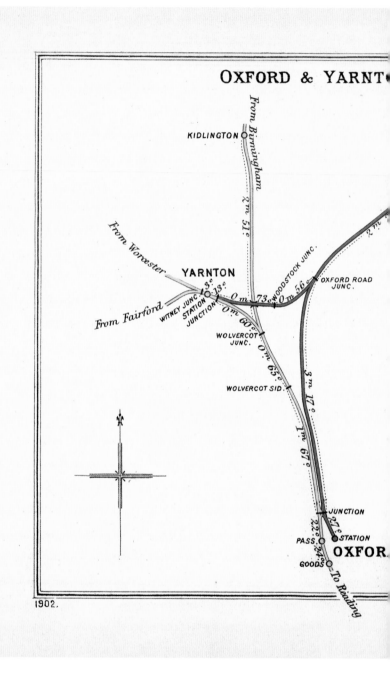

and several parts of Australia still have half-hour or quarter-hour offsets, and the People's Republic of China has rejected time zones altogether (pre-Communist China had five).

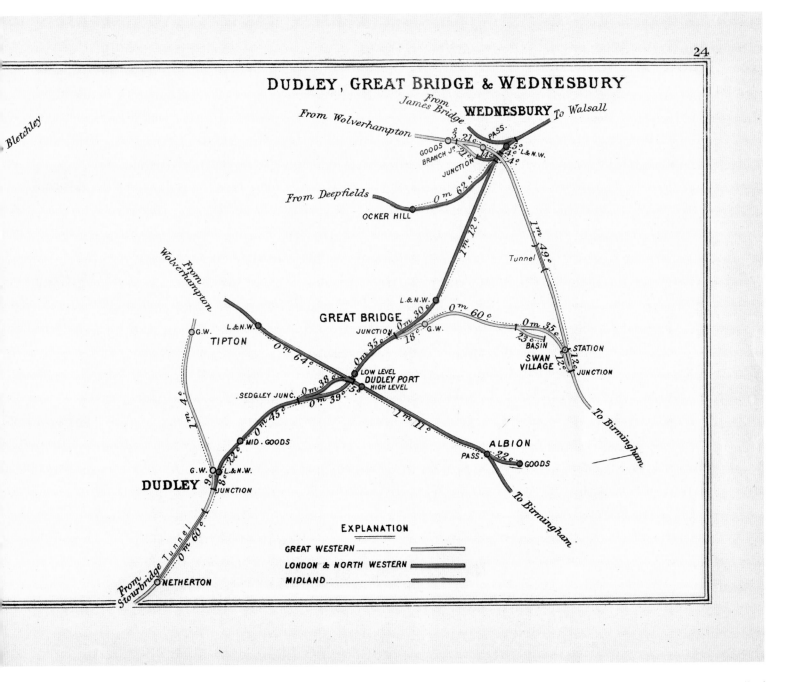

By 1954, due to waves of railway amalgamation followed by nationalisation, the RCH had only one remaining client, the British Transport Commission (BTC), and was wound up the following year. However, the BTC continued almost all of RCH's former activities, including the issuing of maps.

1902b

Mapping beneath the earth's surface

The world's first geological map at a national scale, of England and Wales, was completed in 1812 by William 'Strata' Smith (1769–1839). The son of an Oxfordshire blacksmith, Smith left school by the age of 11 and had worked with decidedly mixed success as a land- and mine surveyor, sea-defence builder and canal-company engineer while surveying his map, which would eventually be engraved and published in 1815 by John Cary (1755–1835). It was in part as a result of the Smith–Cary map's success that the organisation now known as the British Geological Survey – also the first of its kind – was established 20 years later as a branch of the Ordnance Survey.

The Ordnance Geological Survey's (OGS) founding director Henry De la Beche (1796–1855) is best remembered today for his pioneering watercolour picture and subsequent lithograph *Duria Antiquior* ('A more ancient Dorset', 1830), in which an ichthyosaur fights a plesiosaur as a primitive crocodile and turtle look on from the dubious shade of the waterside palm trees, and pterosaurs flap overhead. But De la Beche had demonstrated a superior understanding of geology through an 1830 book of 40 carefully annotated lithographs, more than a quarter of which were in colour. Titled *Sections and Views, Illustrative of Geological Phaenomena*, it included the direct ancestors of the geological section that was provided with the present map. De la Beche hastened to explain that *Sections and Views* was 'not intended to support or oppose any particular theory'. Indeed, he gently mocked the 'complacent' and 'amusing' manner in which geologists had spun theories from 'meagre data', extrapolating the formation of the whole planet 'with all the detail and air of eye-witnesses' based solely on observation of their own local districts. The implication was clear: that the science of geology needed to move beyond the isolated efforts of armchair amateurs, rock hounds and bored clergymen, and be coordinated nationally,

J.H. Blake et al./Geological Survey of England and Wales, *Oxford* (1908)

EXPLANATION of Geological Signs and Colours.

Alluvium

Brickearth

Valley Gravel

Plateau Gravel

Scale 200 feet to One Inch.

h^4 — Upper Greensand

h^3 — Gault (Clay)

CRETACEOUS — UPPER

h^2 — Lower Greensand

h — Shotover Sands (Wealden)

g^{14} — Purbeck Beds (Clay & Limestone)

$g^{13"}$ — Upper Portland Beds (Limestone & Sands)

$g^{13'}$ — Lower Portland Beds (Sands) & Hartwell Clay

LOWER

g^{12} — Kimeridge Clay

$g^{11"}$ $g^{11'}$ — Coral Rag & Oolite $g^{11'''}$ — Ampthill Clay

$g^{10"}$ — Calcareous grit and sand

Corallian

g^{10} — Oxford Clay and Kellaways Beds (Sand and Clay)

JURASSIC

g^9 — Cornbrash (Rubbly limestone)

g^8 — Forest Marble (Clay & Limestone)

g^7 — Great Oolite Series (Limestone and marl)

g^5 — Inferior Oolite (Limestone)

$g^{1\cdot3}$ — Lias (Clay & Limestone shown only in section)

This was among the first British geological maps to be printed in colour. Its predecessors were printed in black and white and hand-watercoloured.

or even at some higher, pan-Imperial or pan-European level. *Sections and Views* was followed in short order by De la Beche's *Geological Manual* (1831), aimed at helping the 'student . . . wandering in a wilderness of crude hypotheses or unsupported assumptions', which was reprinted twice before his appointment as head of the OGS.

Superficially, De la Beche's compatibility with the OS's general ethos seemed unproblematic: the son of a cavalry colonel, he had attended the Royal Military College at Marlow from age 13 to 15, at the height of the Napoleonic Wars. But in fact he was expelled for pro-French views, and 'opposed all forms of aristocratic privilege' (J.A. Secord), despite personally owning a slave plantation in Jamaica and opposing the abolition of slavery. He was also spectacularly divorced, and smeared as 'a great intriguer' and 'thoroughly incompetent' by the man who eventually replaced him as head of the Geological Survey of Great Britain and Ireland (as the OGS was renamed in 1845). Competent or not, De la Beche's success in governmental, indeed quasi-military employment at a time of immense social and political conservatism is evidence of his unique combination of talents: in particular, his ability to communicate scientific ideas clearly and interestingly in both visual and written form.

The practical value of having a government geological survey department was also clear-cut, insofar as the industrial revolution had brought unprecedented demand for coal and thus for methods of predicting where it might be safely and economically extracted from the ground; 'Strata' Smith had often made ends meet as a 'coal-hunter'. But geology – due to its implications for drainage, and therefore for hygiene – was also at the forefront of debates on epidemiology. When William Ormerod [1848] spoke on cholera to the Ashmolean Society, 'Professor Buckland . . . remarked that "the map of Oxford on which Mr Ormerod had marked by colours the prevalence of the disease, was in fact a geological one, the unhealthy districts coinciding with the alluvial soil"' (R.J. Morris). Among other things, the present map clearly shows the special characteristics of what geologists term the Summertown-Radley Terrace, the gravel island to which the develop-

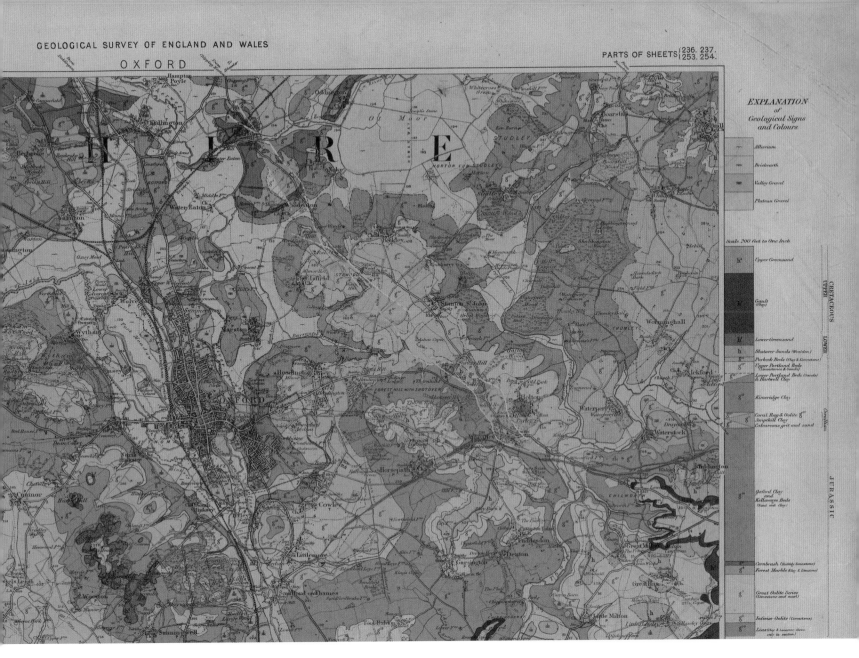

ment of both the original core of Oxford and its northern suburbs was constrained. This is also one of the first geological survey maps to have been printed in colour, with prior generations of maps down to 1900 being produced via the hand application of watercolour to printed OS base maps.

The BGS parted company from the OS in 1965, and is now a part of the Natural Environment Research Council. The scale of this map, 1 inch to 1 mile (i.e. 1:63,360) was used exclusively until 1972, when 1-inch and 1:50,000 scales began appearing side by side. The latter replaced the former completely in 1999. The BGS is now at the forefront of interactive digital mapping, with web-based 1:50,000 and 1:625,000 online maps that allow 'professional and amateur geologists to pull the information into virtual globe software which enables them to manipulate it further and mesh it with other types of data' (BBC News). It advises the British government on a range of geoscience-related issues, and is actively pursuing a transition from '2-D' mapping to '3-D' modelling.

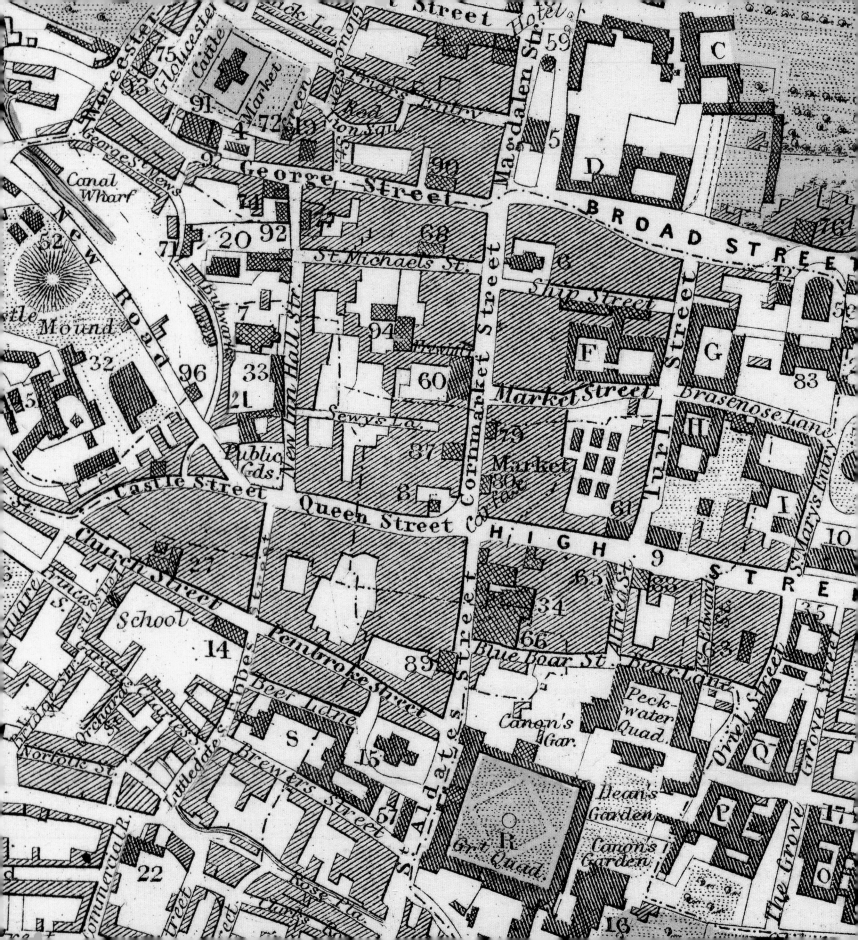

1909

Money for old rope – or pearls before swine?

This map is a salutary reminder of both the sheer cost of engraving, and of the key roles of the profit motive, and chicanery, in a wide array of cartographic enterprises. Produced from the very same *Weekly Dispatch Atlas* plate that was already out of date when Cassell's bought and used it in the mid 1860s [*c.*1862], it has been updated by someone in the employ of George Washington Bacon, who by this point had owned it for 40 years. At the time of its publication in 1909, the resulting map was inescapably an artefact of a bygone age: outmanoeuvred on the aesthetic front by Bartholomew [1895], on the business-model front by Stephens & Mackintosh [1898], and on both fronts by Baedeker [1910]. None of this, however, mattered one iota to George Washington Bacon.

Born in New York City around 1830 to two English parents, Bacon was apparently educated in the United States, for he was regarded as an American when he reappeared in the historical record in early 1860s London. He was styled a map publisher by 1862, and was appointed as a sales agent for Ordnance Survey maps in 1866, but went bankrupt the following year. With a note of shock, David Smith in the *Dictionary of National Biography* notes that the *Weekly Dispatch*/Cassell's maps Bacon bought in 1869 – not one of which had been surveyed later than 1862 – were 'presented as new and up to date' well into the twentieth century. Smith continues:

> Equally out-of-date material was acquired from other publishers. Most remarkably the firm published from about 1885 until the 1920s maps printed from copper plates first used in 1792. Bacon also commonly plagiarized the maps of others and in 1900 was judged to have infringed copyright. . . . He bought in all sorts of maps from other publishers, or simply plagiarized

J.W. Lowry/Bacon's Geographical Establishment, *Plan of Oxford* (1909)

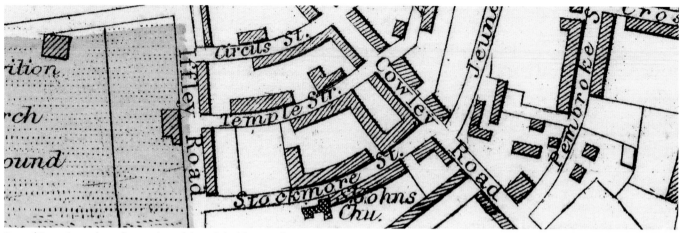

Part of Bacon's southward extension of the original Lowry plate.

them to create touring maps which, although occasionally excellent, were generally of dubious reliability and poor quality. The maximum life was wrung from every product and the same maps were repackaged under different titles in attractively coloured pictorial covers.

The present map's history is rather more complicated than the above narrative would tend to suggest. Bacon's people have added a column to the lettered key at right to reflect the establishment of Keble, Mansfield and Manchester colleges between 1870 and 1893, as well as the rebranding of the 1820s incarnation of Magdalen Hall as Hertford College in 1874. The copying of the original engraver's lettering style in this section would not fool an expert, but neither is it jarringly bad.

The numbered key to mostly non-university related sites has been extended even more dramatically, from 66 items to 99. This does not appear to have been done regularly, however, but in just two stages: with the structures referred to by numbers 97 through 99 (in a different hand to additions 66 through 96) all having been completed between 1893 and 1901. The 'Moved to Iffley Rd.' notation of the Cassell's era has also been corrected to read 'Moved to Cowley Rd.', in precisely the same clumsy manner as the earlier, incorrect

correction. In the map per se, the road-widening of Carfax in 1896 that led to the destruction of the main body of St Martin's Church is reflected, as is the development of Leckford Road (1873–85), Jericho and Park Town. The now-lost Drill Hall seen here on the east side of St Cross Road was described as early twentieth century by archaeologists Ruth Beckley and David Radford, and Bartholomew [1895] labelled the site as 'University Raquet Courts': further evidence of a serious post-1900 attempt to keep the present map's content current.

Most significantly – not least in terms of cost – the *Dispatch* plate has been significantly extended at its southern margin, and newly engraved to cover the recent streets and buildings in the suburb of Grandpont, including St Matthew's Church (consecrated 1891), and Cowley, as far south as Stockmore Street's 1859 'Iron Church' of St John the Evangelist, a minor tourist attraction until its demolition in 1896. In some ways, then, the Bacon Geographical Establishment was living up to its rather pompous name. Taking all his other activities into consideration, Bacon seems merely to have been perpetuating Georgian-era norms to an absurd distance into the modern age, and disguising them with a superficial touch of Barnum-esque showmanship. As such, he can be seen as a metaphor for America herself. He died solvent and happy at his home in Surrey at the age of 91.

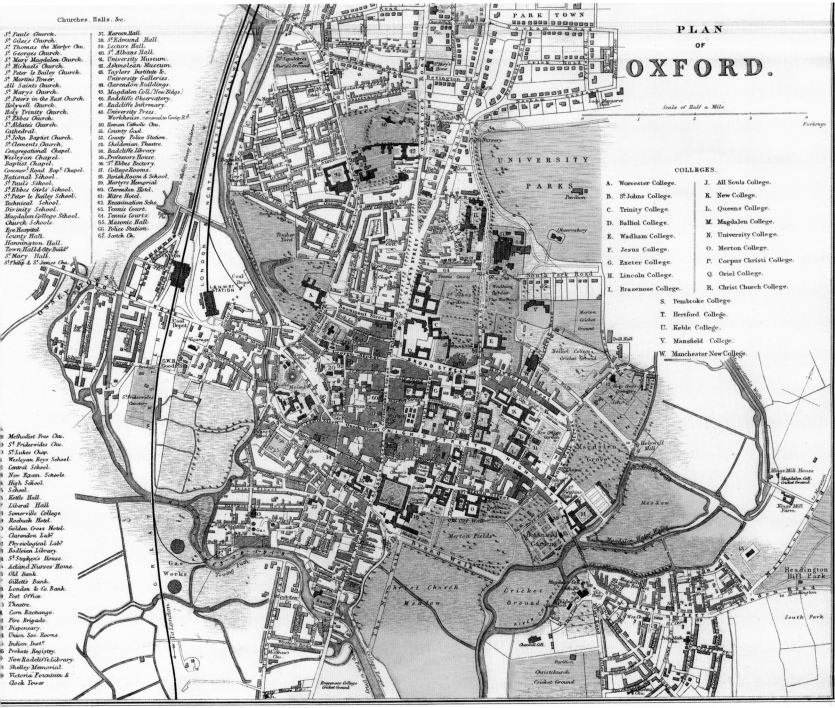

Churches, Halls, &c.

St Pauls Church.
St Giles's Church.
St Thomas the Martyr Chu.
St Georges Church.
St Mary Magdalen Church.
St Michaels Church.
St Peter le Bailey Church.
St Martins Tower.
All Saints Church.
St Marys Church.
St Peters in the East Church.
Holywell Church.
Holy Trinity Church.
St Ebbes Church.
St Aldates Church.
Cathedral.
St John Baptist Church.
St Clements Church.
Congregational Chapel.
Wesleyan Chapel.
Baptist Chapel.
Commer.l Road Bap.t Chapel.
St Pauls School.
National School.
St Ebbes Girls School.
St Peter le Bailey School.
Technical School.
Divinity School.
Magdalen College School.
Church Schools.
Eye Hospital.
County Hall.
Hannington Hall.
Town Hall & City Build.s
St Mary Hall.
St Philip & St James Chu.

37. Marcon Hall.
38. St Edmund Hall.
39. Lecture Hall.
40. St Albans Hall.
41. University Museum.
42. Ashmolean Museum.
43. Taylors Institute &c.
    University Galleries.
44. Clarendon Buildings.
45. Magdalen Coll. (New Bldgs.)
46. Radcliffe Observatory.
47. Radcliffe Infirmary.
48. University Press.
    Workhouse..removed to Cowley R.d
50. Roman Catholic Chu.
51. County Gaol.
52. County Police Station.
53. Sheldonian Theatre.
54. Radcliffe Library.
55. Professors House.
56. St Ebbes Rectory.
57. College Rooms.
58. Parish Room & School.
59. Martyrs Memorial.
60. Clarendon Hotel.
61. Mitre Hotel.
62. Examination Schs.
63. Tennis Courts.
64. Tennis Court.
65. Masonic Hall.
66. Police Station.
67. Scotch Ch.

Methodist Free Chu.
St Frideswides Chu.
St Lukes Chap.
Wesleyan Boys School.
Central School.
New Exam. Schools.
High School.
School.
Kettle Hall.
Liberal Hall.
Somerville College.
Roebuck Hotel.
Golden Cross Hotel.
Clarendon Lab.y
Physiological Lab.y
Bodleian Library.
St Stephen's House.
Acland Nurses Home.
Old Bank.
Gilletts Bank.
London & Co. Bank.
Post Office.
Theatre.
Corn Exchange.
Fire Brigade.
Dispensary.
Union Soc. Rooms.
Indian Inst.t
Probate Registry.
New Radcliffe Library.
Shelley Memorial.
Victoria Fountain &
Clock Tower

Scale of Half a Mile

COLLEGES.

A. Worcester College.
B. St Johns College.
C. Trinity College.
D. Balliol College.
E. Wadham College.
F. Jesus College.
G. Exeter College.
H. Lincoln College.
I. Brasenose College.

J. All Souls College.
K. New College.
L. Queens College.
M. Magdalen College.
N. University College.
O. Merton College.
P. Corpus Christi College.
Q. Oriel College.
R. Christ Church College.

S. Pembroke College.
T. Hertford College.
U. Keble College.
V. Mansfield College.
W. Manchester New College.

Geographical Establishment. Edin.o

Hall

Wadham

St. John's Garden.

Garden

Balliol

Cricket Ground

Savile Rd.

St. John's College

Trinity Garden

Wadham College

Manchester College

Jowett Walk

St Cross Road

Taylor Inst.

Martyrs' Mem.

Trinity College

St. Stephen's House

Music Rooms

Holywell Street

The Slipe

New Coll

Balliol College

St. Mary Magd.

Broad Street

Indian Inst.

Clarendon Building

Sheldonian Theatre

New College

New Coll. Gard.

Magdalen St.

Old Ashmol. Mus.

Bodln. Divinity Libry. School

Hertf'd Coll.

New College Lane

St. Michael's

Ship Str.

Turl Street

Radcliffe

Camera

All Souls College

Queen's College

St. Peter's in the East

Corn-market Str.

Jesus College

Exeter Coll.

Brasenose L.

St. Edmund Hall

Union Rooms

Crewen Ct.

Market Str.

Brasenose College

Lincoln Coll.

Radcliffe Squ.

St. Mary's

High Street

University College

Logic Lane

New Coll. Studs

Magdalen Coll. School

St. Martin's & All Saints

St. Mary Hall

Grove Street

Non- Exam. Schools

King Street

Car- Green Str.

High Street

Carfax

Bank

Alfred Str.

St Edward Str.

Oriel Str.

Merton Street

Logic Lane

Long Wall Street

Municipal Builds.

St. Aldates Str.

Bear Lane

Blue Boar Lane

Peckwater

Oriel Coll.

The Grove

Merton College

St. Alban Hall

Rose Lane

Post Office

Quad.

Corpus Christi College

Pembroke Str.

Beef Lane

St. Aldates

Christ Church College

Cathedral

Dead Man's Walk

Bot. Gard

Pembroke College

Brewer's Street

Merton Fields

1910

A German tourist map of Oxford
on the eve of the World War

There are few better-known names in the history of tourism than Baedeker, the guidebook publisher established in Germany in 1827 as part of a multigenerational publishing empire that stretched back into the eighteenth century, albeit originally spelled Bädeker. Its change of direction was largely the result of its buyout of F.F. Röhling, whose *Handbuch für Schnell-reisende* ('Handbook for rapid travellers') was reissued in revised form by Karl Baedeker (1801–1859). However, the guidebooks published in Britain starting in 1836 by John Murray III (1808–1892) also seem to have played a part in Baedeker's aesthetic decision-making, and in particular his fateful choice of red bindings. Much of the guidebook firm's superb reputation, however, was the result of changes made by Fritz Baedeker (1844–1925), who took the reins in his mid twenties. Fritz's three critical early decisions were to divest from the bookselling business; to move the firm's headquarters to Leipzig, a city arguably as central to German publishing as

London was to British banking; and to facilitate collaboration between two distinguished cartographers: Ernst Debes, who had been based in Gotha, and Eduard Wagner, from Darmstadt. The resultant Wagner & Debes Geographical Establishment, located next door to Baedeker's own offices, would go on to produce maps that *The New Yorker* magazine once praised as the best in the world. You may make your own judgement.

Prior to Fritz Baedeker's time, his firm's guides had concentrated on Germany, Italy, Switzerland, Paris and London, but this lens was soon to be dramatically widened. Before the outbreak of the First World War, Baedeker's guides had covered much of North America, Asia, the Eastern Mediterranean, Russia and Scandinavia. Around 30 per cent of this output would be in the English language. It is not clear whether Baedeker was implicated in Wagner & Debes's decision to produce their antiquarian map reconstructions of twelfth-century Lincoln and Oxford on one sheet, which were

Wagner & Debes Geographical Establishment, 'Oxford', from Karl Baedeker, *Great Britain* (1910)

published in London by Macmillan in 1887; in this case, the Oxford map was similar to – though far less detailed than – the Weller plan shown in the Introduction, above.

This map's use of large contiguous blocks of cool colour is appealing; reassuring. A city that looks fundamentally like all the other cities in the guidebook is *ipso facto* not a place of danger, disease or disorientation. Unlike the lengthy series of maps that began with the *Weekly Dispatch Atlas* [*c.*1862, 1909] and therefore with Hoggar [1850], there is no longer any pretence that this is a map for 'general purposes'. The map-user is to arrive, see the sights, send a postcard and go away again, ideally within the hours of daylight. A rare lapse in the pattern of omissions, the Gloucester Green cattle market, has been labelled at a peculiar angle; perhaps it has been mentioned only as a place particularly to be avoided. Osney Town and St Ebbe's have both been masterfully framed out, along with Folly Bridge – clearly well past its sell-by date, touristically speaking. In effect, the city of Oxford is merely binding matter for educational institutions, and educational institutions stand virtually alone as loci of sightseeing.

In 1914, Oxford's colleges rapidly emptied of students and were transformed into hospitals and officer-training facilities. In all, nearly 15,000 university men served in the war, and one in five was killed. But as Virginia Woolf once remarked, human character itself had changed fundamentally in a 'modernist' direction by the end of 1910; and the devastating brutality of the war was an effect of this change, not its cause. It is doubtful that there was any significant military use of Baedeker guides to Britain by the enemy during the Great War, as neither invasion nor precision bombing was seriously contemplated. In the Second World War, however, Luftwaffe terror bombing of cultural sites in England including Canterbury, Bath, Norwich, Exeter and York commenced in April 1942, and was christened the 'Baedeker blitz' or 'Baedeker raids', apparently because Nazi foreign office spokesman Baron Gustav Braun von Stumm remarked that the German air force would bomb every building in England marked in Baedeker's with three stars. The Baedeker headquarters and entire archive were flattened by the RAF in December of the following year.

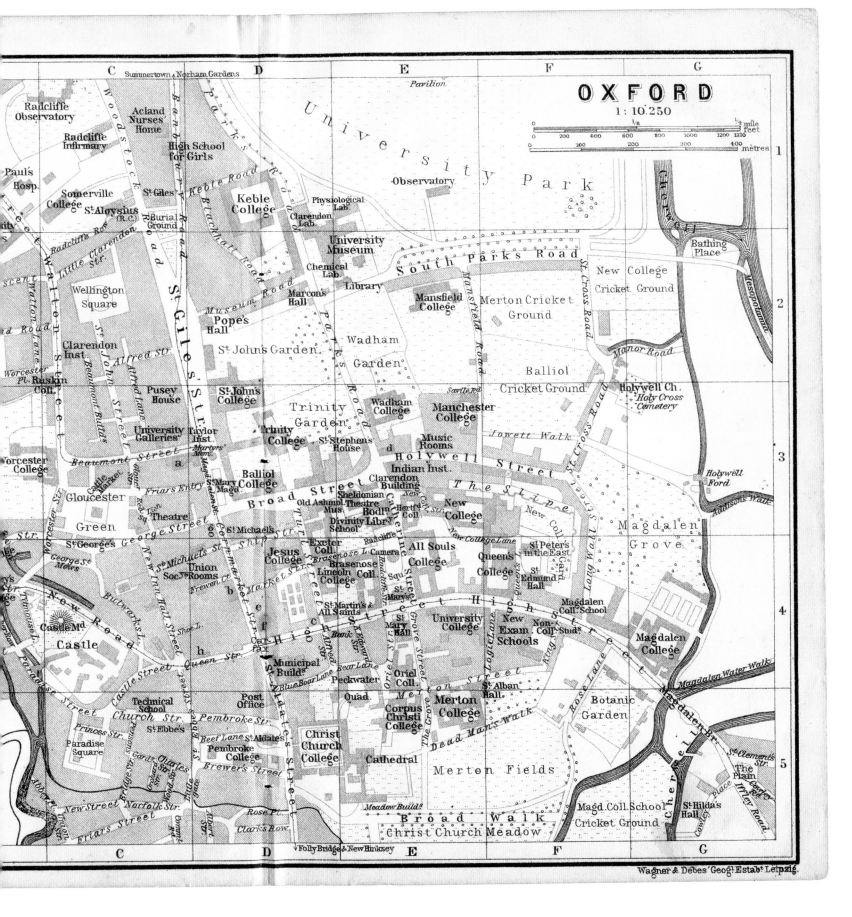

OXFORD

1 : 10.250

VIEW from the Roof of the BODLEIAN LIBRARY

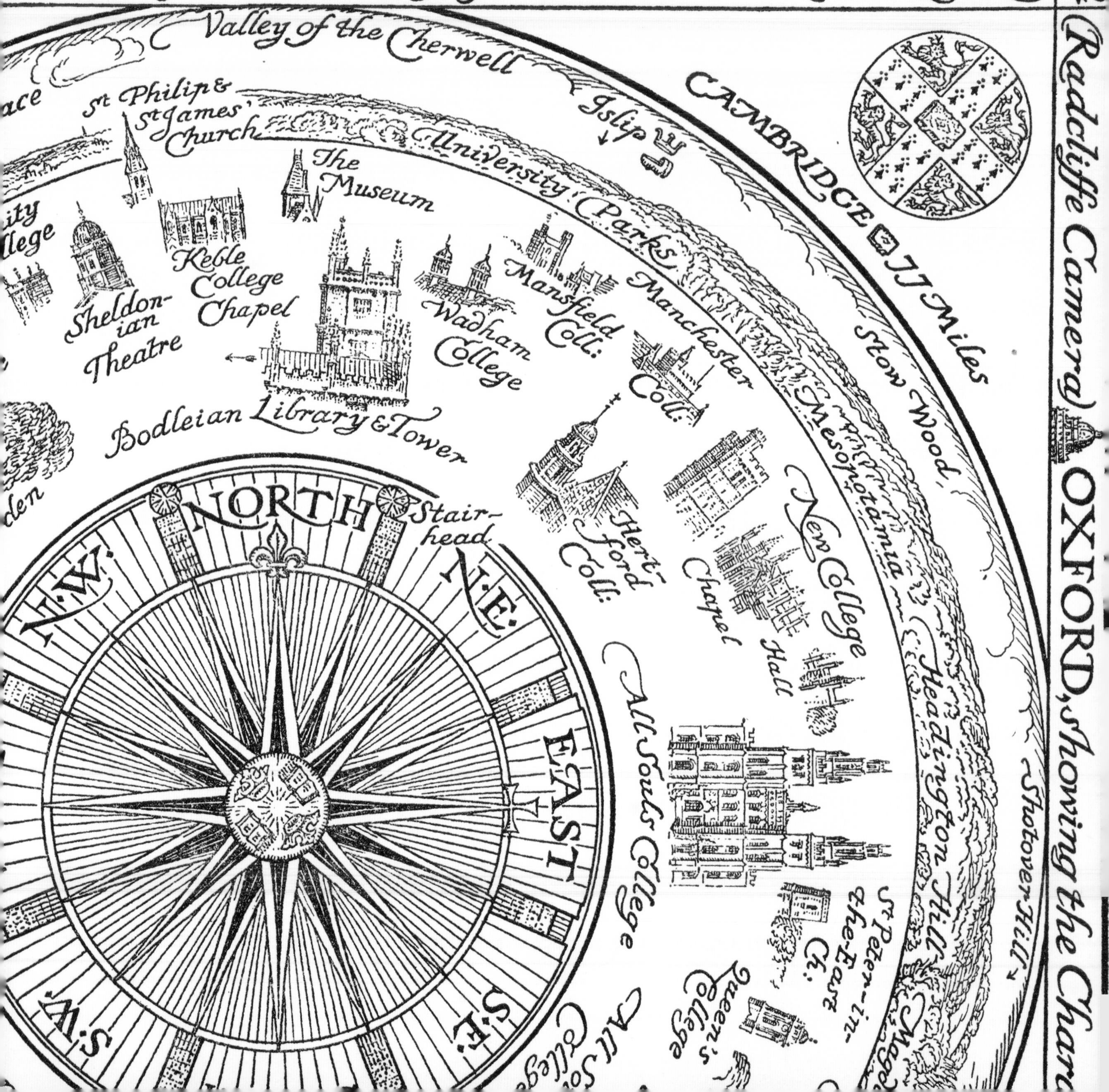

(Radcliffe Camera) OXFORD, showing the Cher...

Valley of the Cherwell

St Philip & St James' Church

The Museum

University Parks

Islip

CAMBRIDGE 77 Miles

Stow Wood

...ity ...llege

Sheldon-ian Theatre

Keble College Chapel

Wadham College

Mansfield Coll:

Manchester Coll:

Mesopotamia

New College Chapel

Hall

Headington Hill

Shotover Hill

Bodleian Library & Tower

Hertford Coll:

Stair-head

NORTH

N.W.

N.E.

EAST

S.W.

S.E.

All Souls College

All Souls College

Queen's College

Queen's College

St Peter-in-the-East Ch:

1917

The shock of the old

More than any other place I have known, Oxford has inspired a regular or perhaps constant looping back to the past, not in a vague or general sense but to specific moments. Simply within the compass of the present book, we have seen Aggas copied by Speed and Loggan, de Gomme (or someone like him) inspire Taylor, Taylor beget Faden, and Faden finally chewed up and spat out again by Moule, himself an obsessive neo-Gothicist. Hoggar begets the *Weekly Dispatch Atlas*, and Cassell's atlases, and Bacon's, while genuine innovators like Ogilby and Williams and indeed Hoggar are damned by faint praise.

Here, we have an item that at first glance seems inspired almost solely by the map of Barker's Oxford panorama of a century earlier [1807], for its stated purpose is essentially the same. But there is no panorama, save what external reality itself can provide; the viewer who puts his hat on or feels a touch of vertigo will ideally, in this case, do so because he really is out of doors and really observing the scene from a great height.

And what lies *beyond* the view? Nothing but other universities, each represented not just in terms of compass direction and distance, but heraldically: my own undergraduate alma mater, Birmingham, with its mermaid, and the respective crosses of Cambridge, London and Bristol. Is this magnanimity? Egalitarianism? Or an assertion that, as the oldest British university, Oxford is at the centre of the universe of universities, with all newer universities – especially Cambridge – revolving around it? Suddenly, older antecedents than Barker come to mind thickly and quickly: not just Pawley, Donne and Cole [1805], but Andreas Cellarius's splendid seventeenth-century charts of the Copernican universe, and the Hereford

Falconer Madan/E.H. New, *Pictorial key to the view from the Roof of the Bodleian Library
(Radcliffe Camera) Oxford, showing the Characteristic Features of the principal buildings & the landscape
as they appear from the Eight Divisions formed by the Buttresses that support the dome* (1917)

Edmund Hort New was a prolific and highly respected practitioner of the Arts and Crafts style in illustration.

Mappa Mundi depicting a round, possibly flat world with the Red Sea actually coloured in red and Jerusalem at the centre. Mansfield and Manchester colleges are here too, tiny asteroids desperately reflecting the light of the medieval and therefore real Oxford from their pseudo-battlemented surfaces, bright as two new pins.

We have already met Falconer Madan [1878], whose motivations for creating new paper ephemera – and for part-automating the answers to out-of-town library visitors' frequently asked questions – are not far to seek. His partner in this map, Edmund Hort New (1871–1931), was an altogether more complex case. From a well-to-do Quaker family in Worcestershire, New trained at the Birmingham Municipal School of Art and thereafter focused on book illus-

tration. By his mid twenties, he was operating in the upper echelons of the Arts and Crafts movement; his career included a stint with William Morris's Kelmscott Press, and one of his least glamorous positions was as the drawing teacher to the future Lawrence of Arabia. The scores of books New illustrated included the 1898 Bodley Head edition of Izaak Walton's *The Compleat Angler*, J.W. Mackail's 1901 biography of Morris, and his own *New Loggan Guide to the Oxford Colleges*. New's masterpiece, however, may have been the immense neo-Jacobean photogravure view *The City & Port of London from the Borough of Southwark showing the River & the Principal Buildings between the Temple & the Tower Bridge A.D. 1919*, at which time he gave his address as 17 Worcester Place, Oxford.

PICTORIAL KEY to the VIEW from the Roof of the BODLEIAN LIBRARY

This is the Top

Radcliffe Camera) OXFORD, showing the Characteristic Features of the

PRINCIPAL BUILDINGS & the LANDSCAPE as they appear from the

Eight Divisions formed by the Buttresses that support the DOME

F. Madan & E.H. New inv.

E.H. New del. AD 1917

Bladon Heath • Round Castle • Begbroke • Inn • 204 • 201 • 194 • Inn

Gosford • 215 • 283 • Inn • Noke • Horton • 193 • 198

Ivy Ho. • 224 • Lock • 230 • 315 • Stud

Yarnton • 210 • Inn • Water Eaton • Manor Ho. • Wood Eaton • Beckley • Roman Villa • 210 • Menr

216 • Oxford Rd Halt • 280 • Inn

YARNTON STA. • Cutslow • 233 • 195 • Manor Ho. • Stowood • Woodperry • 259

Worton • Cassington • 221 • Pear tree Hill • Dukes Lock • 236 • Cemetery • 192 • Elsfield • 419 • 230

225 • 203 • King's • Weir • Pixey Mead • Upper • Halt • 206 • Ho. • Sunnymead • Summertown • Inn • 206 • Stanton St. John • 358 • 338 • Inn

Inn • Hagley Pool • Lower • Halt • Inn • Ferry • Manor Ho • Bayswater Brook • 191

Great Wood • Godstow Nunnery • Port Meadow • Park Town • R. Cherwell • Marston • Barton • Foresth

Wytham • Godstow Lock • Hall • Headington • 203 • Headington Quarry • 292 • 338

Swinford • Abbey • Well • 206 • University Park • Ho. • 298

Wytham Hill • Wytham Park • 478 • Binsey • Inn • Bathing Pl. & Ferry • Headington Hill • New Headington • Shotover H • Hill Ho

Farmoor • Woodend • 245 • Medley Weir • Halt • College • Shotover Hill • 562

Skinner's Bridge • 206 • Botley • 187 • STA • 322

Filchamstead • 227 • Osney • OXFORD • Cathl Holly Br • Workho • Asylum • St. Clements • St Bartholomew's Hospital • 516 • Wheatley

Dean Co. • Cumnor Hill • 378 • Pound • N. Hinksey • Ferry • New Hinksey • Barracks • Horsepath • 379

Chawley • Reservoirs • 284 • Cowley • Military College • Industrial Sch.

Heath Eaton • 359 • Hurst Hill • 520 • 415 • S. Hinksey • Abingdon Rd Halt • Lock • Iffley • 264 • Cowley • Garsington Br Halt • Stay Ba

Cumnor • 385 • Whitebarn Ho. • Hinksey Hill • Egrove • Ch. • 234 • 224 • Northfield Brook • 42

Old Golf Course • 366 • Rose Isle Inn • STA. • Littlemore • Inn • Ho

Bessels Leigh • 355 • 339 • Boars Hill • 444 • Kennington • Inn • Asylum Inn • Sandford on Thames • arsingt

Wootton • 315 • 366 • Bagley Wood Ho. • Little London • Lock • Inn • Manor Ho

Bessels Leigh Manor • 319 • Foxcombe Hill • 370 • 189 • 218

312 • Tubney wood Park • 256 • Bayworth • 306 • 258 • Golf Co. • 198 • Toot Baldon • Chipping

263 • Sunningwell • 254 • Manor Ho • 292 • Inn

Dry Sandford • 240 • 289 • Radley Park • 226 • Baldon Row • Pebble Hill • 289

264 • Pewit Ho. • St Peter's College • Inn • Ho. • March Baldon • Inn Ho.

Tubney warren Ho. • Cothill Hospl • Cholswell Golf Co. • 216 • 213 • Radley • 175 • Nuneham Courtenay • Chislehampton

Oakley Ho. • Gosford • 247 Inn • 219 • Inn • STA. • Camo Court Brook

245 • Inn • 253 • 230 • Shippon • Manor Ho. • 185 • 195 • Northcourt • Wick Hall • 193 • Rectory • Lake • Camo Court • 217

Sheepstead Ho. • St Helen Without • Workho • R.C.Convent • 197 • Nuneham Park • The Mansion • 240 • 175

1930

Motor city

Many places that became 'conurbations' in the Edwardian era reached that state as a result of classic tram-led suburbanisation, in which clerical workers from city-centre industries such as banking, insurance, law and shipping moved ever farther outward in search of decent, affordable housing. Oxford did develop a modest horse-drawn tramway network between 1881 and 1887, supplemented by horse-buses to Iffley Turn, Wolvercote Turn, Cumnor Hill and Headington; and the trams had become double-deckers by 1910. But their electrification – planned for 1907 – was an administrative disaster and had not been executed seven years later, when the now hopelessly misnamed Oxford Electric Tramways Company was granted the exclusive right to run a fleet of 24 city motor-buses instead. In any case, the economy of the city centre remained dominated by the retail and hospitality industries and the university, all of which provided significant amounts of housing for their lower-paid workers, while brewery workers mostly lived in central slum areas within walking distance of their places of employment. Oxford's need for clerks was also small, in comparison to places where the abovementioned high-level service industries predominated.

Nevertheless, and despite the stark absence of a retail centre of its own, the Cowley/Iffley district's population increased by 122 per cent between 1921 and 1931, with 11,000 people moving into the area from other parts of the country. By 1938, the population of Oxford east of the Cherwell surpassed that of the old city and all of its northern, southern and western suburbs combined. This mushroom growth had proceeded not because of, but in spite of, Oxford's transport infrastructure, and was largely due to the efforts of a single person, carmaker W.R. Morris (1877–1963).

From a landless ex-farming family with roots in Witney

John Bartholomew & Son Ltd/Great Western Railway, *The existing routes operated by the City of Oxford Motor Services Co. Ltd . . .* (1930)

and Headington, the teenaged Morris used his £4 of capital to establish a cycle-repair shop in his parents' house at 16 James Street, Cowley. Educated at the Cowley village school, he 'had no formal training except for an evening class in engineering at the Oxford schools of technology, which he attended only twice' (R.J. Overy). After a failure in motorcycle manufacturing in a converted stables in Holywell Street, he established a combined car dealership, car-hire service and garage in Longwall Street. It was Morris's 1913 launch of a renegade, unlicensed motor-bus company to compete with the city's slow and strike-prone horse-tram service that led directly to the transformation of the latter into a motor-bus company the following year. From this point, Morris's rise was so rapid as to almost defy explanation. Having designed his first car as recently as 1912, he took over the disused Cowley Military College [1876] as his manufacturing headquarters, and by the time this map was made he was producing one-third of all British cars, in a factory complex that covered 80 acres and employed 4,000 people. Morris Motors' share capitalisation rose from £104,000 in 1919 to £5 million in 1926. Ironically, the GWR's Garsington Road Halt – which had operated from 1908 to 1915 in an unsuccessful effort to help the railway compete against other companies' new rural motor-bus services – reopened in expanded form as Morris Cowley Station in 1928, to serve the car factory's hordes of workers, many of whom could now commute in from Banbury. Cars made in Cowley for export were also sent by train to Brentford Dock in London.

This map, produced as part of a 1930 agreement between GWR and the former tramway company (renamed City of Oxford Motor Services Ltd in 1920) aimed at 'more efficient and profitable working of road and rail traffic . . . secured by coordination' between the two companies, both of which had omnibuses 'operating in the districts outside the City of Oxford'. Ten years after the banishing of the absurd 'Tramways' moniker, it now returned, as the coordination venture was named the Oxford Tramways Syndicate Ltd. Based on a George Washington Bacon touring map [1909], lifted with Bacon's customary shamelessness from

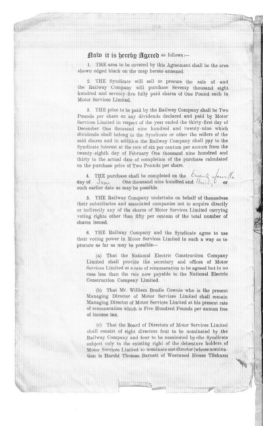

Bartholomew's – and so old that it still labelled the Morris works as 'Military College' – its purple-coloured additions clearly indicate the so-called Tramways' aggressive expansion into rural areas since 1916 that had begun with services to Abingdon. By 1933, backed up by railway money, this would be followed by takeovers of rival rural-bus companies in Aylesbury, Bicester and Watlington.

From 1931, considerable city-planning brainpower was being taken up by the question of how the city's further expansion could be checked, or even reversed, with Thomas Sharp's influential *Oxford Replanned* (1948) recommending that the Morris operation be broken up altogether. Fortunately for the working people of East Oxford, nothing of the kind actually happened, and 'Plant Oxford' is now BMW's manufacturing headquarters for the Mini brand.

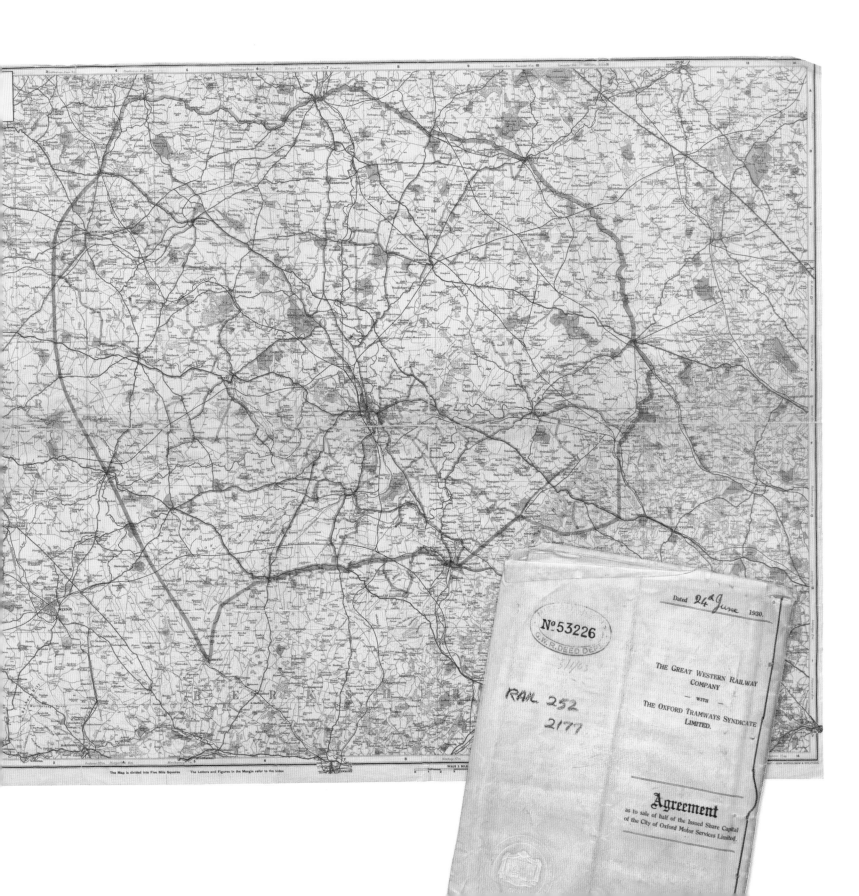

Dated 24ᵗʰ June 1930.

THE GREAT WESTERN RAILWAY
COMPANY

— WITH —

THE OXFORD TRAMWAYS SYNDICATE
LIMITED.

Agreement

as to sale of half of the Issued Share Capital
of the City of Oxford Motor Services Limited.

Sparrowgap
Bridge

EL.
SUB
STN.

Langford Lane

1950

Oxford takes wing

The inception of the Kidlington Aerodrome, now known as Oxford Airport or more controversially as London Oxford Airport, was a 1932 leader in the *Oxford Times* newspaper, which pointed out that 'cities having an airport . . . reap direct benefits' from the country's burgeoning networks of air-mail and air-passenger services, and urged the Council to build one. The construction of a city-owned Municipal Aerodrome was duly agreed the following year. The freeholds on 390 acres of farmland 7 miles northwest of the city centre were secured for just under £20,000 (around £5.6 million at today's prices) from three local landowners, one of whom was the 10th Duke of Marlborough. Alternative names for the chosen site included Campsfield and Thrupp, after hamlets located immediately to its southwest and northeast, respectively.

As with so many other peacetime initiatives, however, the long build-up to the Second World War pushed the project in unanticipated directions. In 1937, two years before the Municipal Aerodrome was first licensed for civil use, the RAF Volunteer Reserve leased part of it for 12 years and established a training flight of Hawker Audaxes, Hawker Hinds and Miles Magisters. The Magister, the first plane designed specifically as an RAF trainer, was built fairly close by, in Woodley, Berkshire. The other two types – both obsolescent biplane bombers – were chosen for training on the grounds that they were one step up in difficulty from both the Magister and the much-loved de Havilland Tiger Moth, which was produced by the Morris works in Cowley.

Soon after the outbreak of the war, a much larger training unit (No. 15 Service Flight Training School) flying more than 100 aircraft, mostly lease-lend North American Harvards, transferred to Kidlington from RAF Brize Norton. By the spring of 1941, RAF Kidlington was clocking up nearly 7,000

J. Campbell Riddell, *City of Oxford – Oxford Airport* (1950) training hours per month, one of the most impressive figures for facilities of its kind. Unsurprisingly, the Luftwaffe attacked the airfield several times, dropping at least two dozen bombs. The training school was struck another blow in January 1941, when Amy Johnson (b. 1903), heroine of peacetime exploits including the first female solo flight from Britain to Australia and winner of the 1932 Segrave Trophy, disappeared en route to Kidlington while delivering a new training aircraft.

Four months later, Prime Minister Winston Churchill came to the aerodrome to interview the 14th Duke of Hamilton regarding the recent capture of Deputy Führer Rudolf Hess, who had flown solo to Scotland in an attempt to meet the Duke and negotiate a peace deal. Hess's expectations that Hamilton might be a Nazi sympathiser or 'peacenik' were ill-founded, however, as the latter had been an RAF officer for 14 years and was actually on duty as a wing commander at Turnhouse near Edinburgh, tracking Hess's plane as it arrived. Beyond this, Hamilton was an unusually accomplished pilot who in 1933 had cheated death by a whisker while making the first flight over Mount Everest, as part of an expedition financed by Lucy, Lady Houston, an eccentric septuagenarian former showgirl, suffragette and inveterate hater of the Labour Party. Hamilton was quickly cleared of any wrongdoing, with the Air Minister describing his handling of the Hess affair as 'in every respect honourable and proper'. Coincidentally, some of the wreckage of Hess's plane was briefly put on public display in St Giles, having been brought south by road for inspection by Oxford's No. 50 Maintenance Unit, RAF, which was closely connected with the Cowley works.

The final German air raid on RAF Kidlington took place in 1941, though training deaths among personnel from Britain and several Commonwealth countries continued; some of the victims were buried at Botley [1893]. As war gave way to Cold War, the armed forces remained, but shared Kidlington with an increasing number of other users, including civilian hobbyists and Oxford University's officer-training flight, which had

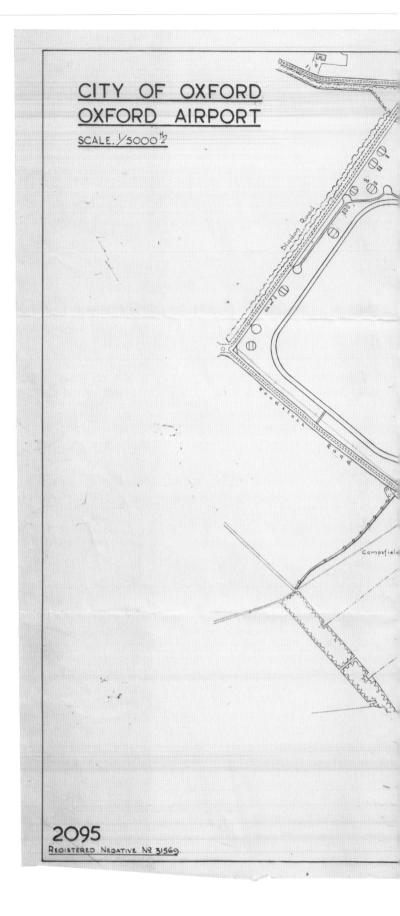

CITY OF OXFORD
OXFORD AIRPORT
SCALE. 1/5000th

2095
REGISTERED NEGATIVE No 31569.

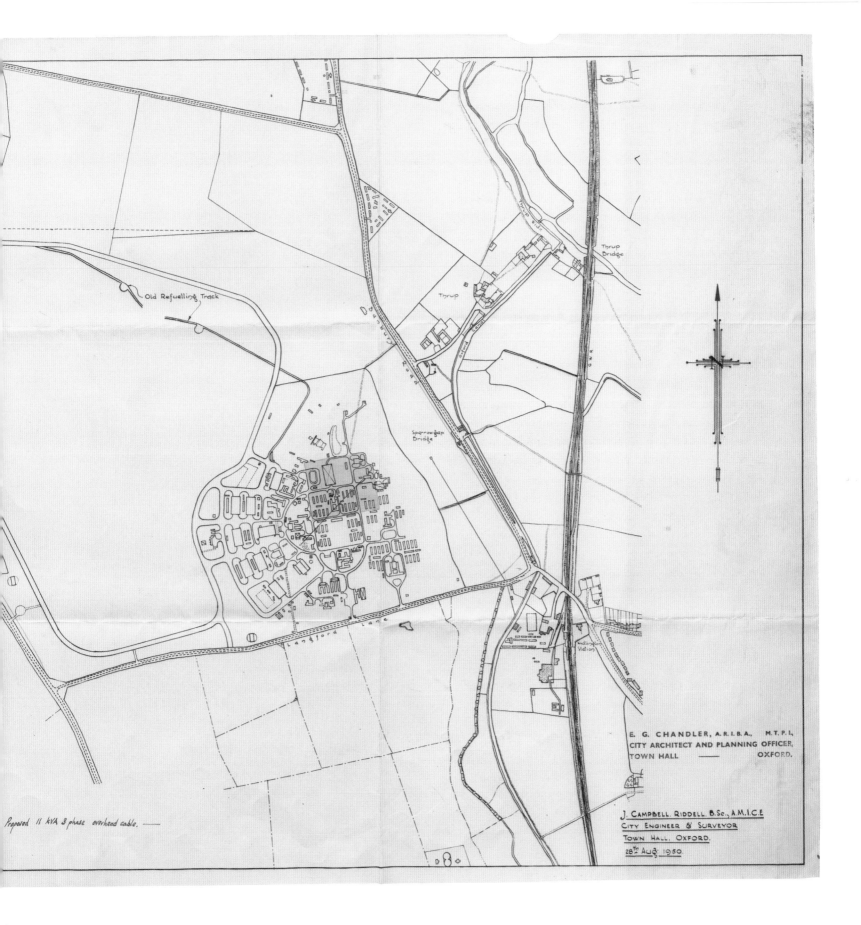

Old Refuelling Track

Thrup
Bridge

Thrup

Thrup

G W R

Danbury Road

Oxford Lane

Sparrowgap
Bridge

Langford Lane

Kidlington
Station

Proposed 11 kVA 3 phase overhead cable.

E. G. CHANDLER, A.R.I.B.A., M.T.P.I,
CITY ARCHITECT AND PLANNING OFFICER,
TOWN HALL ——— OXFORD.

J. CAMPBELL. RIDDELL. B.Sc., A.M.I.C.E.
CITY ENGINEER & SURVEYOR
TOWN HALL. OXFORD.
28ᵗʰ Aug. 1950

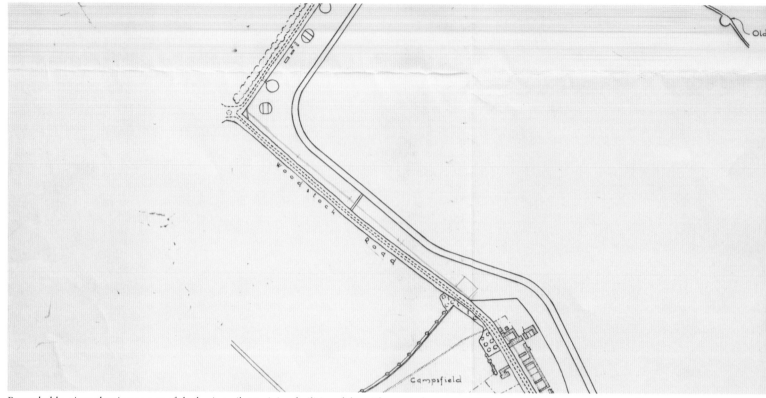

Remarkably, given that it was one of the busiest pilot-training facilities of the mid-twentieth century, Kidlington's airstrips were grass until 1975.

previously been based in Abingdon. Passenger services to the Isle of Jersey commenced in 1949, priced at £8 return, and the last military tenants, No. 96 Maintenance Unit, RAF, departed two years later. Though full civilian control of the airport would not be resumed until 1959, it was in this context of demilitarisation that the present map was produced. Specifically, the licensing of civil aerodromes in the British Empire was authorised by the Air Navigation Act 1920, as amended in 1936 and 1947. The associated regulations still require that OS-based airport maps be filed for licensing purposes; that '[c]hanges in the physical characteristics of the aerodrome including the erection of new buildings and alterations to existing buildings or to visual aids shall not be made without prior approval'; and that licensees immediately notify the relevant authorities of 'any material change' in the landing area's surface or approach characteristics.

Despite the utopian visions of the 1930s, most visitors to Oxford still arrive by surface transport, and the airport is principally important as a training centre, now as in the past. Indeed, it has trained around 20,000 commercial pilots for more than 80 different airlines since the 1960s, when it acquired the UK's first privately owned flight simulator for four-engine jets. It was also the first British flight school allowed to grant both commercial pilots' and helicopter pilots' licences to candidates with no practical experience of flying prior to their courses beginning. Thus, by 1968, despite receiving relatively few passengers, Oxford's airport was the second busiest in the nation after Heathrow in terms of the sheer number of take-offs and landings. This business was a direct outgrowth of the post-war Oxford Aeroplane Club

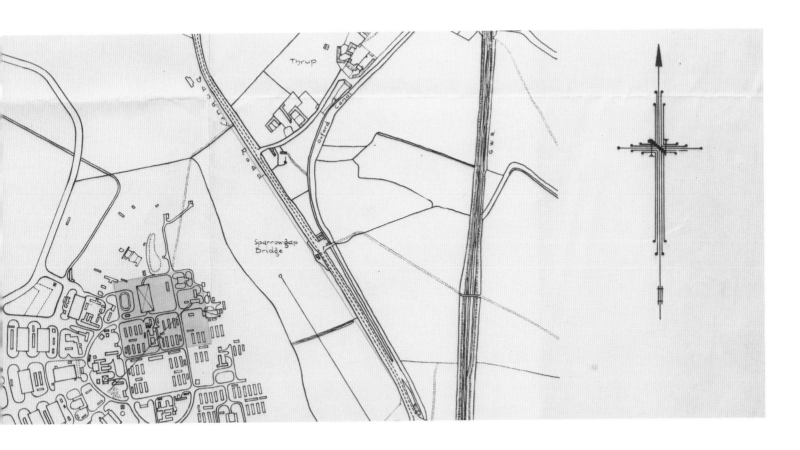

(itself a successor to the amateur Oxford Flying Club that met at Kidlington for a brief period in 1939), and was all the more remarkable in that Kidlington's runway was of grass until 1975.

In 1971, a Kidlington-based aircraft dealership called CSE Aviation Ltd supplied and kitted out the Piper Aztec in which Sheila Scott OBE (1922–1988) became the first person to fly solo over the North Pole in a light aircraft; ten years later, CSE bought the airport's freehold for £1.4 million, representing a profit for Oxford City Council of around 45 per cent on what they had paid for the site originally, adjusted for inflation. Today, the airport as seen here would be scarcely recognisable, due to a spate of major runway extensions and new construction since 1988, leading it to have a much smaller number of much larger buildings. Training still accounts for more than

a third of its total activity, and recent attempts to offer passenger services between Oxford and Edinburgh have been beset by administrative problems.

The Duke of Hamilton's friend Lady Houston, who contributed generous sums to the Schneider Trophy seaplane races as well as the Everest expedition, was reportedly so appalled by the Abdication Crisis of 1936 that she starved herself to death. Hamilton, though himself educated at Balliol, was Chancellor of the University of St Andrews from 1948 until his death in 1973. The remains and Airspeed Oxford aircraft of Amy Johnson, who was probably downed by 'friendly fire' over the Thames Estuary, have never been located. Polly Vacher MBE (b. 1944), described as a 'resident' of the airport on its website, topped Scott's feat in 2003–04, by flying solo over both poles.

1965

A new system of mapping for aerial spying

Over the course of the twentieth century, Oxford University contributed more than its fair share of personnel to military mapping efforts, not least among them Colonel T.E. Lawrence of Jesus College and Arabia. The resultant web of connections became more elaborate after 1940, when enemy bombing led to the Topographical Section of the Naval Intelligence Division being evacuated to the university's School of Geography. Part of Naval Intelligence's Geographical Section – which since the 1910s had produced map-rich handbooks on the geography, geology, history and ethnology of various parts of the world – the Topographical Section passed from naval to inter-services control due to increasing demand for combined-operations planning over the course of the Second World War. In this context, it is perhaps less surprising that one of the more ambitious cartographic experiments of the pre-digital age was launched in 1961 by Oxford University's Soil Science Labora-

tory in cooperation with the UK's Military Engineering Experimental Establishment (known as MEXE), located in Christchurch, Hampshire.

As explained in MEXE report no. 945, circulated in October 1969, the project's goal was the creation of a simple system whereby the information from published geological maps of varying ages and qualities could be integrated with recent air photographs at any scale between 1:8,000 and 1:50,000, to create highly accurate 1:50,000 or 1:63,360 printed maps 'for predicting terrain conditions at inaccessible sites': a thinly veiled reference to countries behind the Iron Curtain. If MEXE were to be able to test the new system's accuracy, however, 'accessible' terrain was a must, and so a domestic location (centred on Oxford) was chosen for the prototype map presented here. Although the final report made no overt mention of the military requirements that underlay

R. Webster, P.H.T. Beckett, A.O. Barrie and F.W. Gibbs/Military Engineering Experimental
Establishment, *A classification system for terrain – a facet map of the Oxford area* (1969)

the initiative, they are not particularly difficult to imagine, and probably would have included prediction and long-range targeting of the routes of overland convoys hauling supplies and reinforcements for a Warsaw Pact ground invasion of Western Europe [1972].

The crucial basis of the project was the classification of all terrain into the smallest possible number of meaningfully distinct types, each of which was termed a 'land facet'. Each facet type had a shared set of lithological, soil-type, landform, elevation and drainage characteristics that, taken together, would have tended to make it easy to identify and demarcate in spy-plane photos. Facet types were assigned Arabic numerals 1 through 22, with sub-types identified by lowercase letters or small Roman numerals; 'Dry valleys' were apparently of special interest to the project team, and were to be separately printed in purple.

The initial plan was for the facet information gleaned from photos at varying scales from 1:8,000 to 1:28,000 to be transferred onto OS 1:25,000 base maps using a machine called a Vertical Sketchmaster. This relied on

[t]he camera lucida principle . . . a semitransparent mirror used in such a way that the eye receives two superimposed images, one from the photograph and one from the map. The operator simultaneously views the map through the semitransparent mirror and the photograph by reflection from the first-surface mirror and through the semitransparent mirror . . . Thus, the two images are superimposed, allowing the operator to trace detail from the photograph to the map or from the map to the photograph if their positions are reversed. (D. Paine and J. Kiser)

Unfortunately, MEXE found the results of the Sketchmaster process to be satisfactory only when the aircraft's camera *and* the subject terrain were both almost perfectly level – and even then, 'only for a small central working field'. The operators also complained of eye strain.

The 'main difficulty' of the entire operation, according to MEXE, lay in '[t]ransferring facet boundaries from air photographs onto a base map, particularly where map scales differed', which after the failure of the Sketchmaster process had to be 'done by eye'. However, one might have added the further criticism that many or most of the 22 land-facet categories seemed to be derived a posteriori from deep knowledge of central England in particular, making their applicability to East Germany or Czechoslovakia, let alone the Volga Uplands, questionable at best. Unsurprisingly, given this set of problems, the Facet Map initiative was deemed a failure: 'For most purposes, a transparent overlay would be as useful, and . . . more easily prepared.'

One year after the project was abandoned, MEXE merged with the Fighting Vehicles Research and Development Establishment, successor to the Admiralty's 1915 Landships Committee that had developed the tank; and the merged entity was later combined with others to form the 9,000-employee Defence Evaluation and Research Agency (DERA). The town of Christchurch then became part of Dorset as a result of the local-government boundary changes of 1974 that also brought Abingdon, Didcot and Hinksey, among many other places, into Oxfordshire from Berkshire. The Christchurch-based elements of DERA became part of defence company QinetiQ Group Plc upon DERA's part-privatisation by the Blair government.

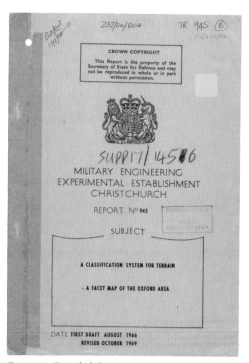

Opposite. Detailed descriptions of land-facet types. *Above.* Cover of MEXE report no. 945.

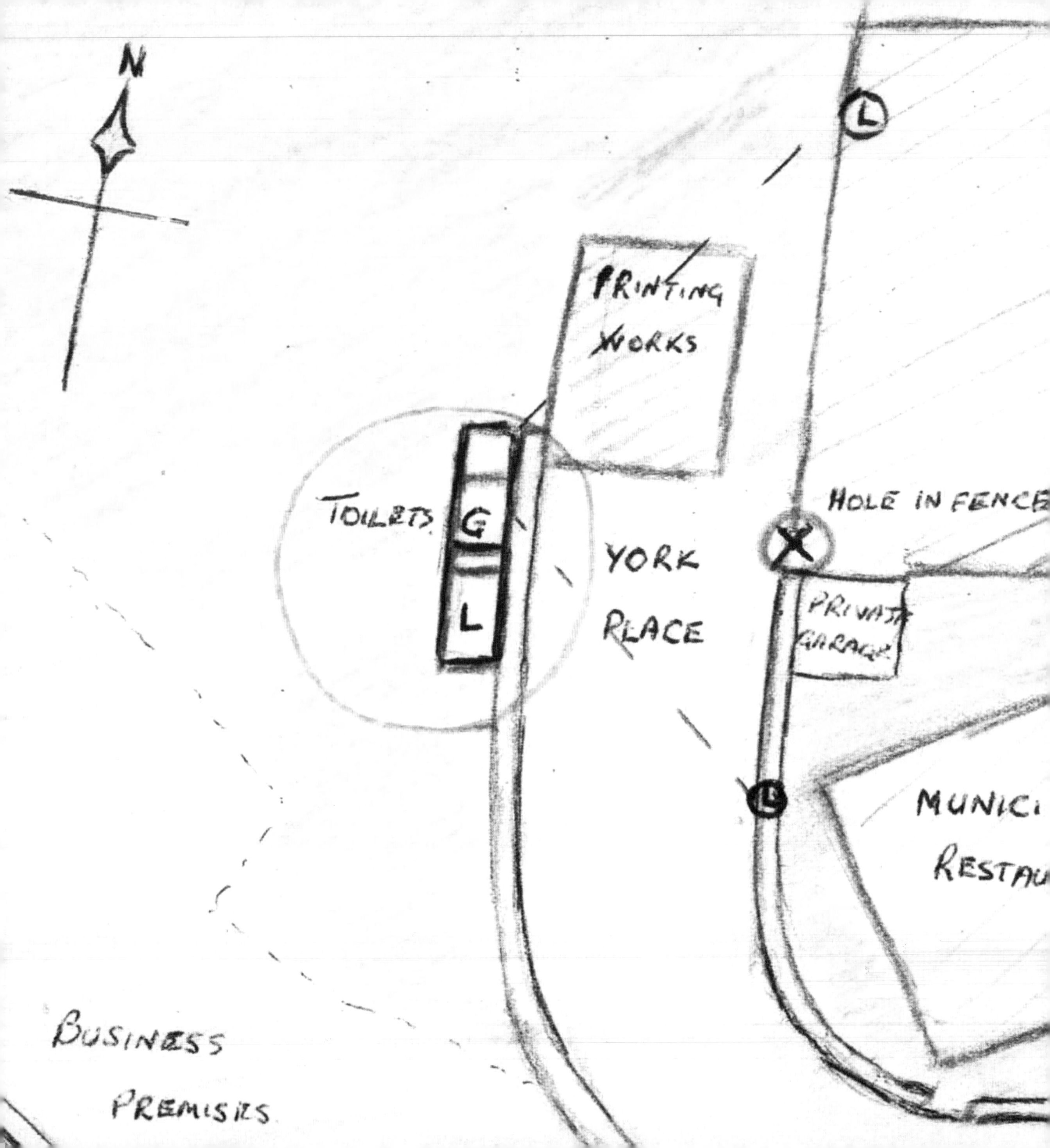
N
PRINTING WORKS
TOILETS
G
L
YORK PLACE
HOLE IN FENCE
PRIVATE GARAGE
MUNICI
RESTAU
BUSINESS PREMISES

c.1968

Oxford friends

Prior to the Reformation, homosexuality was primarily dealt with as a sin and prosecuted in ecclesiastical courts, but this changed with the passage of the Buggery Act 1533, which made anal intercourse with a man, woman or animal a civil offence punishable by hanging and confiscation of all property. Attempted buggery merited two years' imprisonment, assuming the convicted person first survived their exposure on the pillory. After being watered down under Edward VI and repealed under Mary I, the act was reinstated by Elizabeth I in its original, most stringent form. Georgian-era arguments by Jeremy Bentham and others that there was no real harm in homosexuality fell on deaf official ears, and when the act was repealed in 1828, it was only so that it could be replaced with another, clarifying that the death penalty could be applied even in cases where there was no proof of ejaculation. However, fellatio – even where one of the parties was underage – was not first made illegal until 1885, 50 years after the last executions for buggery, and a quarter of a century after the death-penalty nature of the offence was changed to penal servitude for ten years to life. Though the penalties had lessened, securing convictions was made easier in the era of Oscar Wilde by a much lower burden of proof: the crime of 'gross indecency', which the 1885 act did not define further, was very much in the eye of the beholder.

From this point through to the 1960s, high social status was no longer an effective protection against arrest, as demonstrated not least by the celebrated eight-day trial of New College-educated Lord Montagu of Beaulieu in 1954. At the end of the same year, there were 1,069 men in prison in England and Wales for violating the 1885 statute. Home Secretary Sir David Maxwell Fyfe, who had been an undergraduate at Balliol in the 1910s, described male homosexuality

Oxford City Police, *Plan of area of St. Clements showing York Place & location of toilets* (n.d.)

as a 'plague' and pledged to rid 'England' of it – perhaps under the impression that it did not exist in his native Scotland. In the paranoid atmosphere of the Cold War, a perceived correlation among Oxbridge education, homosexuality and communism led to a special singling-out of high-status gay men by the authorities. This was the case even or especially after the Maxwell Fyfe-sponsored Wolfenden Report of 1957 recommended that homosexuality be fully decriminalised – presumably not the answer the Home Secretary was expecting. Oxford was enormously overrepresented on the 15-member Wolfenden Committee, which was chaired by Magdalen College-educated Sir John Wolfenden and included the City Recorder and the university's Regius Professor of Moral and Pastoral Theology. The only dissenter from the report's landmark finding that all sexual acts between 'consenting adults in private' should be legal was a prosecutor from Glasgow. Partial decriminalisation followed ten years later, but may actually have led to more arrests, as the new law made it clear that sex other than in private houses, or involving more than two men, was still illegal.

This sketch-map was prepared as part of a police crackdown on male homosexual 'importuning' in and around the St Clement's Street Car Park. It is difficult to gauge how commonplace such maps were, but we are fortunate that this document from the latter days of coordinated official persecution happened to find its way into the National Archives at Kew.

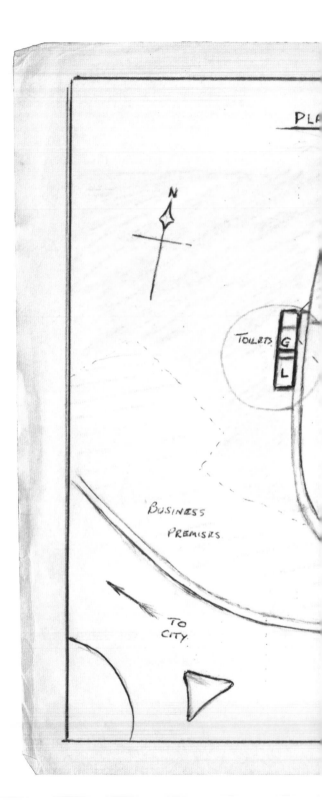

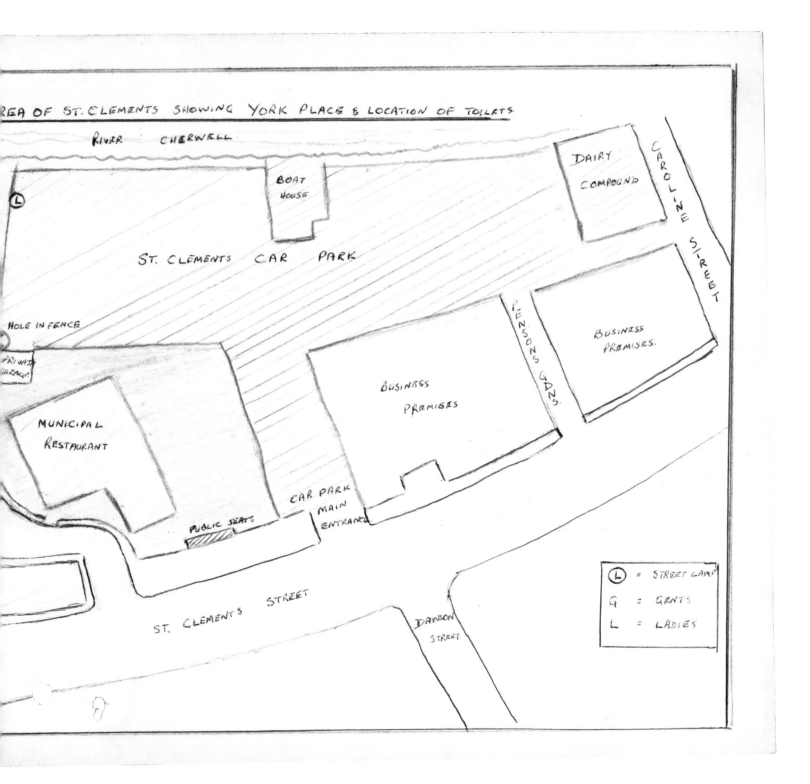

AREA OF ST. CLEMENTS SHOWING YORK PLACE & LOCATION OF TOILETS.

RIVER CHERWELL

BOAT HOUSE

DAIRY COMPOUND

CAROLINE STREET

ST. CLEMENTS CAR PARK

HOLE IN FENCE

PRIVATE GARAGE

MUNICIPAL RESTAURANT

PENSONS GDNS.

BUSINESS PREMISES.

BUSINESS PREMISES

PUBLIC SEATS

CAR PARK MAIN ENTRANCE

ST. CLEMENTS STREET

DANSON STREET

ⓛ	=	STREET LAMP
G	=	GENTS
L	=	LADIES

1972

Mapping for a Soviet occupation

The quality of Soviet military cartography, which at its height employed tens of thousands of people, was extremely high. Though often based on information from maps published in or by the enemy countries being depicted, human spying was also used – particularly with regard to small but tactically critical variations in features' height above sea level. Possible evidence for such activity in this 1:10,000 map of the Oxford area is the fact that its contours are metric, 'at a time when Ordnance Survey contour information . . . was still displayed in imperial units' (N. Millea).

Showing key industrial and administrative targets in black and violet, the present map was produced at a particularly dangerous moment for the Western allies, with the United States heavily committed to a major war in Vietnam that it was imminently to lose; France pursuing its own policy, having effectively withdrawn from NATO in 1966; and an economically fragile Britain largely failing to translate the decoloni-sation of Africa into a stiffer military presence at home. Indeed, the troop strength of the British Army of the Rhine actually fell by some 30 per cent during the 1960s. Four Warsaw Pact armies' brutal repression of a pro-democracy movement in Czechoslovakia in 1968 had met with merely token protest on our own side of the Iron Curtain, and by the time this map was compiled in 1972, a Western preference for détente and de-escalation led some in the Warsaw Pact to think that it would be possible to make further conquests in Europe without triggering even a 'limited' nuclear exchange.

In some respects, the 1973 Yom Kippur War – a full-scale armoured invasion of US ally Israel by Syria and Egypt – was a field-test of this idea: with the Arab side applying Soviet battlefield doctrines and weaponry, often under the direction of embedded Soviet officers, and receiving some 75,000 tonnes of war materiel from Warsaw Pact countries by air and sea. Israeli air and naval forces regularly exchanged fire with Soviet

Soviet General Staff, *Oksford* (1973)

239

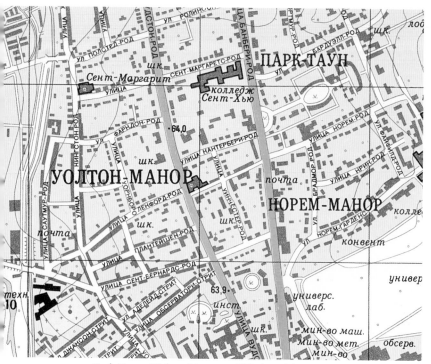

Park Town, Walton Manor and Norham Manor.

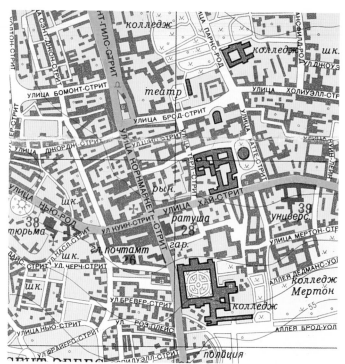

The colour-coding of University College as a governmental target may reflect an overestimation, based on its name, of its importance relative to the university's other colleges.

naval and civilian surface vessels, and one of the latter, the *Ilya Mechnikov*, was sunk. Israel was resupplied from the United States, to the tune of 40,000 tonnes, including hundreds of tanks and dozens of nuclear-capable fighter-bombers. Though nuclear weapons were very publicly fitted to Israeli warplanes, the defenders' better training, superior conventional weapons and higher motivation to win rendered use of 'the bomb' unnecessary. America's role in the war was controversial within NATO and led directly to severe economic dislocation as Arab countries refused to supply the US with oil. But Israel's remarkable victory convinced many on both sides in the Cold War that Western Europe might be able to blunt a Warsaw Pact blitzkrieg without 'tactical nukes' (the defensive use of which had been an article of faith for NATO since the mid 1950s) – or even roll it back and make small territorial

gains among the Soviet satellite states in Central Europe. Nonetheless, Soviet mapping in anticipation of a street-by-street conquest of the United Kingdom would continue through the 1980s.

Curiously, the general framework of Soviet military cartography was conceived in 1890s Germany, and formalised four years prior to the Russian Revolution as the International Map of the World project, headquartered in London. This utopian initiative's goal was the international standardisation of mapping based on a scale of 1:1,000,000, a division of the globe into a set of 2,500 segments measuring four degrees of latitude by six of longitude, and – ironically, given the product now before us – universal use of the Roman alphabet for cartographic labelling.

Ярнтон
Сент-Бартоломью
Манор-Хаус

Ред-Барн
Пертри-Хилл
Пертри-Хилл

Уотер-Итон
Сент-Фрайдсуайд
Катслоу

Саутфилд-Коттедж

ур.Окси-Мил
Дьюкс-Лок-Хаус

Саутфилд

Нэтслоу
Сескет

плотина Кингс

АППЕР-

Манор

Саннисайд-Истейт

мост Черуэлл
Нью-Манор
Хилл

ур.Марстон-Коммон

ВУЛВЕРКОТ
ЛОУЭР-

САННИМИД

Те-Авеню

МАРСТОН-

ур.Вулверкот-Коммон

Годстоу
мост Годстоу

Годстоу
шл.Годстоу

Нортерн-Медоу
мост Марстон

Виктория-Армс

Уайтем

САММЕРТАУН

радиаторный
8

спорт.пл.

НЬЮ-МАРСТОН

ур.Порт-Медоу

Темза (Айсис)

граница

ПАРК-ТАУН

Сент-Маргарет
Сент-Маргарет

колледж
Сент-Джон

Сент-Маргарет

сторожка Марли

УОЛТОН-МАНОР

НОРЕМ-МАНОР

Дейм-Маргарит-Холл

Бинси

университетский
парк

Те-Лайма-Перч-Инн
Медли-Манор

плотина Медли

ДЖЕРИКО

конвент

сторожка Ботли

колледж
Сент-Катрикс

ботан.сад

БОТЛИ

ОСНИ

театр

колледж Мертон

колледж Магдалин
мост Магдалин

мост Ботли
мост Осни

колледж Вустер

колледж
Сент-Хилда

СЕНТ-ЭББЕС

БОТЛИ-ПАТНИ

2016

Climate change and the 'internet of things'

Our lifetimes have witnessed revolutionary transformations in how maps are made, why and by whom. In the 1970s, small groups still toiled in private, or indeed in secret, using cartographic techniques – and in some cases, business models – that had barely changed since the Georgian era. Today, a host of new possibilities are exploding at the nexus of satellite photography, mobile networks, artificial intelligence, drone technology, web-based collaborative tools, inexpensive wireless remote-sensing devices and, crucially, a whole array of machines that can communicate geographic information directly with one another. Some maps, in other words, are being made by everyone, and others by no one. Elsewhere I have critiqued the 'post-human turn' in cartography, but in a broader sense, it is just one aspect of the 'internet of things' (IoT): a term coined in 1999 by Birmingham-born tech pioneer Kevin Ashton to describe 'a global infrastructure for the information society, enabling advanced services by interconnecting (physical and virtual) things based on existing and evolving interoperable information and communication technologies' (United Nations). Potentially sinister implications of this exultant enmeshing of the hitherto separate realms of the high-tech, the low-tech and the natural are not far to seek. However, there have been many positive developments too, especially involving sensor networks for environmental-monitoring and early-warning systems, often with cartographic outputs.

An excellent example is this flood-monitoring map of the Oxford area, designed 'to enable people to take action when water levels rise' (BBC News). The project was initiated in 2013 by the Oxford Flood Network (OFN), a community group co-founded by Ben Ward because the Environment Agency's river-level data were insufficiently detailed to allow them to protect their homes from flooding: a perennial feature of life in the city, but particularly acute in January and February 2014. After OFN began deploying sensors and

Flood Network/Nominet, *Live river levels (beta)* (2016)

243

The map currently updates at ten-minute intervals, and a continuously updated version is planned.

reporting the collected data via the internet, they were joined in the effort by Nominet, the company known chiefly for its administration of UK internet domain names, but which has a strong research-and-development interest in the IoT as part of a wider commitment to 'ensuring the internet is a force for good'. Now running a company called Flood Network, Ward reports that low-power, low-cost ultrasound sensors

can be installed under bridges, overhangs, or even under floorboards, and report back water levels and temperature every 15 minutes to the map. . . . The products are aimed at community flood action groups and local authorities who need more information about flooding than is currently available and can alert people and organisations to take action earlier. The data that's collected is useful to hydrologists to model flooding in the future and improve flood risk maps or plan alleviation schemes.

Environment Agency sensors are also linked to the map, which currently updates at ten-minute intervals. A continuously updated version is planned, though the sensor network's 'intermittent, aperiodic, asynchronous timeseries data . . . is fiddly to handle' (Nominet). One test using a hexacopter drone in place of a fixed sensor was deemed a success, and further such explorations may be in the offing.

In addition to the sidebar with 'sparklines' showing change in river levels over time, the map features a 'traffic light' system that indicates current levels, from clear (normal), through green and amber, to red (high water). A 4-mile, £120-million Oxford flood-relief channel is tentatively scheduled for construction from 2018, but even in the unlikely event that it is a complete success, the present map looks set to fill a vital niche for at least the next several years.

Nominet chief executive Russell Haworth told BBC News: 'If this can work in Oxford, it can work anywhere.' Certainly, parallel initiatives in Asia for tsunami, earthquake and

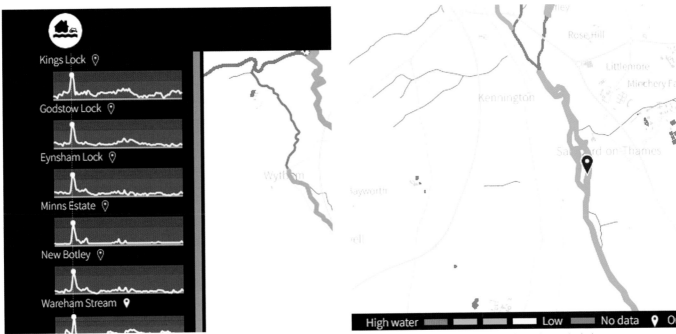

'Sparklines' show changes in water levels over time in multiple locations.

A 'traffic light' system for river levels is also included.

radiation-leak warning show considerable promise. Whole 'smart cities' have been planned, notably in South Korea and China, featuring integration of transport, power, water, educational, medical, transport and even law-enforcement systems, among others; and it has been estimated that by 2020, the number of 'things' connected to the IoT worldwide will be 20–50 billion. Ward stresses, however, that the 'smart city' concept will only work to the extent that it is demystified and becomes something that large numbers of people participate in. Professor Sir John Krebs of the UK's Committee on Climate Change, meanwhile, expects flooding to pose ever-increasing risks to bridges, many of which carry IT and electrical connections as well as people and vehicles. What Sir John calls the resultant 'cascade of risks' arguably places the physical robustness of sensor networks at the forefront of our civilisation's technological needs, at least in the medium term while the root causes of climate change are being addressed. As Nominet's blog on the flood-mapping project put it:

Cold, frosts and dampness tend to kill equipment. . . . [D]ull but important issues such as fixings become all important: how exactly do you fix a sensor to a disused 60cm cast iron pipe? . . . [H]ow do you realistically achieve a 250m connection across wooded areas? [H]ow do you remotely reboot a Raspberry PI gateway that is held securely in someone else's property? . . . [H]ow big do the buttons on a mobile app need to be when your fingers have gone numb from standing in a wet muddy field in December? The key thing to remember about the Internet of Things is that it is where the physical world meets the digital world. The physical world is complex and messy.

Perhaps we have not evolved quite as far as we think we have beyond the type of surveying that killed James Brindley in 1772 [1768]. But in any case, Oxford, and maps of Oxford, will remain on the muddy front line for many years to come.

Further reading

Books

Bendall, S. (ed.), *Dictionary of Land Surveyors and Local Map-Makers of Great Britain and Ireland, 1530–1850*, 2nd edn. (London: British Library, 1997).

Boase, C.W., *Oxford* (London: Longmans Historic Towns, 1887).

Clark, P. (ed.), *The Cambridge Urban History of Britain, Vol. 2: 1540–1840* (Cambridge: Cambridge University Press, 2000).

Corbett, M. and Norton, M., *Engraving in England in the Sixteenth and Seventeenth Centuries, Part III: The Reign of Charles I* (Cambridge: Cambridge University Press, 1964).

Crossley, A. (ed.), *A History of the County of Oxford: Volume 4* (London: Victoria County History, 1979).

Harvey, P.D.A., *Maps in Tudor England* (London: University of Chicago Press, 1993).

Hewitt, R., *Map of a Nation: A Biography of the Ordnance Survey* (London: Granta, 2010).

Hind, A.M., *Engraving in England in the Sixteenth and Seventeenth Centuries, Part I: The Tudor Period* (Cambridge: Cambridge University Press, 1952).

Hind, A.M., *Engraving in England in the Sixteenth and Seventeenth Centuries, Part II: The Reign of James I* (Cambridge, Cambridge University Press, 1955).

Hurst, H., *Oxford Topography: An Essay* (Oxford: Clarendon, 1899).

Kain, R. and Oliver, R., *British Town Maps: A History* (London: British Library, 2015).

Oliver, R., *Ordnance Survey Maps: A Concise Guide for Historians*, 3rd edition (London: Charles Close Society, 2013).

Sherwood, J. and Pevsner, N., *The Buildings of England: Oxfordshire* (London: Penguin, 1974).

Tyacke, N. (ed.), *The History of the University of Oxford, Vol. 4: Seventeenth Century Oxford* (Oxford: Clarendon, 1997).

Woodward, D. (ed.), *The History of Cartography, Vol. 3: Cartography in the European Renaissance* (Chicago and London: University of Chicago Press, 2007).

Worms, L. and Baynton-Williams, A., *British Map Engravers: A Dictionary of Engravers, Lithographers and their Principal Employers to 1850* (London: Rare Book Society, 2011).

Articles and Reports

Barley, M.W. (ed.), *CBA Research Report No. 14: The Plans and Topography of Medieval Towns in England and Wales* (Leamington: Council for British Archaeology, 1975).

Beckley, R. and Radford, D., *Oxford Archaeological Resource Assessment 2011: the Modern Period (1800-1950)* (Oxford: Oxford City Council, 2012).

Elwood, S., Goodchild, M.F. and Sui, D.Z., 'Researching Volunteered Geographic Information: Spatial Data, Geographic Research, and New Social Practice', *Annals of the Association of American Geographers 102* (2012), 571–590.

Fletcher, D., 'Map or Terrier? The Example of Christ Church, Oxford, Estate Management, 1600-1840', *Transactions of the Institute of British Geographers 23(2)* (1998), 221–237.

Harley, J.B., 'Silences and Secrecy: The Hidden Agenda of Cartography in Early Modern Europe', *Imago Mundi 40* (1988), 57–76.

Martin, G.H., 'Road Travel in the Middle Ages: Some Journeys by the Warden and Fellows of Merton College, Oxford, 1315–1470', *Journal of Transport History,* New Ser., *3(3)* (1976), 159–178.

Morris, R.J., 'Religion and Medicine: the Cholera Pamphlets of Oxford, 1832, 1849 and 1854', *Medical History 19(3)* (1975), 256–270.

Rhodes, J. and Munby, J., *Castle, Canal and College: Worcester Street Car Park and Related Areas, Oxford. Historic Context Study and Conservation Plan* (Oxford: Oxford Archaeological Unit Ltd, 2008).

Tittler, R., 'Political culture and the built environment of the English country town, c.1540–1620' in Hoak, D. (ed.), *Tudor Political Culture* (Cambridge: Cambridge University Press, 1995), 133–156.

Websites

Bodleian Libraries – Catalogues and Finding Aids, http://www.bodleian.ox.ac.uk/weston/finding-resources/ catalogues/.

British Library – Maps, Plans and Views, http://www.bl.uk/subjects/maps/.

Catalogue of British Town Maps, http://townmaps.data.history.ac.uk/.

Library of Congress – Geography and Map Division, https://www.loc.gov/maps/.

Map History – History of Cartography Gateway, http://www.maphistory.info/.

Measuring Worth – Purchasing Power of British Pounds from 1270 to Present, https://www.measuringworth.com/calculators/ppoweruk/.

National Archives of the United Kingdom, http://discovery.nationalarchives.gov.uk/.

National Library of Scotland – Bartholomew Archive, http://digital.nls.uk/bartholomew/.

National Library of Scotland – Map Images, http://maps.nls.uk/.

Nominet Research Blog, http://www.nominet.uk/researchblog/.

Old Maps Online, http://www.oldmapsonline.org/.

Oxford Dictionary of National Biography, http://www.oxforddnb.com/.

Oxford History, http://oxfordhistory.org.uk/.

Oxfordshire County Council – Maps at Oxfordshire History Centre, https://www.oxfordshire.gov.uk/cms/content/maps-oxfordshire-history-centre/.

Oxoniensa – Journal of the Oxfordshire Architectural and Historical Society (OAHS), http://oxoniensia.org/.

Unveiling of Britain, http://www.bl.uk/onlinegallery/onlineex/unvbrit/.

Illustration sources

pp. x and xiv Boston Public Library

p. xiii Author's collection

1568: De Agostini/The British Library Board, 11314589

1578: Bodleian Library, University of Oxford, no shelfmark

c.1600: Oxfordshire County Council – Oxfordshire History Centre, POXO116926

1605: The British Library Board, Maps C.7.c.20.(2.), f.43

1646: Bodleian Library, University of Oxford, MS Top.Oxon.b.167

1648: Bodleian Library, University of Oxford, G.A.Oxon a.41(14)

1673: The Board and Trustees of the National Library of Scotland A.42.b.11

1675: The British Library Board, Maps C.6.d.8, plate 80.

1695: Bodleian Library, University of Oxford, C17:70 Oxford (121)

1724: Government Art Collection, GAC3527

1733: Bodleian Library, University of Oxford, G.A.Oxon a.41(31)

1750: Bodleian Library, University of Oxford, Gough Maps Oxfordshire 13

1759: Bodleian Library, University of Oxford, Gough Gen Top 200 [1759]

1762: The Board and Trustees of the National Library of Scotland, EME.s.41

1768: Bodleian Library, University of Oxford, J. Maps 224 [85]

1771: The British Library Board, Maps K.Top.34.33.3.a.

1773: Bodleian Library, University of Oxford, Gough Oxford 140 facing p.[1]

1786: Bodleian Library, University of Oxford, MS C17:70 Oxford (45)

1789: Bodleian Library, University of Oxford, (E)C17:70 Oxford (66)

1805: Library of Congress, Washington DC

1807: Bodleian Library, University of Oxford, G.A.Oxon a.41 (unnumbered)

1819: Oxfordshire County Council – Oxfordshire History Centre, QSD/AD, Vol. D

1830: Oxfordshire County Council – Oxfordshire History Centre, QSD/A, Vol. E

1831a: Author's collection

1831b: Bodleian Library, University of Oxford, J Maps 279 [42]

1832: Oxfordshire County Council – Oxfordshire History Centre, QSD/A, Vol. E

c.1834: Bodleian Library, University of Oxford, Oxford C(17:70 (32)

1834: Oxfordshire County Council – Oxfordshire History Centre

1835: Author's collection

1837: Bodleian Library, University of Oxford, G.A. Oxon a.41(50)

1838: Warwickshire County Record Office CR1590/P267

1844: National Archives RAIL 1075/89/18

1848: Author's collection

1850: Bodleian Library, University of Oxford, (E)C17:70 Oxford (1A)

1853: Oxfordshire County Council – Oxfordshire History Centre, QSD/AD, Bk. 11

1855: Bodleian Library, University of Oxford, G.A.Oxon a.41(62)

c.1862: Author's collection

1872: Bodleian Library, University of Oxford, C17:70 Oxford (33)

1876: National Archives MR 1/846/35

1878: Bodleian Library, University of Oxford, G.A.Oxon.a.41(77)

1883: Bodleian Library, University of Oxford, C.17.70 Oxford (7)

1893: Bodleian Library, University of Oxford, G.A.Oxon.a.41, 83

1895: Author's collection

1898: Author's collection

1900: Bodleian Library, University of Oxford, J. Maps 279 [60]

1902a: Author's collection

1902b: Oxfordshire County Council – Oxfordshire History Centre, CJ/IX/vii/1

1909: Author's collection

1910: Author's collection

1917: Bodleian Library, University of Oxford, J. Maps 279 [56]

1930: National Archives RAIL 252/2177

1950: National Archives, DR 4/156

1965: National Archives, DR 4/156

c.1968: National Archives, HO291/1060

1972: Bodleian Library, University of Oxford, C17:70 Oxford [154]

2016: Oxford Flood Network/Nominet. Contains public sector information licensed under the Open Government Licence v3.0.

Index